GUIDE TO SKILLS, TOOLS & TECHNIQUES

family handyman

GUIDE TO SKILLS, TOOLS & TECHNIQUES

Chief Content Officer Jason Buhrmester
Content Director Kirsten Schrader
Creative Director Raeann Thompson
Associate Creative Director Kristen Stecklein
Editor Christine Campbell
Manager, Production Design Satyandra Raghav
Assistant Art Director Samantha Primuth
Senior Print Publication Designer Sanjeev Dhiman
Deputy Editor, Copy Desk Ann M. Walter
Copy Editor Rayan Naqash
Contributing Editor Rachel Maidl
Electrical Consultant John Williamson
Plumbing Consultant Bret Hepola, master plumber,
All City Plumbing, Minnetrista, MN

A FAMILY HANDYMAN BOOK

1610 N. 2nd St., Suite 102
Milwaukee, WI 53212-3906

ISBNS
979-8-88977-119-7 (Hardcover)
979-8-88977-160-9 (Paperback)

Component Number
118300137H

For more *Family Handyman* products and information,
visit our website: *www.familyhandyman.com*

Printed in China
1 3 5 7 9 10 8 6 4 2 (Hardcover)
1 3 5 7 9 10 8 6 4 2 (Paperback)

Photo Credits
Text, photography and illustrations for *Guide to Skills, Tools & Techniques* are based on articles previously published in *Family Handyman* magazine (*familyhandyman.com*).
Cover photo, tools: Floortje/Getty Images
Dot background used throughout this book: VectorHotShot/Getty Images

WARNING
All do-it-yourself activities involve a degree of risk. Skills, materials, tools and site conditions vary widely. Although the editors have made every effort to ensure accuracy, the reader remains responsible for the selection and use of tools, materials and methods. Always obey local codes and laws, follow manufacturer's operating instructions, and observe safety precautions.

SAFETY FIRST—ALWAYS!

Tackling home improvement projects and repairs can be endlessly rewarding. But as most of us know, with the rewards come risks. DIYers use chain saws, climb ladders and tear into walls that can contain hazardous surprises.

The good news is that armed with knowledge and the right tools and procedures, homeowners can minimize the risks. As you go about your projects and repairs, stay alert for these hazards:

ALUMINUM WIRING

Aluminum wiring, installed in about 7 million homes between 1965 and 1973, requires special techniques and materials to make safe connections. This wiring is dull gray, not the dull orange characteristic of copper. Hire a licensed electrician certified to work with it. For more information, go to *cpsc.gov* and search for "aluminum wiring."

SPONTANEOUS COMBUSTION

Rags saturated with oil-based paints and stains, or oil finishes like Danish and linseed oil, can spontaneously combust if left bunched up. Always dry them outdoors, spread out loosely. When the oil has thoroughly dried, you can safely throw them in the trash.

VISION AND HEARING RISKS

Safety glasses or goggles should be worn whenever you're working on DIY projects that involve chemicals, dust and anything that could shatter or chip off and hit your eyes. Sounds louder than 80 decibels (dB) are considered potentially dangerous. Sound levels from a lawn mower can be 90 dB, and shop tools and chain saws can be 90 to 100 dB.

LEAD PAINT

If your home was built before 1979, it may contain lead paint, which is a serious health hazard, especially for children 6 and under. Take precautions when you scrape or remove it. Contact your public health department for detailed safety information or call (800) 424-LEAD (5323) to receive an information pamphlet. Or visit *epa.gov/lead*.

BURIED UTILITIES

A few days before you dig in your yard, have your underground water, gas and electrical lines marked. Just call 811 or go to *call811.com*.

SMOKE AND CARBON MONOXIDE (CO)

The risk of dying in reported home structure fires is cut in half in homes with working smoke alarms. Test your smoke alarms every month, replace batteries as necessary and replace units that are more than 10 years old. As you make your home more energy-efficient and airtight, existing ducts and chimneys can't always successfully vent combustion gases, including potentially deadly carbon monoxide (CO). Install a UL-listed CO detector, and test your CO and smoke alarms at the same time.

FIVE-GALLON BUCKETS AND WINDOW COVERING CORDS

Anywhere from 10 to 40 children a year drown in 5-gallon buckets, according to the United States Consumer Products Safety Commission. Always store these buckets upside down, and store ones containing liquid with their covers securely snapped.

According to Parents for Window Blind Safety, hundreds of children in the U.S. are injured every year after becoming entangled in looped window treatment cords. For more information, visit *pfwbs.org* or *cpsc.gov*.

WORKING UP HIGH

If you have to get up on your roof to do a repair or installation, always install roof brackets and wear a roof harness.

ASBESTOS

Texture sprayed on ceilings before 1978, adhesives and tiles for vinyl and asphalt floors before 1980, and vermiculite insulation (with gray granules) may contain asbestos. Other building materials made between 1940 and 1980 could also contain asbestos. If you suspect that materials you're removing or working around contain asbestos, contact your health department or visit *epa.gov/asbestos* for information.

CHAPTER 01

Tool Guide

CHAPTER 02

Carpentry

CHAPTER 03

Flooring

CHAPTER 04

Electrical

CHAPTER 1

Tool Guide

23 Things Every DIYer Should Own

Whether you're a novice or an expert, these tools are crucial for getting jobs done at home

By Rachel Brougham

MIRAGEC/GETTY IMAGES

PLIERS

A few pairs of pliers come in handy when you need to grip, turn or pull something, such as a screw or nail. Add both locking and combination pliers to your must-have list.

ADJUSTABLE WRENCH

An adjustable wrench allows DIYers to work with all sizes of nuts and bolts. And while you can buy sets of wrenches in various sizes, an adjustable wrench is a good investment, especially if space or budget constraints are an issue.

CLAW HAMMER

So many projects require the use of a hammer. Use them for woodworking projects, hanging artwork and putting together furniture. And claw hammers are a good choice because not only do they drive nails, you can use the claw to remove nails as well.

UTILITY KNIFE

There's a good reason a utility knife is considered one of the most versatile tools in the toolbox. They can be used on many projects, including cutting drywall, removing carpeting and even exposing popped nail heads.

LEVEL

Add a level to your kit and you'll have an accurate guide when it comes to positioning items both vertically and horizontally. A basic foot-long level will get the job done and fit in most toolboxes.

SCREWDRIVERS

Every DIYer should have a few screwdrivers on hand, including flat-head, Robertson, Pozidriv and Phillips types. And having screwdrivers in a few different sizes will help you deal with a variety of screw heads.

TAPE MEASURE

A tape measure is a must-have when you need accurate, precise measurements. You don't need anything fancy. Look for one that is retractable and lockable to get the job done.

LED FLASHLIGHT

LED flashlights are a good choice for any DIYer because the batteries and bulbs last much longer than standard flashlights. LED flashlights can also come in handy during storms, so it's not a bad idea to have a few on hand.

EXTENSION CORDS

Every homeowner needs an extension cord at some point, and having a few around will make life a lot easier. Extension cords come in handy when using power tools. This includes power saws, shop vacuums and leaf blowers.

EXTENSION CORDS: BILL OXFORD/GETTY IMAGES

SHOP VACUUM

You'll get any mess cleaned up quickly with a shop vacuum. Look for a wet/dry model that can be used to clean up liquids as well as dirt, dust and debris.

ROTARY TOOL

A rotary tool, such as the Dremel, can be used in a variety of tasks, including grinding, cutting, sanding and buffing. While the average DIYer will already have several hand tools that will do the same work, a rotary tool and the use of its attachments will get that work done quicker.

PLASTIC TARP

A plastic tarp will serve a variety of functions. Rake leaves onto the tarp to haul them to the compost bin, or use it to cover outdoor items such as patio furniture to protect them from harsh weather.

BUNGEE CORDS

Bungee cords aren't just for mountaineering. So keep a few bungee cords around to stop items in your trunk from rolling around or falling over. They make it easy to strap down items and secure them to the top of your car.

SAFETY GLASSES

Safety glasses are a must-have for everyone because when you're working, you should always protect your eyes. Keep a couple pairs around your work area so they are within easy reach. They also make a great gift for handy family members and friends.

GLUE

Have a bottle (or two or three) of wood glue around for making repairs or even as a quick-fix for suturing wounds. Also keep gel-type superglue (cyanocacrylate glue, or CA) on hand for attaching small pieces that would be hard to clamp. Glues comes in a few different brands, including Super Glue, Gorilla and Krazy Glue.

WD-40

Don't be caught without some WD-40 in your work space. It's a multiuse lubricant that is great for freeing up rusty or stuck hinges, bolts and reducing squeaks in latches. There are dozens of ways to utilize this convenient product.

TOOLBOX

You need to keep all those tools and supplies organized somehow so you can find them when you need them. You'll thank yourself for the storage. Plus, a toolbox will allow you to easily bring your tools with you no matter where you go.

HANDSAW

If you have just one saw, make it a handsaw that can be used in basic woodworking projects. When you buy a handsaw, remember that bigger teeth will cut faster. Saws have variations on teeth per inch (TPI), which also influences its potential cutting ability.

SHOP VACUUM: ILEXIMAGE/GETTY IMAGES;

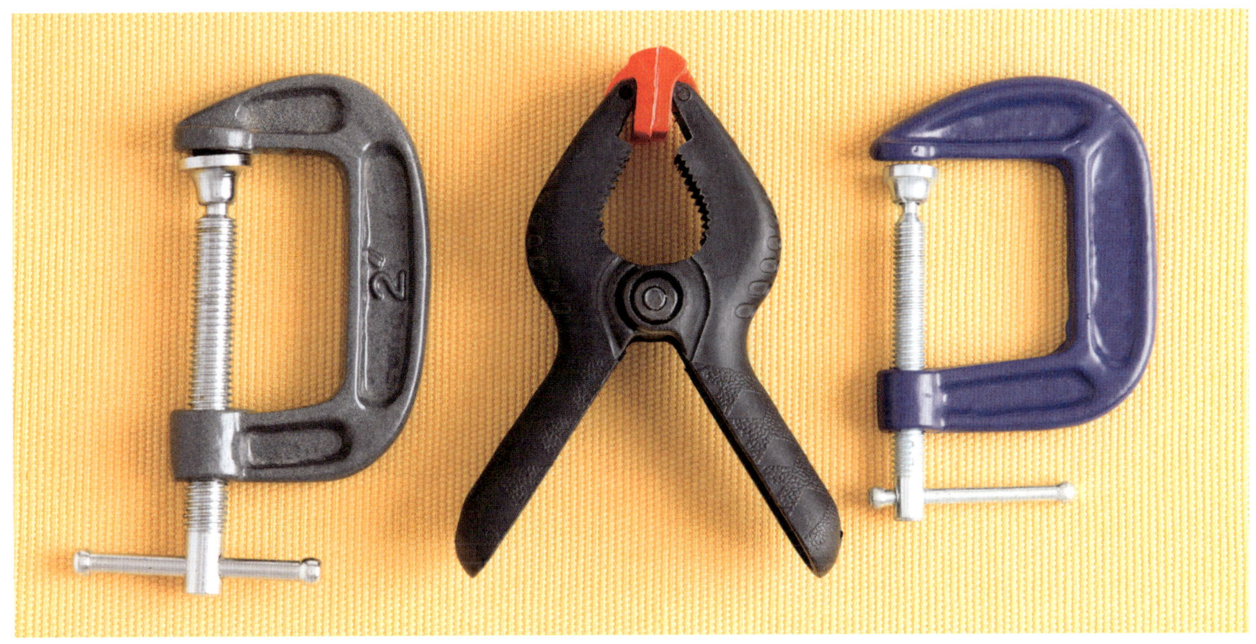

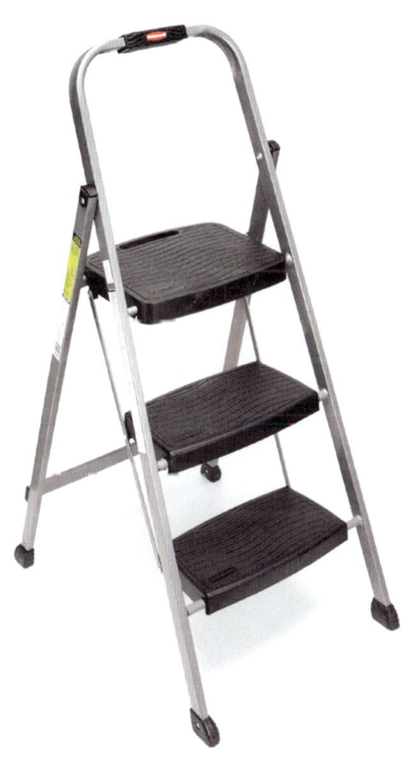

CLAMPS

Clamps help you hold or secure objects so they don't move while you're working with them. There are a variety of clamps available, including C-clamps, pipe-clamps and handscrew clamps.

TAPE

Keep a roll of electrical, Teflon and duct tape in your toolbox. You can use electrical tape for electrical work, while Teflon is used for plumbing projects.

A MIX OF HARDWARE

DIYers should always have a collection of screws and nails available. Try storing hardware in a container with separate compartments so you can keep everything organized.

SCRAPER

Use a scraper to remove flaky or old surfaces, such as a popcorn ceiling, vinyl flooring or wallpaper. Just look for a scraper with a comfortable handle.

STEP STOOL AND LADDER

At some point, you'll need a steady, sturdy platform for projects such as cleaning gutters or trimming trees. And a step stool is a great choice for when you just need a little boost. Caution: When using an extension ladder, remember the highest safe standing level is four rungs from the top.

Jigsaw Basics

Learn how to use this less-intimidating, versatile saw with tips from pros

A jigsaw excels at cutting curves in lumber and sheet goods of every type, and it can be used to make straight cuts too. Compared to a circular saw, it's quieter, lighter and—because the blade moves in a more "relaxed" up-and-down motion—safer and more user friendly. With the right blade, it can be used to cut metal, plastic pipe and tile.

THINGS TO KNOW:

- The narrower the blade, the tighter the curve it can cut. The more the TPI, the smoother the cut.
- When making a cut in the center of a board or panel, drill a ¾-in. starter hole first, insert the blade and then proceed.
- For best results, cut slightly outside your cut line. Then you can use a power or hand sander for final shaping.

GET THE RIGHT JIGSAW FOR YOU

Some jigsaws have handles; some don't. Many pros prefer the no-handle, "barrel-grip" style because they feel they have better control with their hands closer to the action. Folks with smaller hands often complain about the barrel being too large to grab.

PRO TIP Pushing as hard as you can on the jigsaw doesn't necessarily make it cut faster; sometimes the exact opposite is true. And pushing too hard into a curve can cause you to veer off your line, burn the material or break a blade. Ease off on the pressure until the jigsaw cuts smoothly with little vibration.

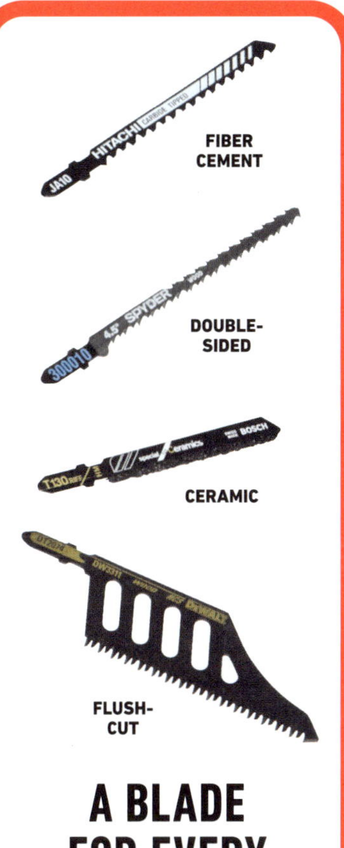

A BLADE FOR EVERY OCCASION

There are a couple of basic things to know about blades for jigsaws: The larger the teeth, the more aggressive and rougher the cut. And the narrower the blade you have, the tighter the turns it can make.

Match the type of blade with the material you're cutting—don't use a wood blade to cut metal. Manufacturers have taken most of the guesswork out of blade selection—read the description of the blade to know what it does. It is usually written on the blade itself. Buy a combo pack, and you'll be ready for most jobs.

DRILL ACCESS HOLES

If you need to cut out a hole in the center of the work surface, drill a hole slightly bigger than your jigsaw blade in two opposite corners. That way, you can make four neat cuts starting from the two holes.

MAKE A METAL SANDWICH

Jigsaws are great at cutting sheet metal, but it's difficult to clamp the material down so the saw blade doesn't rattle the material up and down instead of cutting through it. One way to solve this problem is to sandwich the metal between two ¼-in. sheets of plywood. Once the plywood is clamped down, the metal has nowhere to go, so you get a fast, easy, clean cut.

MAKE RELIEF CUTS FOR SHARP TURNS

There's a limit on how sharp a curve a jigsaw can cut, and that depends on the blade—the narrower the blade, the sharper the turns it should make. If you try to force the blade into a turn tighter than it's capable of, you'll either veer off your line or break the blade.

If you're not sure about a particular shape, mark it out on a piece of scrap and practice on that. If you have a curve you know is too tight, make relief cuts. The sharper the curve, the more relief cuts you'll need. And be sure you don't cut past your line. Play it safe and leave at least a blade's width of material between the relief cut and your pencil mark.

PRO TIP Typically, there's an SPM (strokes per minute) "sweet spot" where the jigsaw cuts the fastest and cleanest and with the least vibration. Try different speeds by changing pressure on the trigger. Once you find the best speed, set the adjustable speed dial so you can pull the trigger all the way while maintaining the desired SPM.

CUT WITH THE "GOOD" SIDE DOWN

Most jigsaw blades cut on the upstroke, so chips and splinters occur mostly on the top of the wood. If you value one side of a board more than the other, make sure you keep the good side face down, and mark and cut the less important side. You can buy "reverse cut" or "down cut" blades that do cut on the downstroke. These blades are used when you want as little tear-out on the top surface as possible. Cutting out a sink hole in a laminate countertop is one common use for reverse-cut blades.

CUT ANYTHING

The main mission of a jigsaw is to cut curves in wood, and it's easy to overlook its other abilities. Instead of trudging along with your hacksaw, grab your jigsaw to quickly cut steel, copper or any metal. You can also cut heavy plastic and tougher stuff such as ceramic tile or fiber cement siding. The key to success is to match the blade to the material.

PROTECT THE WORK SURFACE

When making a cut, firmly hold down the saw to keep the blade from chattering, and even then, it may vibrate a bit. The combination of downward force and vibration is tough on the work surface. Reduce damage by applying a layer or two of masking tape to the base of the jigsaw. Remove the tape when you're done so it doesn't leave a sticky residue on the base.

PRO TIP Be sure the blade is up to speed before you start your cut. If you start the saw with the blade touching your material, it can grab hold and rattle the material, possibly damaging it. And let the saw come to a complete stop when you pull it from the material mid-cut. If you don't, you might experience the dreaded "woodpecker effect," when a moving blade bounces off the surface, leaving behind pockmarks and a bent blade.

King of Cuts: Circular Saws

A superstar of every garage and shed, this saw makes quick work of any size project

What a hammer is to hand tools, a circular saw is to power tools; it's a must-have tool for DIYers. It shines when it comes to cutting 2×4s and other boards to length and is unequaled when it comes to cutting plywood and paneling. The standard 7¼-in. circular saw can cut material up to 2 in. thick and can make angled cuts up to 45 degrees. With the right blade, it can even be used to cut metal, concrete and nail-embedded lumber. For occasional use, a small cordless circular saw will suffice.

THINGS TO KNOW:

- Always wear hearing and eye protection.
- Be sure to keep the base plate (aka shoe) resting firmly on your workpiece as you cut.
- Position your board so the cutoff can drop away freely. In the case of plywood, make sure the piece you're cutting is well supported so it doesn't "pinch" or bind the blade.

GET THE RIGHT SAW FOR YOU

When shopping for a circular saw, consider corded (more powerful) vs. cordless (more convenient), weight and balance, steel shoe (less expensive) vs. aluminum shoe (more durable) and extras such as an integrated work light and easy adjustments.

Steel shoes are common on less expensive saws, and they have a few downsides. First, they can bend if you drop the saw. And a bent shoe can cause your saw to cut poorly. Also, the rolled edge on a steel shoe can be a problem when using a thin straightedge like a rafter square for a saw guide. The saw can slip over the top of the guide and ruin the cut. We tend to prefer aluminum or magnesium shoes with crisp, square edges. Most of the expensive saws in this group have excellent shoes.

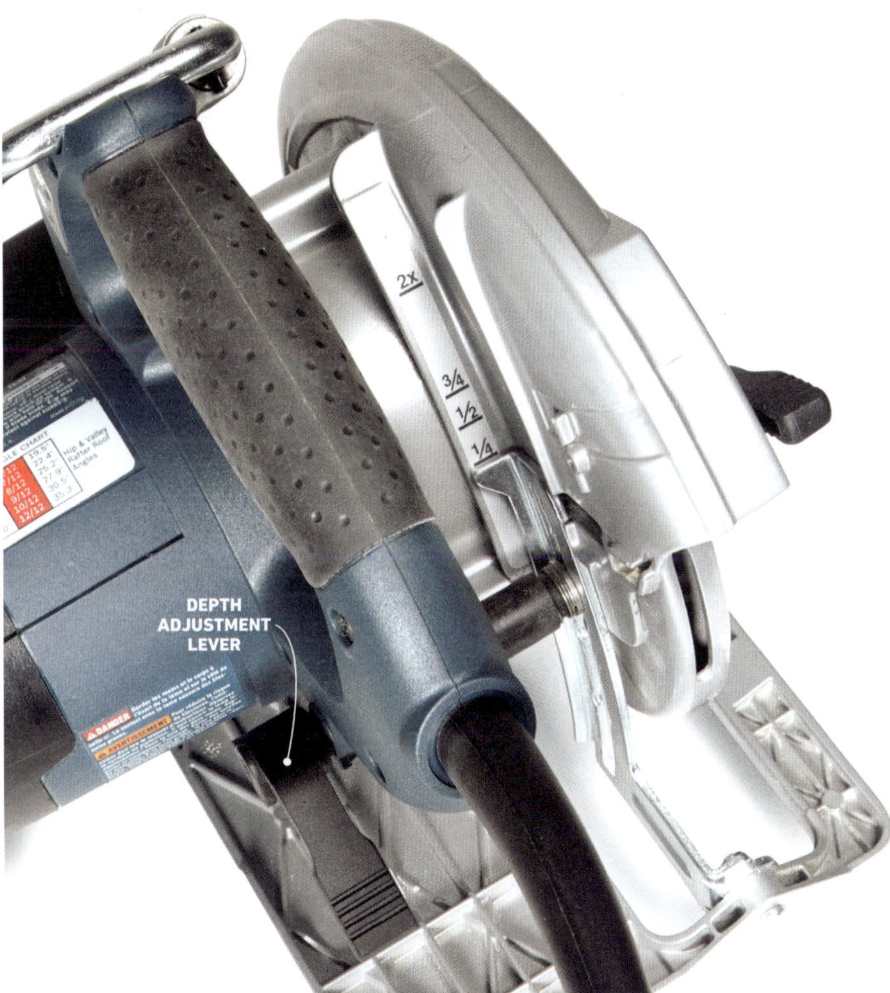

EASY DEPTH ADJUSTMENT

Changing the depth of cut on a circular saw requires you to loosen a lever and move the shoe up or down. There are two depth-adjusting features worth comparing in this group of saws. First, some saws have what we are calling an "outboard" lever; that is, the lever is located to the left of the handle where it's more accessible. We like this feature. Also, while most saws have some type of cutting-depth scale, the Bosch, Craftsman, Makita, Ridgid and Skil saws have exceptional scales that are easy to read. Bosch has gone one step further and included detents at common depth settings, making it quick and easy to go from cutting a 2×4 to cutting ½-in. plywood while maintaining the perfect blade depth.

SCRAP SIDE
OF BOARD
"V" MARK

ACCURATE MARKS

To get an accurate cut with a circular saw, you have to start with an accurate mark. Stretch out your tape measure, place your pencil at the correct measurement and make two marks that form a "V," with the tip of the "V" pointing at the exact measurement. A "V" is more accurate than a single line, which can stray slightly to the right or left and throw off your cut mark.

LIGHT UP THE CUT

A perfect cutting line won't do you any good if you can't see it. So before you start cutting, take two seconds to check the lighting. Even in the best-lit workshops or the sunny outdoors, you or your circular saw can cast shadows that make it hard to see your cutting mark. Change the angle of the board or reposition your work light so the line won't disappear into the shadows as you cut.

CAUTION What do earmuffs, safety glasses and dust masks have to do with cutting accurately with a circular saw? Well, it's tough to watch the cutting line with your eyes squinting and blinking through a storm of sawdust. And protection against noise, dust and splinters will make you more comfortable and more patient—and less likely to make a sloppy, rushed cut.

SHOULDER THE CORD

On most corded circular saws, an electrical plug will snag on the edge of plywood, and that'll throw off your cut. To prevent snags, drape the cord over your shoulder. Eliminate this problem by using a cordless saw.

WATCH THE BLADE, NOT THE GUIDES

Every circular saw has notches or marks on the front of the shoe to indicate where the blade is going to cut. Unfortunately, they get covered with sawdust or the whole thing gets bent out of whack, which throws off the guide. Watch the actual blade and line as you cut. All it takes is a light puff of air every few seconds to clear the sawdust.

SCORE A CLEAN CUT

Circular saws usually splinter the wood that's facing up and cut cleanly on the side that's facing down. So when you're cutting veneered plywood, position the material "good side down" so the teeth of the blade are pushing the veneer up against the core rather than ripping it away. Pushing the saw more slowly than normal also helps reduce splintering. If you need both sides splinter free, mark your cut by scoring the veneer with a sharp utility knife, then cut just a hair to the "waste side" of the line. Any splintering occurs on the waste piece. A quick swipe with sandpaper will clean up any little fuzzies left behind.

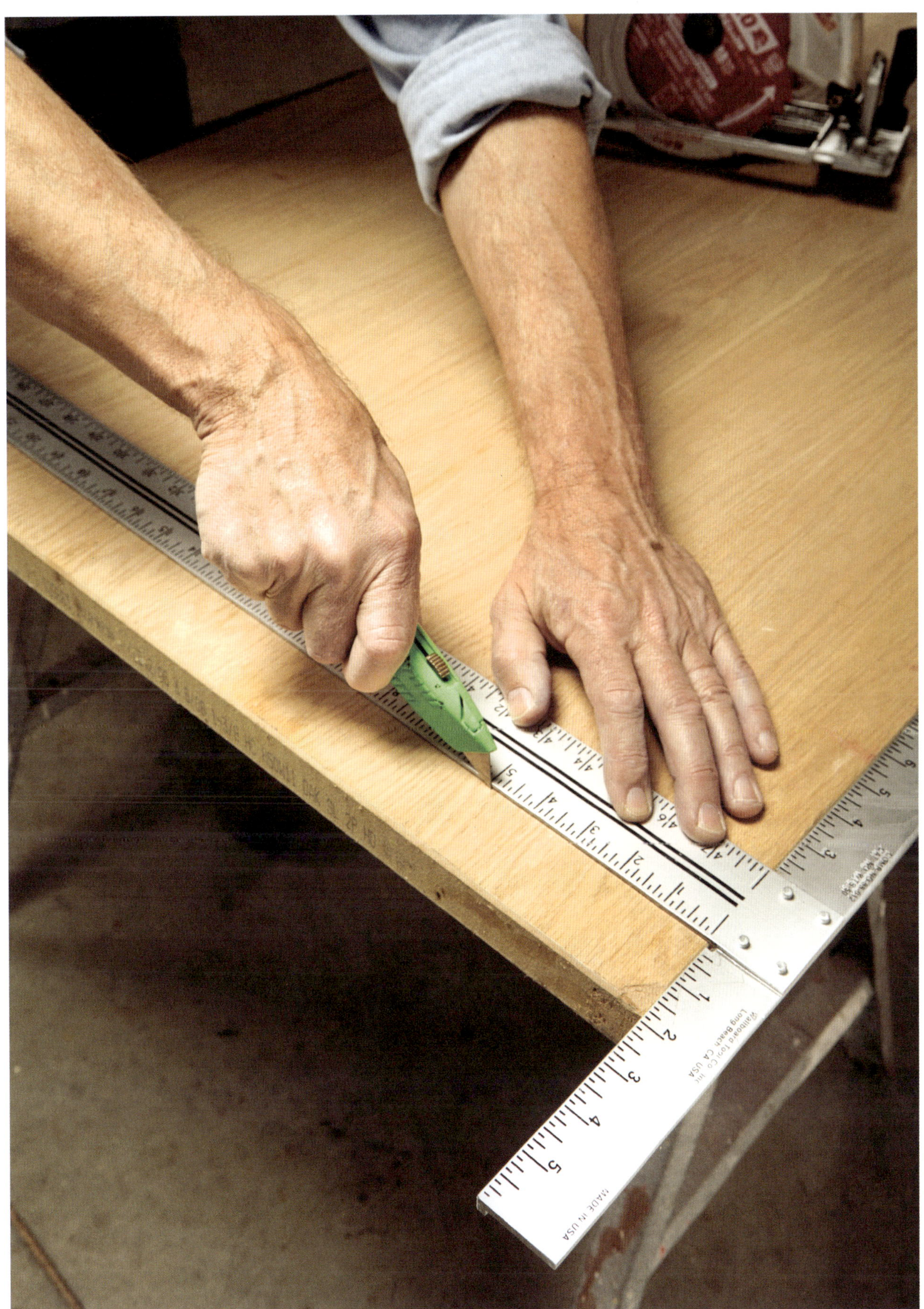

Rotary Tools in the Rotation

Discover all the jobs these multitaskers can accomplish

This tool, often referred to by the brand name Dremel, operates like a high-speed minidrill, but oddly enough is rarely used as a drill. The chuck (or collet) can grasp a variety of bits that can be used for carving, sanding, engraving and polishing. Cordless versions are adequate for light use and when pursuing small-scale hobby work. Accessories range from flexible shafts to jigsaw attachments. Always wear safety glasses when using a rotary tool.

A rotary tool is useful for:

- Removing burrs from pipes or other metals after cutting.
- Engraving names and initials on tools and other frequently "borrowed" items.
- Removing finishes or sanding wood in hard-to-access places.

CUT STUBBORN PARTS

A rotary tool is often the best solution when corrosion causes metal parts to get stuck. With a rotary tool, either slice off the stubborn metal part or cut slits in it so you can break it off (p. 27).

VACUUM-POWERED ROTARY TOOL

The Dremel rotary tool has no motor and is powered solely by the suction of a vacuum! If you want to keep dust to a minimum while sanding, this is the tool.

FIX A DOOR THAT DOESN'T LATCH

Instead of moving the strike plate, slightly enlarge the latch opening in the strike plate. A rotary tool does this quickly and easily. Use a carbide-cutting bit specifically designed for metal cutting. Judge the part of the strike plate that needs grinding by testing when the latch catches. If you have to push down to latch the doorknob, then the top of the strike plate hole needs grinding. If the door has to be pushed in, then grind the outside edge of the strike plate hole. You don't want the latch slopping around inside a huge opening, so don't grind away half the strike plate. Remove only small amounts of metal and then test the door. Repeat the process until the door latch effortlessly catches the strike plate.

CUT HOLES IN TILE

A rotary tool is a great, safe way to cut through tile. Set the depth of the tile-cutting bit shallow to avoid hitting plumbing or wires in the wall cavity. Whenever possible, use grout lines for two sides of the hole because they're much easier to cut through. Drill starter holes in two opposite corners with a glass-and-tile drill bit.

CAUTION
Grinding metal can throw sparks and fragments into the air, so wear safety glasses with side shields or full goggles when grinding. Otherwise, use a small round file for this project.

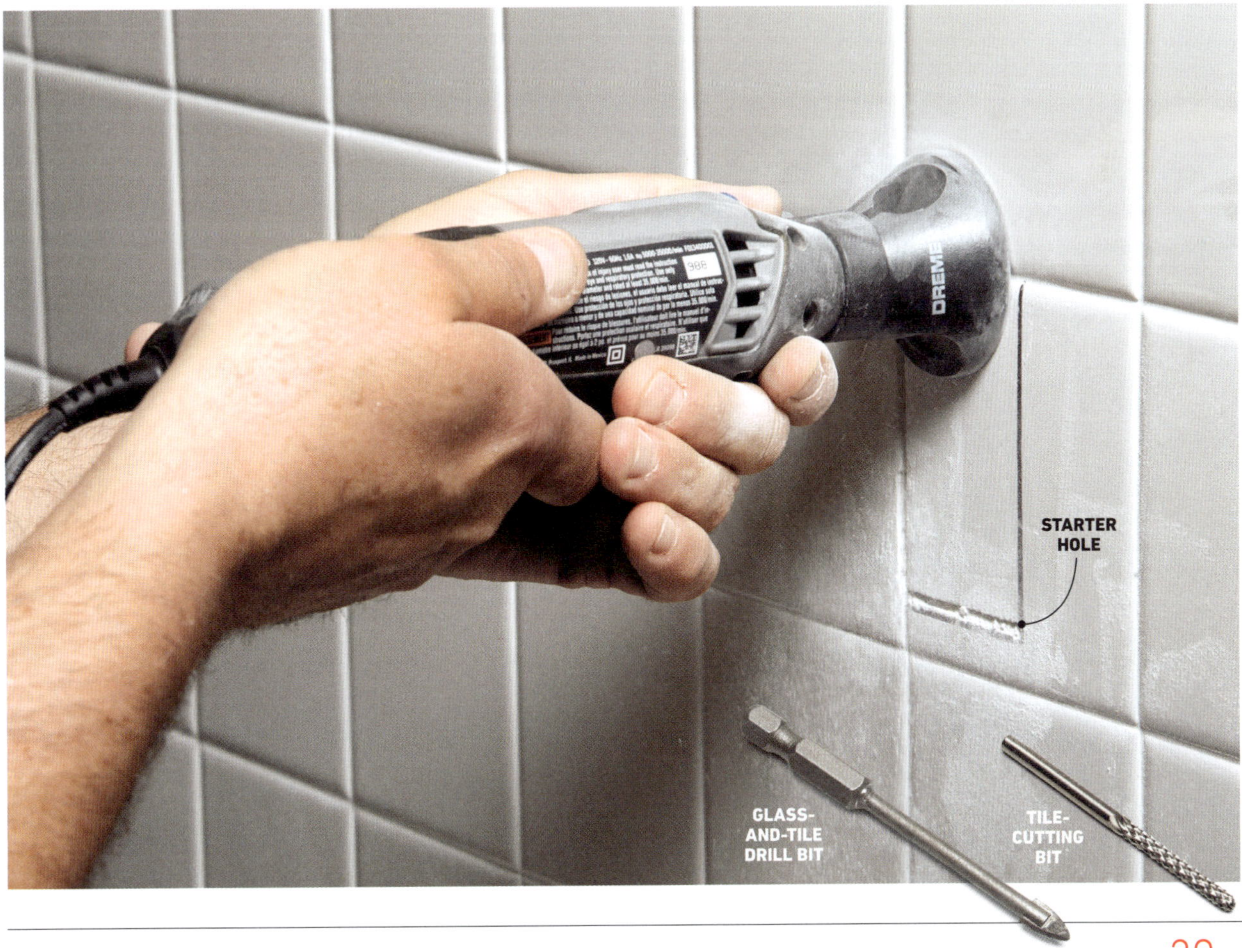

STARTER HOLE

GLASS-AND-TILE DRILL BIT

TILE-CUTTING BIT

DISHWASHER RACK REPAIR

Dishwasher rack tines break off or lose the protective coating at the tips, and then you get rust spots on your dishes. But you can fix this with help from a rotary tool. Buy a bottle of vinyl repair paint and a package of replacement tips to match your rack from any appliance parts store or online. Cut off the rusted tips with a rotary tool and cutoff wheel. Then retip the tines **(Photo 1)**. To patch a rusted area around a broken tine, first clean off the rust **(Photo 2)**.

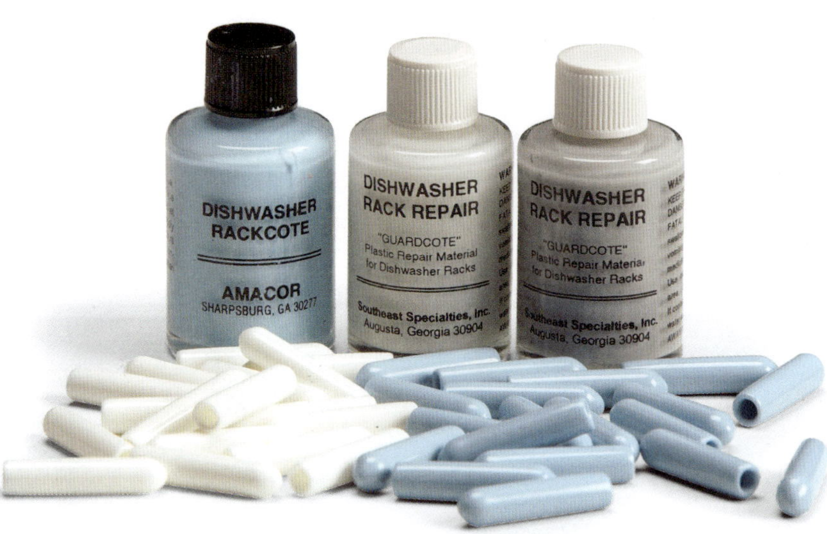

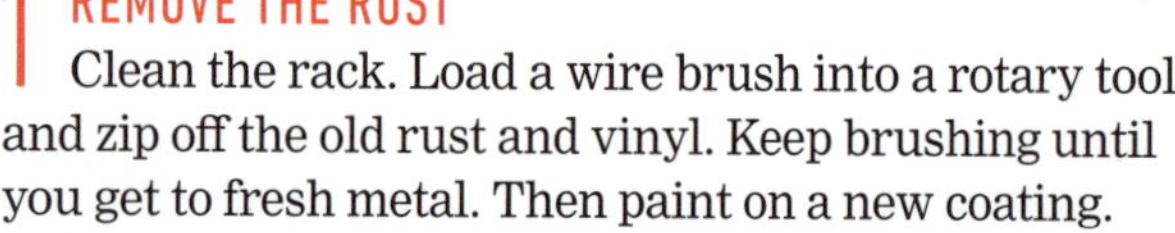

1 REMOVE THE RUST

Clean the rack. Load a wire brush into a rotary tool and zip off the old rust and vinyl. Keep brushing until you get to fresh metal. Then paint on a new coating.

2 FRESHEN UP WITH PAINT

After cutting damaged tines, paint the new tips. Coat the freshly cut tip with vinyl paint. Then slip a new vinyl tip over the tine.

DUST-SUCKING ROTARY TOOL

Nothing works better at cutting holes in drywall than a rotary tool. It's also true that nothing fills a room with dust faster. Look for dust collection attachments for your tool if yours doesn't have one. Adding one can reduce airborne dust by up to 90%. Rotary tools also work on wood, cement board and tile, among other materials.

CUT STAINLESS STEEL WITH A GRINDING DISC

There are many types of stainless steel, and some hard varieties are challenging to cut. For small jobs like cutting stainless steel backsplash tiles, a rotary tool fitted with an abrasive metal-cutting disc works fine.

ROTARY TOOL
ABRASIVE DISC
STAINLESS STEEL

DUST-SUCKING ROTARY TOOL: ROBERT BOSCH POWER TOOLS GMBH

DREMEL
MULTI-MAX
MM40

All About Oscillating Tools

This is the Swiss Army Knife of power tools—compact, versatile and able to get into areas and perform tasks like no other

This barrel-shaped tool has a short vibrating shaft, to which a variety of accessories can be attached for cutting, scraping or sanding. An oscillating multitool is often used for repairs and remodeling. Most DIYers find it particularly useful for:

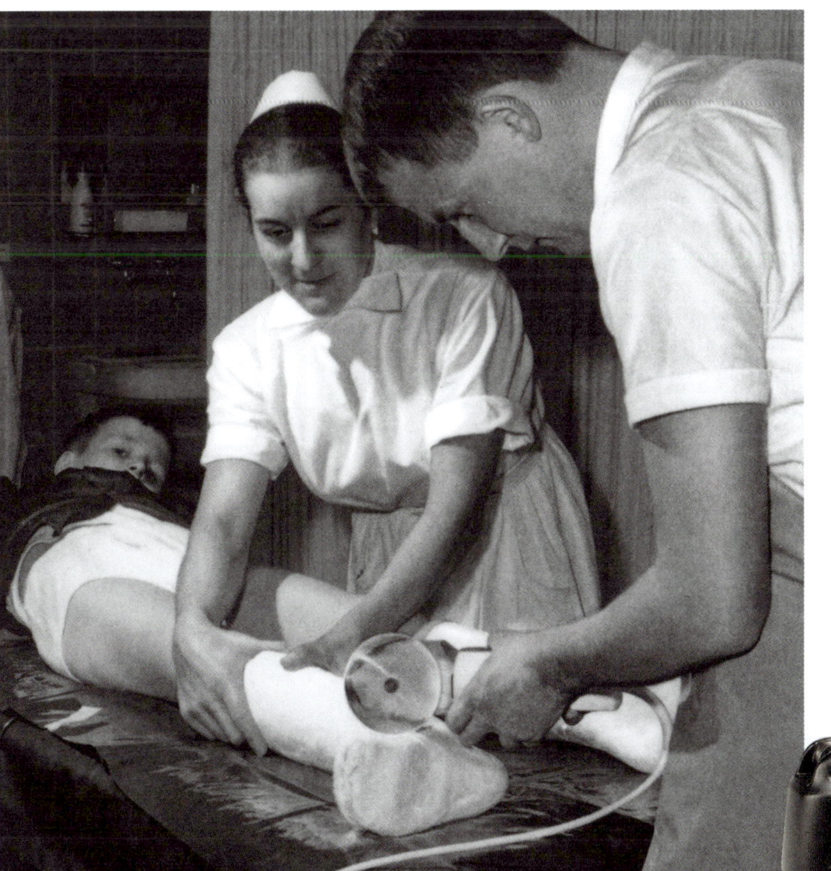

HOSPITAL: FEIN POWER TOOLS

- Cutting off pipes and rusted bolts in tight spaces.
- Sanding or scraping in tight corners when refinishing furniture or floors.
- Removing old grout, caulk and floor adhesives when you're remodeling.

FROM HOSPITALS TO JOB SITES

In 1968, Fein patented the oscillating "plaster cast saw," which could slice through a cast without harming the patient's skin. That medical tool evolved into the do-anything tool we know today. Fein still makes pro-grade oscillating tools, and many pros swear it's still the best choice.

PRO TIP Don't burn up the blade. Heat kills blades. Occasionally swing the blade back and forth out of the cut to clean out dust. And don't press too hard.

GET INTO TIGHT SPOTS

When access is tight or you need to make a flush cut, an oscillating tool fitted with a metal-cutting blade will solve the problem. Corroded mounting nuts on toilets or faucets are easy to cut off with an oscillating tool. You can also use an oscillating tool to cut plumbing pipes, bolts on cars, nails and other metal objects in places where a larger tool wouldn't fit. Just make sure the blade is intended to cut metal.

HOW IT WORKS

An oscillating tool works with a side-to-side movement. The oscillation is very slight (only 3 degrees) and very fast (about 20,000 SPM), so it feels more like vibration. A saw blade is shown, but the tool also works with scrapers and sanding pads.

CUT STUBBORN PARTS

An oscillating tool works great for cutting toilet bolts that are rusted or corroded.

OSCILLATING TOOL

PRO TIP Oscillating tools are usually sold as kits with varying assortments of accessories. Considering the high cost of blades, checking the contents of the kit is worthwhile. Don't just look at the number of pieces, though: A 30-piece kit might include 25 low-cost sanding pads.

REMOVE OLD CAULK

Slice through the old caulk along walls and floors with an oscillating tool equipped with a flexible scraper blade. This often works better than a utility knife.

THE BEST WAY TO REMOVE GROUT

If you have grout that's stained or moldy, the best tool for the job is an oscillating tool fitted with a diamond blade. An oscillating tool won't damage any tiles or whip up a dust storm. You'll need at least two diamond blades, depending on the size of the job. Switch to a scraper blade for your oscillating tool to scrape away caulk at the inside corners.

PRO TIP Blades are a big expense. Oscillating tool blades are pricey and wear out fast. Over the life of your oscillating tool, you'll probably spend more on blades than on the tool itself.

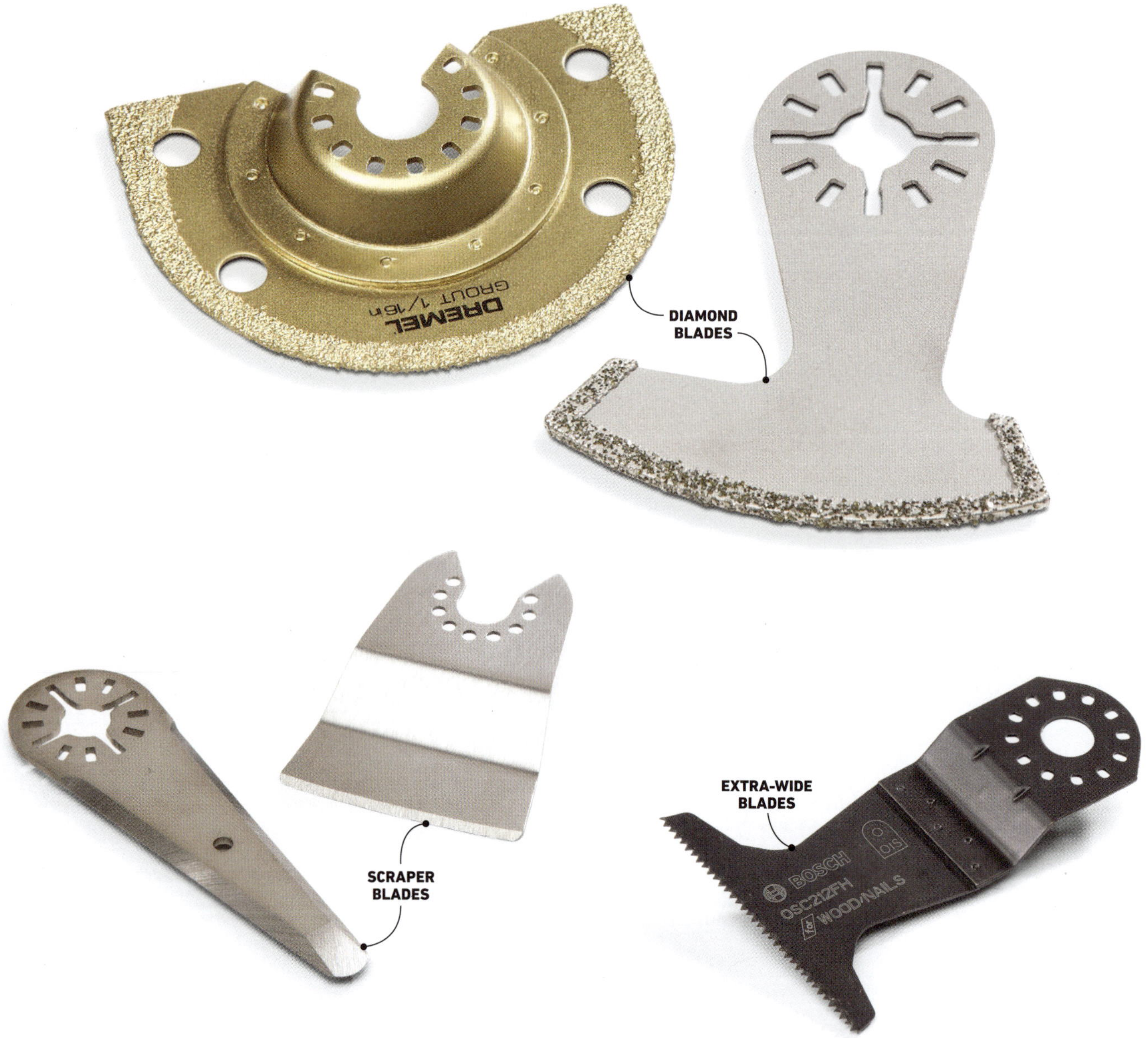

DIAMOND BLADES

SCRAPER BLADES

EXTRA-WIDE BLADES

CAUTION Most blades sold in stores are meant for soft materials like wood and plastic. Cutting metal can destroy them in a few seconds. For metal cutting, be sure to buy blades labeled "bimetal," "titanium" or just "metal."

SPECIAL OSCILLATING TOOL BLADES

Great for grout removal. A carbide is fine for small jobs. For larger jobs, a diamond blade saves you money because it lasts two to three times as long. Both types come in 1/16-in. and 1/8-in. thicknesses to match grout widths. When you can see sparks, you know that the outer edge of the blade is worn out, even though there may be plenty of grit left on the sides of the blade.

Scraper blades. These blades come in lots of styles: stiff or flexible, sharp or blunt, straight or offset. This long, thin version is good for digging caulk out of joints. The other blade works well for scraping patches of dried construction adhesive off of the floor.

Extra-wide blades. Extra-wide blades like the 2½-in. version above are perfect for cutting round stuff like pipe because they don't slip off a curved surface the way narrow blades do. For other jobs, narrower blades are usually best: They plunge-cut better and put less strain on the motor.

FASTER FLOORING PREP

With a scrap of flooring as a guide, an oscillating tool also makes a straight, clean cut. The only downside is the noise. (Oscillating tools are loud!) Hearing protection is a good idea.

A flush-cutting blade is best for undercutting doorjambs. The raised center lets the blade sit flat on a guide scrap. With a flat blade, the tool's bolt head protrudes below, so the blade can't ride over a guide.

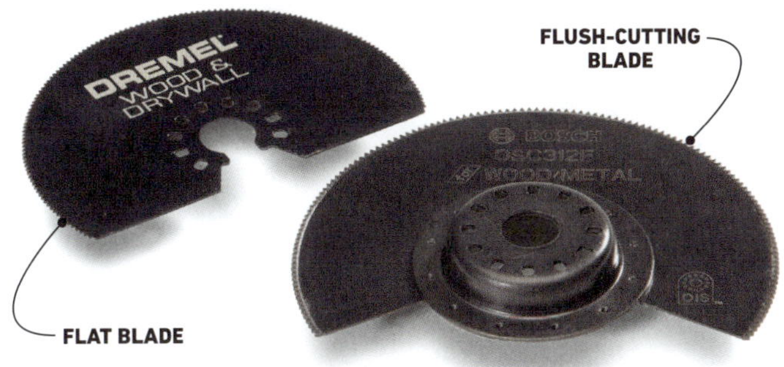

STANLEY
BOSTITCH

Tack It with Brad Nailers

The different types of trim nailers on the market and how to stay safe when working

A brad nailer (aka a trim nailer) is a "gun" used for driving small finish nails ranging in length from ½ to 2 in.; it can be cordless, electric or pneumatic. If you are installing trim, building furniture, assembling picture frames or tackling any other project that requires more than a few dozen nails, a brad nailer is well worth the investment. They not only increase speed, but since they drive nails in a single pop and eliminate the jarring of hammering, they also can improve accuracy.

THINGS TO KNOW:

- Always wear sight and hearing protection.
- Keep your free hand and your body out of the projected path of nails.
- Press the nosepiece, which contains a small "safety" tongue that must be depressed, firmly against the workpiece before pulling the trigger.

TOOL WEIGHT MATTERS

If you're installing crown molding overhead, a few pounds could make the difference between aching shoulders and a pain-free job.

THE NAILS

Brad nailers are categorized by the thickness or gauge of the nails they can shoot: The bigger the gauge number, the smaller the nail (seems backward, doesn't it?). Nailers that shoot the biggest nails, 15 and 16 gauge, are usually called finish nailers. While midsize 18-gauge nailers are called brad nailers. The smallest nailer, the 23-gauge, is usually called a pinner or micropinner.

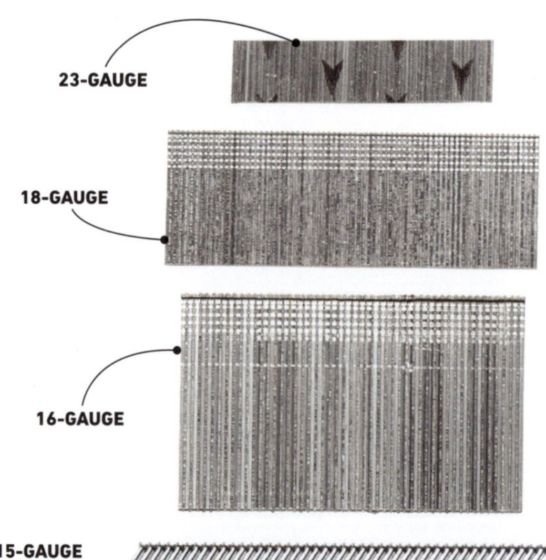

BARE TOOL OR KIT?

Most cordless brad nailers are available as kits containing a battery and charger. If you own other battery-powered tools, you'll save money if you can find a brad nailer that uses the same battery. Otherwise, the kits are usually a better deal.

USE A BRAD NAILER FOR PERFECT MITERED CORNERS

It's hard to beat a brad nailer for perfect miters, especially if you're not skilled with a hammer. Brad nailers allow you to hold the moldings in perfect alignment while you pin them in place. If you can afford only one nailer, buy one that shoots thin 18-gauge nails up to 2 in. long. Where more strength is needed, such as for nailing door jambs, 15- and 16-gauge nailers are good. But the thicker brads make larger, more conspicuous holes and can crack thin moldings. Use shorter brads to nail the molding to the jamb, and long brads along the any of the outside edges.

1 PIN PERFECT JOINTS

In a perfect world, you could nail the trim flat to the wall and the miter would look great. But in reality, minor variations in level between the jamb and the wall often interfere. To solve this problem, start by pinning the inside edge of the trim, making sure the miter joint is pressed tight together. Then, while the miter is still tight, drive a pair of brads through the outside corners at opposite angles to pin it.

2 SECURE A GAP

If there's a slight gap between the molding and the wall, don't press the trim tight to the wall and nail it; the miter joint might open up. Instead, slip a thin shim between the molding and the wall. Then nail the outside edge of the trim. If the gap and shim are visible, fill the crack with caulk before painting.

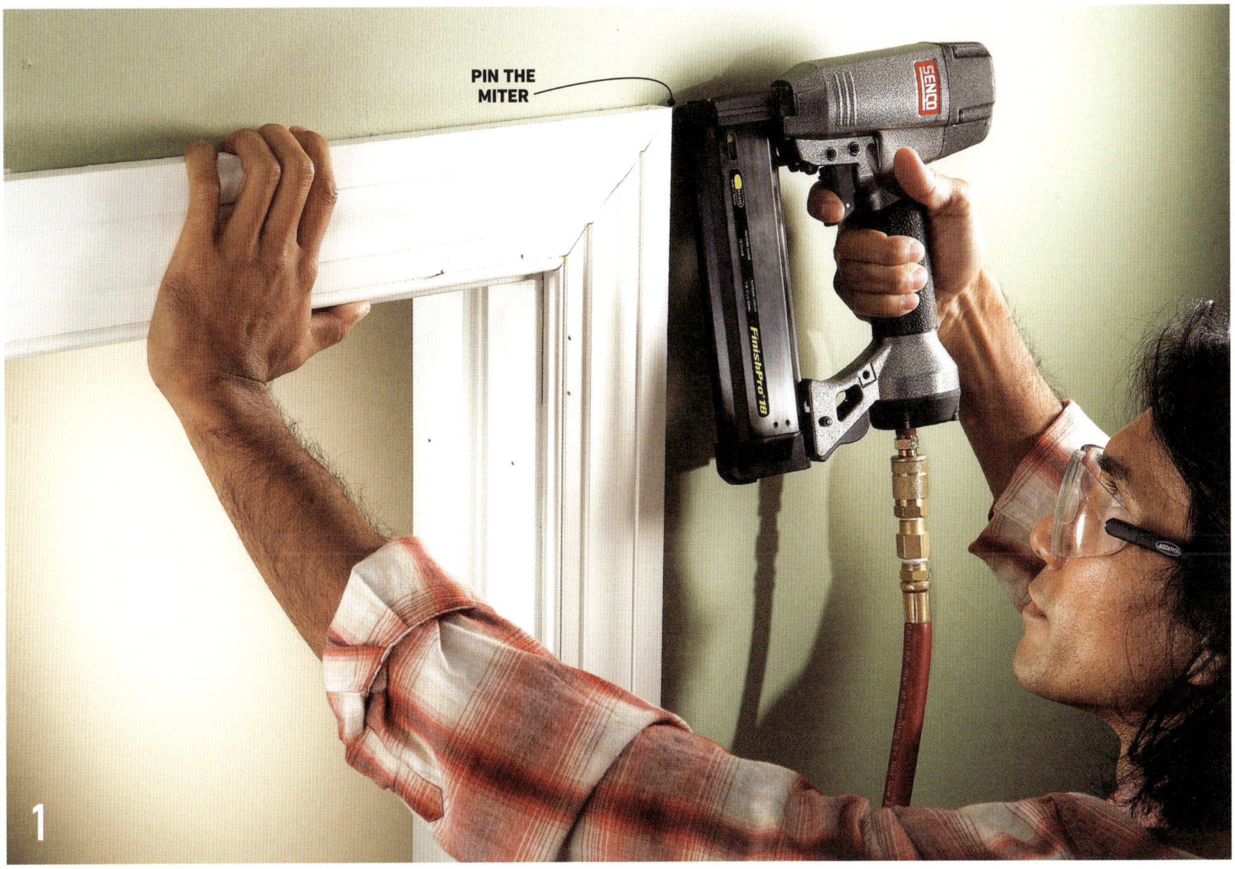

PIN THE MITER

1

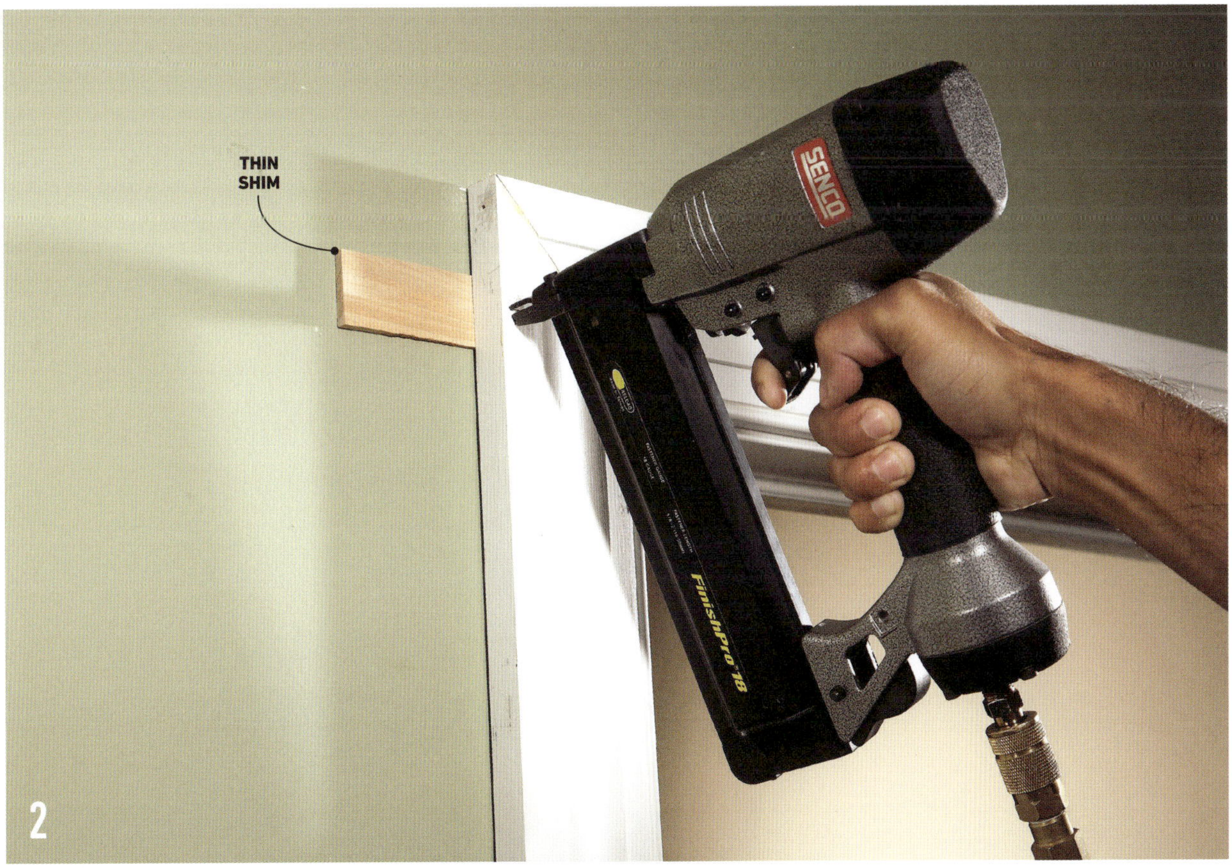

THIN SHIM

2

CHAPTER 2

Carpentry

TAB1962/GETTY IMAGES

TOOL SPOTLIGHT

11 Essential Tools for Carpenters

I've been a carpenter for 40-plus years, but the tools I use daily haven't changed much from day one. Here's a look at my must-haves.

By Gary Striegler

CHISEL

I own chisels from ¼ to 1¼ in. wide, but I carry one ¾ in. wide every day. A chisel is a cutting tool, but at times I've used mine as all sorts of things, such as a pry bar, putty knife and paint can opener. I buy middle-of-the-road quality but make sure it has a metal cap for when you need to hit the chisel with a hammer.

UTILITY KNIFE

I still like a utility knife with a retracting blade, not the folding ones. I think simpler is better, so skip the quick-change models. I use it for cutting drywall, floor paper and plastic, and shaving wood and pencil sharpening. Be sure to always buy high-quality replacement blades. By the way, it's also my go-to tool to remove tricky splinters.

VICE GRIPS

Vice grips aren't for carpentry, but I use my small vice grips to adjust and repair all sorts of carpentry tools. For everything from super quick repairs on a nail gun to getting the leverage to pry off the cap off a glue bottle, the 5-in. vice grips that I keep in my nail apron save me a lot of trips to the truck.

PRY BAR

No one is perfect, so occasionally I have to take something apart, and of course there's always demo work. Most of my work is trim carpentry, so I carry a small, flat bar all the time. The thin edge helps me remove trim with minimal damage. Some pry bars come with scrapers which work pretty well. They can also be sharpened with a belt sander or used as a putty knife too.

CLAW HAMMER

I still drive a few nails today, but mainly I use my hammer with a chisel or nail set. A hammer can also be a demolition tool or for making adjustments that take more force than a bare hands can provide. I choose a curved claw model with a steel handle. The size depends on the task, but a 16 oz. one is a good sized multipurpose hammer.

SCREWDRIVER

Sometimes I wear a lot of hats. I might install doorknobs, adjust cabinet hardware, repair a tool and set appliances all in one day. I carry a screwdriver that's a multipurpose tool. Look for sets with Phillips, slotted, star and square bits that can easily be removed and swapped out. Ones that have different sized nut drivers are also very handy. I like mine in particular because it perfectly fits one of the slots in my apron.

TAPE MEASURE

A tape measure is my most used tool. They come in lots of widths and lengths but 25 ft. long and 1 in. wide works for most jobs. I like the standard slide lock. Don't be tempted to go cheap—a rigid blade and reliable spring are important. A basic tape measure will show 16-in. centers, plus feet and inches down to ¹⁄₁₆ in. Any more information than that can just be confusing and much harder to read.

BLOCK PLANE

If you do any trim carpentry or finish work, a good block plane is a must. I use mine to fine-tune trim joints, ease sharp edges and remove saw kerfs. A good low-angle block plane will cost almost as much as all your other tools combined, but the cheap ones aren't worth unwrapping. A quality plane is worth the investment and will last a lifetime if you take care of it correctly.

DIAGONAL CUTTING PLIERS

These are a mainstay for electricians, but I use mine all the time for removing nails when something goes wrong, repairing cords or on demo work. I use them to grab a nail and work it back and forth until it breaks off, or to just cut a stubborn nail off. A good pair should be about 8 in. long. That'll allow you to get into tight spaces with plenty of leverage to spare.

BLOCK PLANE: KAKMYC/GETTY IMAGES;

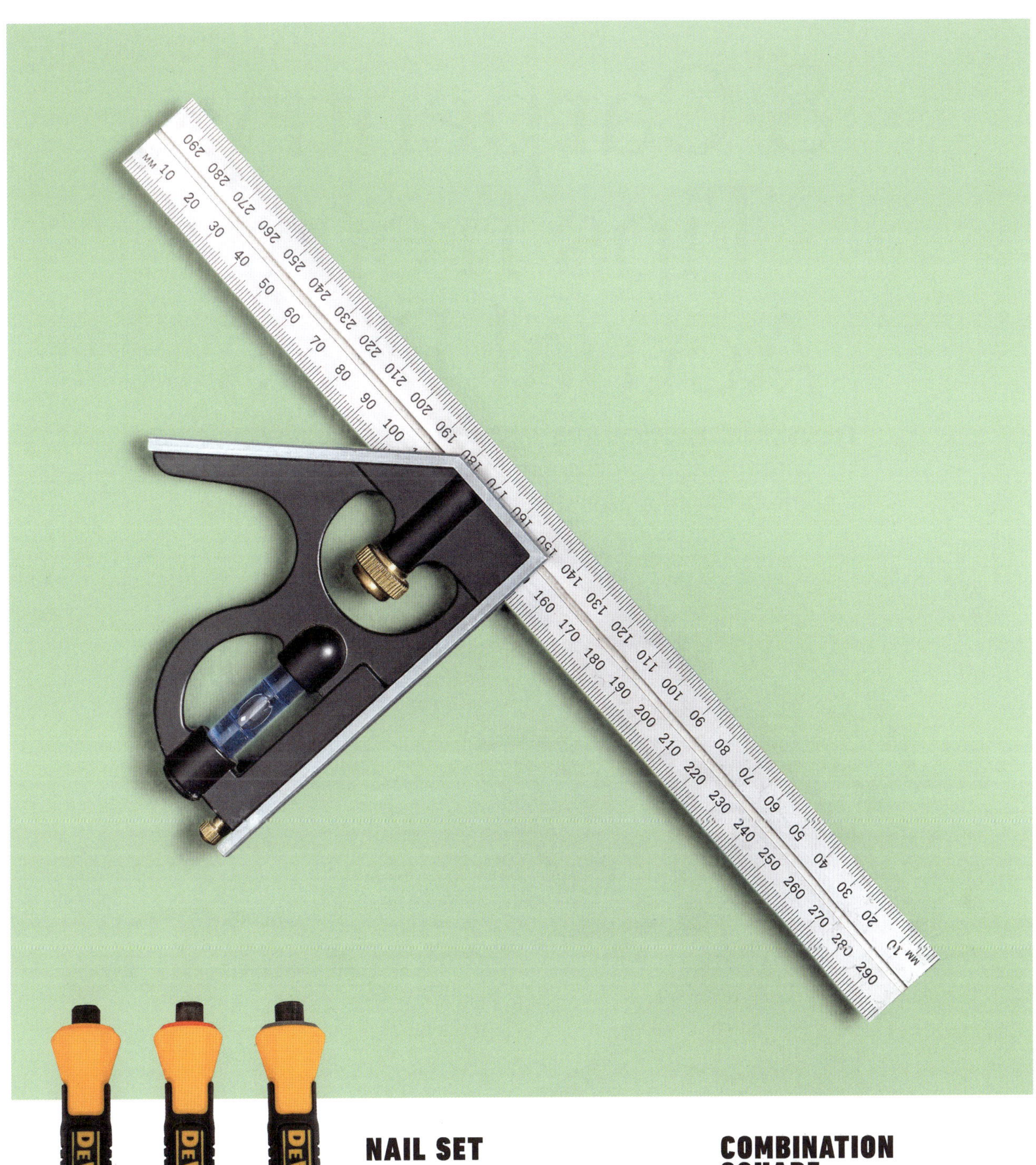

NAIL SET

You almost have to buy these in a set, but the one I carry is 3/32 in., included in the DeWalt 1/32, 2/32 and 3/32 in. Bi-material Nail Set. Everyone uses nail guns, but they aren't perfect—often you still must set a nail into the wood. I also use it to pop up hinge pins and to mark the starting point for a drill bit. I have even used mine to punch a nail through wood on demo work.

COMBINATION SQUARE

A good combination square is a multipurpose tool. It marks the most common cuts, square and 45 degrees. But since it's adjustable I also use mine as a marking and depth gauge; I always check that a saw is set up to cut square. They come in several sizes but I use one that's small enough to fit in my nail apron.

NAIL SET: VIA AMAZON

8 Carpentry Tips from Actual Pros

We asked carpentry pros who have spent years sawing through 2×4s and pounding nails to pass along some of the best tips they've learned on the job site

By Harrison Kral

2

3

TRIM GUN: PHOTOVS/GETTY IMAGES

1 USE THIS FORMULA TO ORDER FRAMING MATERIALS

You don't need a math degree to estimate framing materials for walls. Here's a formula that works every time, no matter how many doors, windows or corners your walls have:

- One stud per linear foot of the walls.
- Five linear feet of plate material (bottoms, tops and ties) per linear foot of wall.

It will look like too much lumber when it arrives, but you'll need the extra stuff for corners, blocking, braces and frames for windows and doors. Set aside any crooked material for short pieces.

2 PRACTICE ON TEST PIECES FOR THE PERFECT MITER

Fine-tuning a miter for a perfect fit is often a trial-and-error process. Practice on smaller test pieces and work on eliminating imperfections until you get your miter saw set to exactly the right angle, then cut the actual parts.

3 BUY A TRIM GUN

Many carpenters likely haven't hand-nailed a piece of interior trim in 25 years. Why? Because air-powered trim guns make the results so much faster, better and neater. No splits, no predrilling, no knocking the piece out of place as you hammer, and only small, barely noticeable holes to fill. If you're going to buy just one size, the most versatile choice is the one that shoots ⅝-to-2-in. 18-gauge brads.

4

5

4 MARK, DON'T MEASURE

Holding trim in place and marking it is more accurate than measuring, and is often faster and eliminates mistakes. This is good advice for other types of carpentry work too, such as installing siding, laying shingles and even framing.

5 WRITE MEASUREMENTS DOWN

Stick masking tape to your tape measure or sand down the side for a convenient "notepad" perfect for jotting down shapes and numbers. That way you won't forget your measurement on the way to the saw.

6 USE THE TOENAIL TRICK TO POSITION LUMBER

Travis Larson, a woodworker and carpenter, shares a handy timesaver:

"On my first job as a framing carpenter, I was beating on a stud to try to coax it into position. The stud just bounced back. A veteran framing carpenter walked over and drove a big nail at an angle through the edge of the stud. The last two blows moved the stud into position, where it stayed. Now I use the toenail trick when I need to adjust stubborn lumber."

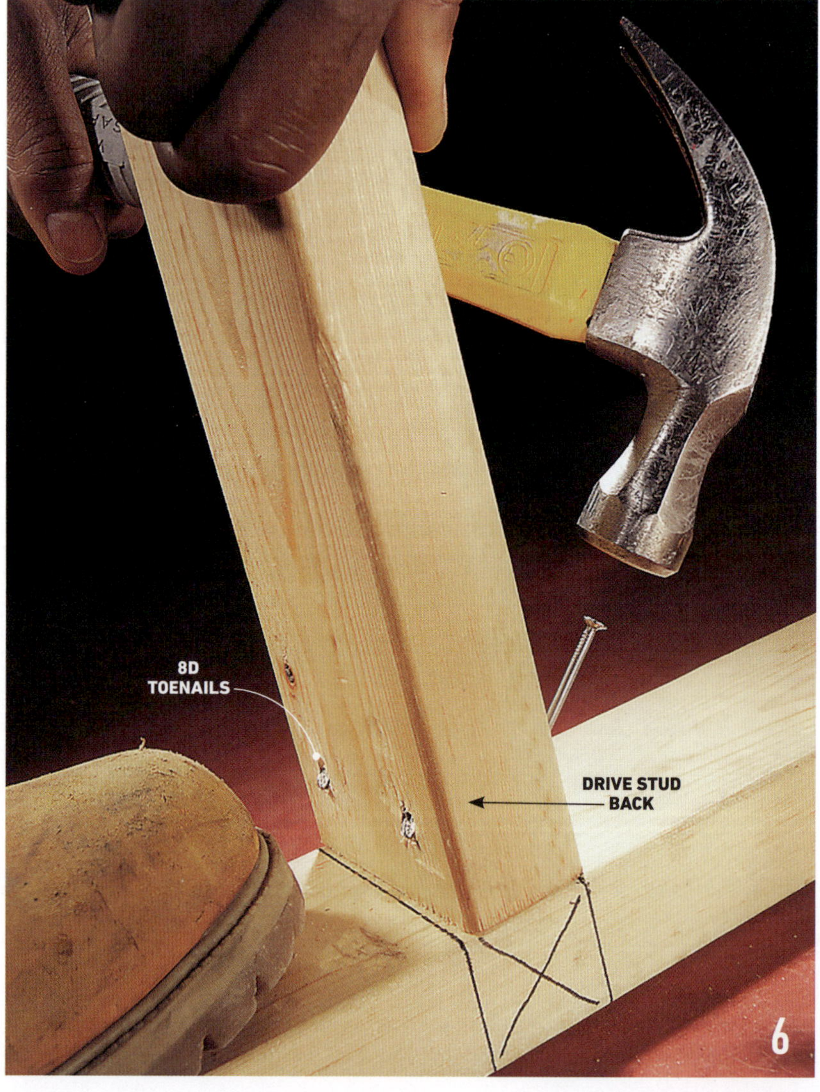

6

7 ALWAYS CARRY A MULTIPURPOSE HAMMER

Whether you're doing rough construction or fine finish work, the best all-around hammer is a smooth-faced 20-oz. hammer with a straight claw. You can use the claw to drive under walls for easier lifting, embed it in framing, and even to do extremely crude chiseling. But best of all, it's a better shape for pulling nails than the curved claw style.

8 USE NIPPERS TO PULL NAILS

Keep a pair of "nippers" in your pouch whenever you're doing trim carpentry or removing trim from a wall. When you pull the trim, use them for pulling the nails through the back of the trim.

How to Drill into a Stud

How much wood are you allowed to cut out of a stud?

By Rebecca Wright Brown

Two benefits come with building or remodeling with wood studs. The studs provide the strength and framework for the structure, and the empty spaces between the studs serve an important function too: If you know how to drill into a stud safely, they provide a veritable vertical freeway to run pipes, vents, drains, wires and ductwork.

The drawback? When you have to run pipes, ducts or wires horizontally, you often have to notch or drill holes—sometimes big ones—into a stud to get them to their destination. But you can't just drill and saw away. There are rules you have to follow for drilling and notching studs. Some rules help ensure the structural integrity of a wall. Others are aimed at protecting the pipes and wires that could be damaged by screws, nails and other fasteners driven into a wall.

NOTCHING AND BORING STUDS

There are lots of building codes dictating just how large a hole or notch you can cut, and building codes allow you to drill bigger holes and cut bigger notches in non-load-bearing walls than in load-bearing walls. The technical yet important rules are:

- Holes in bearing wall studs (exterior and interior walls that bear the weight of the roof and/or other stories) must not exceed 40% of the stud width.
- Notches in bearing wall studs may not exceed 25% of the stud's width.
- Holes in the non-bearing walls can't exceed 60% of their width.
- Notches in non-bearing walls can't exceed 40% of their width.
- The edge of a hole must be at least ⅝ in. from the edge of a stud.

To appease the plumbing gods, building codes have made at least one notable exception. In bearing walls, you can bore 60% size holes as long as you double up the studs and don't drill into more than two successive pairs of the doubled-up studs. This allows you to run a short section of "drain, waste,

POWEROFFOREVER/GETTY IMAGES

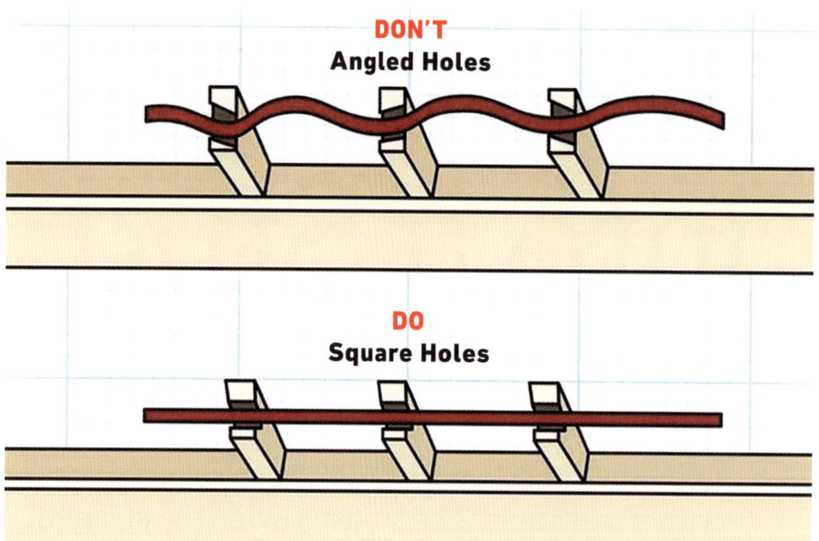

vent" (DWV) pipe through any 2×4 wall without beefing up the whole wall to 2×6 dimensions.

There are other, less specific guidelines:

- When possible, notch a stud near the top, rather than at the bottom.
- Don't locate holes and notches near large or loose knots.
- Don't group too many in the same area of the stud.
- Finally, notch only when necessary; holes weaken the wood less than notches.

In areas with high winds, earthquakes or tornadoes, wall strength is even more important. Studs with too much "meat" removed tend to bow and warp. Your building inspector will be on the lookout for overzealous notching and boring, so follow the rules.

In reality, few walls ever just collapse during everyday duty from being riddled with too many holes and notches. But there are many cases in which unprotected or inadequately protected pipes and wires have been nicked and punctured by screws and nails. That's what you should watch for.

PROTECT WIRES AND PIPES

The National Electrical Code requires holes with nonmetallic cable (often called Romex) or flexible metal-clad cable (the type with the wires already in it) be set back 1¼ in. or more from the edge of a stud to protect the wires from nails and screws. The 1¼-in. screws and nails used to secure ½-in. drywall penetrate the studs about ¾ in.

Most electricians keep their inspector happy by drilling ¾-in. holes dead center on a 3½ in. wide stud. This gives them a hole large enough to run two electrical cables and leave 1⅜ in. of the protective wood on each side. If they need to run more wires, they'll drill more holes directly above the others. If a hole comes any closer than 1¼ in., your inspector will make you install a ¹⁄₁₆ -in. thick protective metal plate to be safe.

Mechanical codes for heating, ventilation and cooling (HVAC) and plumbing systems also dictate that holes containing pipes be set back 1¼ in. from the edge of a stud to protect the pipes from fasteners. Those that come closer need to be covered by metal plates; for big pipes, use a long protective plate.

Note: Building codes vary by state and can change over time. Check in with local regulations before starting a major project.

TIPS FOR LESS DRILLING

Electricians and plumbers spend lots of time drilling big holes, so they know a few tricks to make the job easier.

1. Before beginning a project, plot out where large pipes and ducts will run and determine how you'll get them there.
2. Wherever possible, run large pipes and ducts vertically into unfinished attics or basements. Then, install elbows and run the pipe or duct horizontally below the floor joists or above the ceiling joists.
3. Build 2×6 stud walls where DWV pipes and holes exceed the limits described above.
4. Rent a right-angle drill and use Selfeed or hole saw bits for boring large holes. The right angle drill allows you to drill holes square to the stud face. Holes drilled at an angle will wind up oval.
5. Keep the holes centered on the studs and a consistent height off the floor.
6. Drill holes into a stud at least ¼ in. larger, especially for hot water pipes. If you don't, they'll make annoying creaking sounds as they expand, contract and rub along studs.
7. Joist hanger manufacturers sell wrap-around reinforcer plates. Ask your inspector if they are permissible in special situations.
8. When boring electrical holes, keep them square to the stud for easier wire installation or pulling. It may seem trivial, but angled holes "catch" the wire and keep you from pulling wire through more than two or three studs at a time. Holes in a straight line let you pull wire through an entire wall length of studs at once time.

ILLUSTRATION BY FAMILY HANDYMAN

18 Tips to Be a Wall Framing Hero

What you need to know to build your structure straight, strong and fast

By Jeff Gorton and Mark Peterson

THE BASICS

Wall framing always looks simple and straightforward, but a mistake here, such as a wall that's too short or a window opening slightly too small, wastes lots of time and effort later. We'll show you simple techniques designed to ensure accurate results. Keep in mind, though, that carpentry practices and jargon vary from region to region—and even from one carpenter to the next. So don't be surprised if some of the labels and marks we show aren't exactly what you'd encounter on a local building project. The basic concepts are the same, and with this information your next framing project should go smoothly and error free.

1 SNAP LINES AND SET THE PLATES IN PLACE

Eliminate mistakes by chalking a full-size map of your walls directly on the floor. First mark the inside edge of the wall at each corner and snap chalk lines. Mark the location of interior walls as well and snap chalk lines on both sides of interior wall locations to ensure correct plate positions. Double-check all of your layout lines to make sure the walls are parallel, the corners are at right angles and the dimensions match the plans. Then measure and cut a top and bottom plate for each wall as shown. Double-check lengths by setting the plates in their exact position on the chalk lines.

2 MARK WINDOWS AND DOORS FIRST, THEN LAY OUT THE STUDS

Find the center of each window and door opening. Then divide the "rough opening" (given on your plan or in the window literature) by two and measure left and right of the center mark. Write a "T" to the outside of both marks to indicate trimmer locations. Measure over 1½ in. and draw another line. Mark an "X" outside these marks for the full-height king studs.

With the openings marked, lay out the stud locations **(bottom photo)**. The goal is to position your studs every 16 or 24 in. so that the edges of 4×8 sheets of plywood align with the centers of studs. Subtract ¾ in. from the first layout mark. Then hook your tape on a partially driven nail at this mark, and mark at each 16- or 24-in. multiple. Make an "X" on the same side of each layout mark to indicate the stud position. Mark studs that land between the window or door trimmers with a "C" to indicate cripples rather than full-height wall studs.

2
EDGE OF ROUGH OPENING
CENTER OF OPENING
OPPOSITE EDGE OF ROUGH OPENING

15¼"
16" MARK
EDGE OF FIRST STUD
32" MARK
KING STUD MARK
TRIMMER MARK

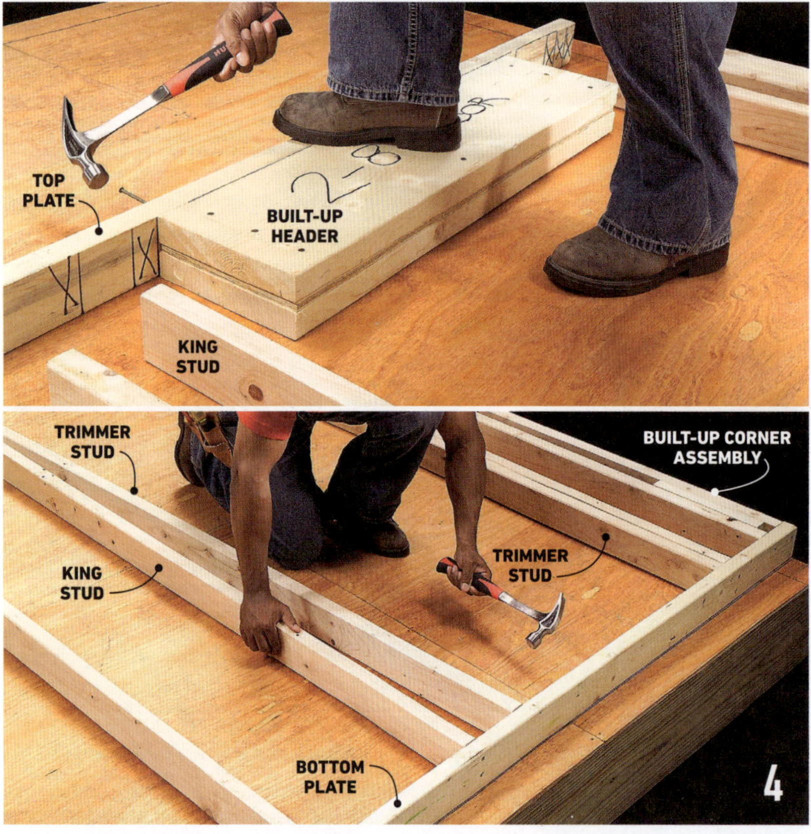

3 TRANSFER THE LAYOUT MARKS TO THE BOTTOM PLATE

Set the plates side by side and transfer the marks from the top plate to the bottom plate using a square. Some carpenters mark only the edge of the plates. We show marking the wide face, which will help you align twisted studs. Tack the pairs of plates together with 8d nails after marking them so they don't get separated and mixed with other plates. Then set them aside until you're ready to build that wall.

4 NAIL FULL-HEIGHT HEADERS TO THE TOP PLATE

Calculate the header lengths by adding 3 in. to the rough opening width. Also add 6 in. to headers that require two trimmers on each side. Cut the header parts and nail them together. Label the headers.

In many plans, headers are positioned against the top plate. If yours are, begin wall assembly by positioning and nailing these "full-height" headers to the top plate with 16d nails **(left, middle photo)**. Then lay full-length studs between the plates and nail king studs to the headers and to the top and bottom plates **(bottom left photo)**. Nail in each of the full-height studs as well as corner assemblies. Note: Sight down each stud before you nail it in and orient any bow (crown) upward. Next, install all the trimmers **(bottom left)**.

5 ADD CRIPPLES ABOVE HEADERS AND UNDER SILLS

In wall plans that have openings with cripples above the header, cut and nail together the king studs and trimmers first. When you're done, position and nail them to the plates. Set the header on the trimmers and nail through the king studs to hold it in place. Measure and nail the cripples into place **(top right photo)**. You have to toenail the bottom of the cripples to the header.

Window openings are just like doors but with the addition of a rough sill. Mark the top of the sill by measuring down from your header. You should use the rough opening height for this dimension. Cut the lower cripples and place one under each end of the sill as a temporary support while you toenail the sill to the trimmers with a pair of 8d nails at each end. Align the cripples with the layout marks and nail through the sill and bottom plate to hold them in place. Use pairs of 16d nails. Know that some carpenters like to double the rough sill, especially on openings wider than about 3 ft. If that's the way you prefer to do it, remember to allow for the thickness of a double sill when you are cutting out your cripples.

TIMESAVING TIPS

Here are some great framing tricks after you nail the basics. They'll make life easier for everyone who follows you. You'll be a rock star in the eyes of the general contractor, electrician, plumber and especially the drywall crew, long after you're done.

6 NAIL THE TIE PLATE OVER STUDS

Do a favor for the electricians, mechanical guys and plumbers by nailing the tie plate to the top plate over the studs only. That way they'll never encounter nails when drilling or cutting holes.

7 SNAP LONG LINES HALF AT A TIME

Keep long lines straight by having a helper in the middle hold down the line with a finger. Take the time to snap each of the sides separately.

8 ROUNDED VS. SQUARE LUMBER

Ask for square-edge lumber instead of rounded if you can. Here's why:

- Tape measures grab and hold onto the wood better.
- More accurate measuring.
- You have better sight lines for crowning.
- Easier to line up to pencil marks and chalk lines.
- Final product looks much more professional.

9 SLOPE WINDOWSILLS WITH A PIECE OF SIDING

Even if you're doing your best to follow best practices for proper waterproofing, water can still find its way onto the wrong side of a window. It's a good idea to slope the sill in the rough opening to help unwanted water find its way back out.

You could slope the sill itself, which requires cutting all the cripples at a slight angle and causes the sill to protrude a bit on each side. Instead, rip down and install a tapered piece of lap siding. Make sure to frame the rough openings a little larger to account for the width of the siding. And, of course, cover it with flexible flashing before installing the window.

10 HANDY FRAMING TOOL

This V-Line Clamp is the perfect tool for snapping lines on plywood—especially angled ones when the chalk line hook won't hold its place. Just clamp it to the mark on the edge of the plywood and hook it on the end of the chalk line. It even works on super-sharp angles.

11 USE WANED WOOD WISELY

"Wane" refers to the edges of lumber that are partially bark or missing altogether. When you're sistering waned boards together, have those edges facing in. Also avoid using the waned areas on outside or inside corners for walls because you'll be missing important nailing surfaces for drywall, corner bead and trim.

12 A BETTER WAY TO INSTALL CEILING BACKERS

Here is the best way to both anchor and provide ceiling drywall backers for walls that run parallel to trusses or joists.

Run 2×4 blocking between the trusses 1½ in. above the bottom of the truss. Then center and install a 2×8 backer where the top of the wall will be built. When you do build the walls, there will be plenty of wood on either side of the 2×8 for anchoring drywall, and you can be confident the drywall will stay in plane with the rest of the trusses.

Another benefit is that you can install a continuous moisture barrier across the backing before installing the wall with no cuts and no taping.

13 OFFSET THE BLOCKS

When you're installing fire blocking on a wall, it's tempting to snap a line and keep all the blocks on one plane. But don't do it. Blocks are easier to install if you stagger them as shown because you can fire the nails almost straight into the ends instead of angling them. If you think a straight line of blocks looks nicer (for the short time they're visible), think again. Blocks will rarely be installed perfectly straight, but a staggered line tricks the eye and looks more uniform. If you're covering seams in the sheathing, then install the blocks in a straight line.

14 BUY PRO MARKERS

If you're a pro, you probably buy professional-grade tools. Markers should be no exception. Professional-grade markers last much longer than standard ones.

14

LEVER BOARD
ANCHOR BLOCKS
BRACE
NAIL
LEVER BLOCK
15

16
DAP
Silicone
CAULK

15 STRAIGHTENING WALLS

Here are the most common methods for straightening walls:

1. Attach a long 2-by brace to a stud near the top of the wall.
2. Nail two anchor blocks to the floor framing at the end of the brace. Add two more lever blocks a couple of feet in from the anchor blocks.
3. Fasten the lever board to the brace with a few closely spaced nails.
4. Have someone sight the wall top plates for straightness while you lever the wall until it's straight.
5. Hold it in position and nail the end of the brace to the anchor blocks.

16 AVOID SQUEAKS

Many floor squeaks are caused by joists slightly rubbing against joist hangers. Even perfectly installed joist hangers can develop squeaks over time. Completely eliminate the possibility by adding a bead of silicone caulk to the inside edges and the bottom of the hanger before dropping in the joist.

17 LAY DOWN A MULCH PATH

A mulch path near door entrances on muddy job sites helps keep the mud out of the house. Buy the cheapest mulch or wood chips you can find. It can all get graded into the yard when the project is done. Be sure to buy several extra bags to freshen up the path once in a while.

18 DON'T FORGET THE BACKERS

Before you leave the job, run around and install backers for handrails, bathroom grab bars and other hardware. Take photos and send them to the job supervisor. This will ensure that everyone is on the same page and earn you a few bonus points with the boss.

17

18

Seal Windows and Doors to Stop Drafts

Five simple steps to keep your home comfortable and energy bill low

By Gary Wentz

If your windows or doors are a source of chilly drafts all winter long, the problem could be worn-out seals, weatherstripping or thresholds. Then again, sloppy installation might be to blame. When cold weather arrives, hold the back of your hand near the edges of windows or doors to track down the source of leaks. If you feel cold air flowing out from behind the trim, chances are the spaces around the window and door jambs weren't properly sealed.

1 CUT THROUGH PAINT
Slice through paint where the trim meets the wall and jamb. Put a new blade in your utility knife and make several passes over heavy paint buildup.

2 POP OFF TRIM
Pry away the trim gently with a flat pry bar. Be sure to protect walls with a shim or a scrap of wood as you gradually work the trim away from the wall.

Plugging these leaks is a job that takes time: You have to pull off the interior trim, seal around the jambs and then reinstall the trim. But if your doors and windows are otherwise fairly airtight, the payoff can be big too. Stopping drafts not only makes your home more comfortable but also cuts energy bills, as air leaks are a major source of heat loss in most homes.

First investigate further: Remove one piece of trim from a window or a door. To prevent chipping or tearing paint, cut through the paint first **(Photo 1)**.

Caution: Lead paint chips are hazardous. If your home was built before 1978, call your local health department for info on testing chips and handling lead paint safely.

Slip a stiff putty knife under the trim and lift it just enough to insert a flat pry bar. Don't simply force up one end of the piece. Instead, work along the length of the piece, moving your pry bar and lifting the trim off gradually **(Photo 2)**. At mitered corners, watch for nails driven through the joint. To prevent these nails from splitting mitered ends, pry up both mitered pieces together. Then pull them apart. When you're removing nails from the trim, pull them through the back side to avoid damaging the face of the trim **(Photo 3)**.

With the first piece of trim removed, examine the space between the jamb and the wall framing. If the drywall covers the space, trim it back with a utility knife. If you see only a few loose wads of fiberglass insulation or no insulation at all between the jamb and framing, it's likely that all your windows and doors are poorly sealed.

To seal the gap, remove the remaining trim and inject foam sealant **(Photo 4)**. Some sealants will push jambs inward as they expand, so be sure to use one that's intended for windows and doors (check the label). We chose DAPtex Plus because it's easy to clean up with a damp rag. Most expanding foams are nearly impossible to clean up before they harden.

Let the foam harden and trim off any excess foam with a knife before you reinstall the trim. Position each piece exactly as it was originally and tack each one up with only two nails **(Photo 5)**. When all the pieces are in place, check their fit. With only a couple of nails in each piece, you can make a few small adjustments by holding a block against the trim and tapping it with a hammer. Then add more nails.

If your trim has a clear finish, fill the nail holes with a matching colored filler such as Color Putty or DAP Finishing Putty. With painted trim, it's best to fill the holes with regular spackle and then repaint.

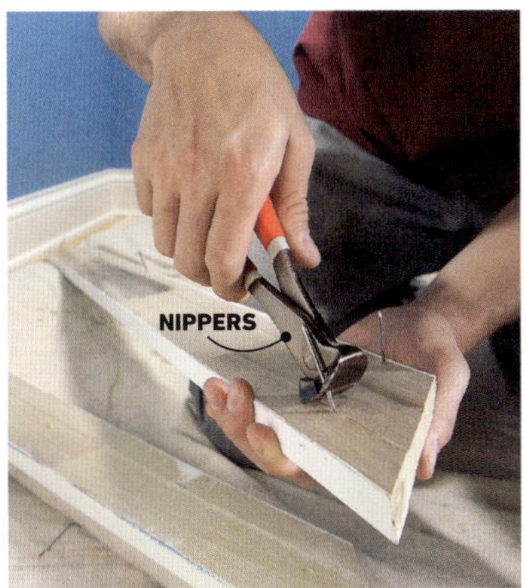

3 REMOVE OLD NAILS Pull nails out through the back side of trim with a nippers or a pliers. Also write the location of each piece of trim on the back side.

4 SEAL WITH FOAM Pull insulation from between the jamb and the wall framing. Seal the gap around the jamb with foam sealant.

5 REINSTALL WOODWORK Tack each section of trim exactly in its original position with a couple of nails. Ridges in the wall paint can help you align each piece perfectly. Make sure the parts fit together tightly at the corners before you add more nails.

Caulk Smarter

The best tips for a smooth, mess-free seal every time

By Family Handyman Staff

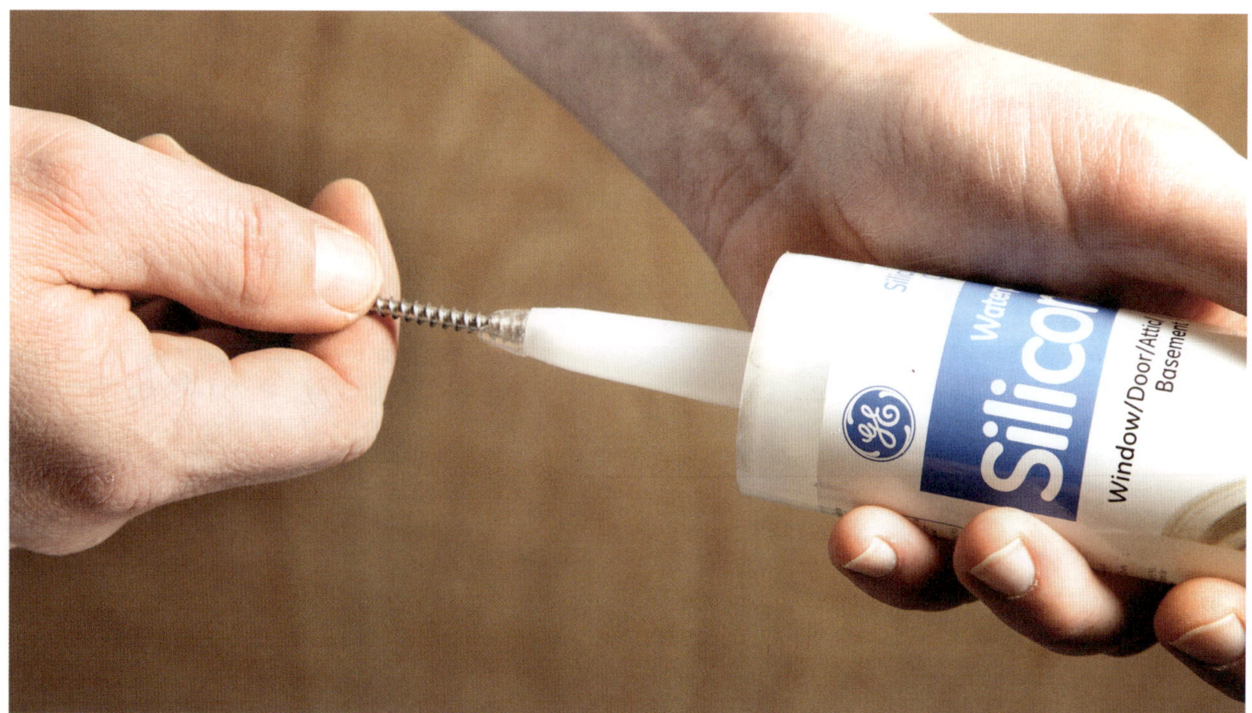

CLEAN THE SPOUT WITH A SCREW

It seems you can never seal the cut tip of a partial tube well enough. Sometimes a plug will form in the tip. Try using a large screw with aggressive threads to remove the plug. This tip works best with silicone products.

CHOOSE THE CORRECT CAULK FOR THE JOB

The selection in the caulk aisle at home centers is mind-boggling, but actually choosing the right one is pretty simple. Most of the caulk on store shelves is basically one of four types: elastomeric, polyurethane, latex or silicone. Here is when to use which type.

- **Siding, windows and doors:** Polyurethane is best. It can be painted. It doesn't shrink. It stays flexible. It adheres better than silicone, and it doesn't attract dust and dirt the way silicone does.
- **Roofing:** Use an elastomeric or rubberized product. This stuff won't dry out in extreme conditions, and it sticks to just about everything.
- **Interior trim:** Use latex if you're sealing gaps and nail holes in trim that are going to be painted. It cleans up easily and dries fast. It's also easy to tool—and cheap.
- **Kitchen and bath:** This is where silicone products shine. Silicone tools well. It can be purchased with antimicrobial additives, and can be easily removed and replaced when it gets grungy.

TAPE BEFORE CAULKING

Apply painter's tape to control your caulk lines. Apply the caulk, smooth the joint with your finger and immediately remove the tape.

CHOOSE THE RIGHT CAULK GUN

The most expensive caulk gun on the rack isn't necessarily the best. Look for a gun with a cradle. Tubes seem to fall out of the guns with the rails. Choose guns with ratchet action rather than friction action and don't consider a gun that doesn't have a hook. Forget about gun-mounted tube cutters—use a utility knife. And if all other things are equal, buy the gun with the longer tube poker. Some aren't long enough to work on every kind of tube.

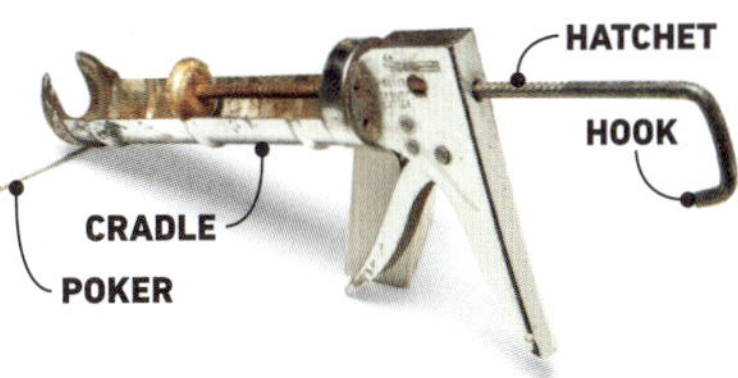

CUT TIPS OFF STRAIGHT

You probably learned to cut the tip at an angle. That works OK in some situations, but an angled tip limits the position the caulking gun has to be in. With a straight tip, you can swivel the gun out of the way of obstacles and caulk right up to an inside corner. And if you have various-size gaps to fill, cut the tip small and do the small gaps first, then cut it bigger for the larger gaps.

DON'T USE YOUR WRISTS

Every golfer knows that the best way to keep a putter moving in a straight line and at a consistent speed is to control it with the upper body. It's the same concept with caulking. Use your upper body, or even your legs, to move the tube along the seam. Avoid using your wrists.

SALVAGE A WET TUBE

The new guy left the case of caulking out in the rain again (it's always the new guy). Those soggy tubes are now going to split open under pressure. Before that happens, wrap some duct tape around the tube. You can also salvage tubes with house wrap tape, masking tape, stretch wrap, shipping tape—it all works. Just use whatever is handy.

AVOID GLOBS ON LONG RUNS

When you have a long bead to run and you can't get it done in one shot, don't start again where you left off. Instead, start at the other end and meet in the middle. It's hard to continue a bead once you've stopped without creating a glob. Also try to keep the meeting place somewhere other than eye level.

FAST CAULKING

A common mistake is to cut off too much of the caulk tube tip, leaving a hole that's way too big for most interior caulking work. When you're filling small cracks to prepare for painting, cut the tip carefully to keep the hole tiny—about $^{1}/_{16}$ in. dia. The tiny hole lets out just enough caulk to fill typical small-to-medium-size cracks. For larger cracks, make a second pass or keep a second caulk gun on hand, loaded with a tube that has a slightly bigger hole. Keep the caulk gun moving quickly along the crack as you squeeze the trigger. This, combined with the small opening in the tip, will give you a nice caulk joint that needs very little cleanup. A quick swipe with a dampened fingertip will leave a paint-ready joint.

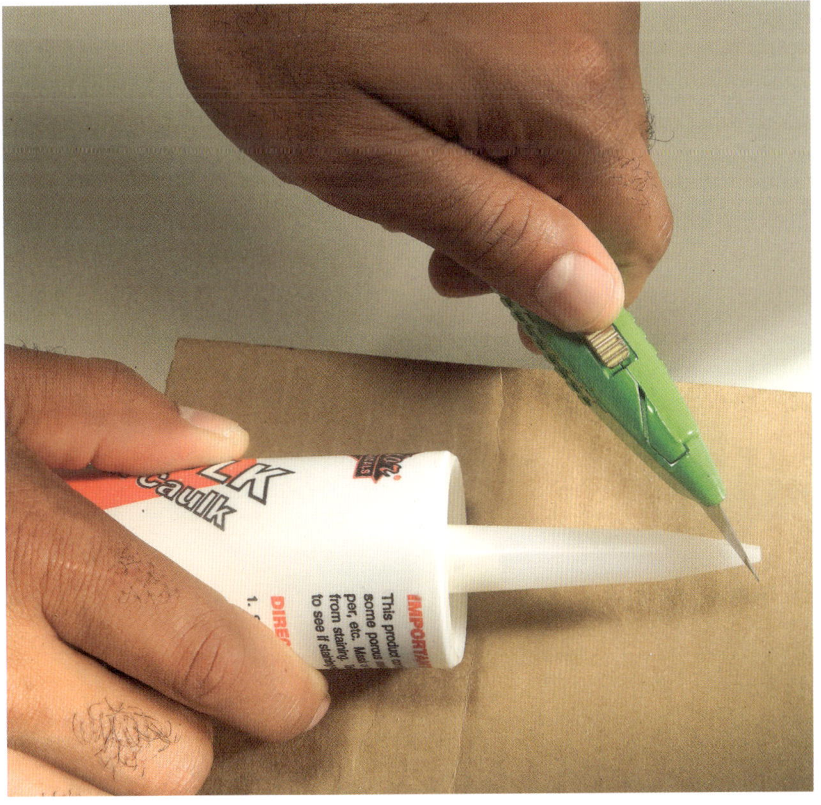

PUSH THE CAULK, DON'T PULL

Try to push the caulk into the gap rather than drag it over it. This greatly increases the odds the caulk will adhere to both surfaces because it forces caulk into the gap—pulling doesn't. One exception to this rule is when both surfaces are flush. When caulking flush surfaces, if you try to push the tip too hard, it will skate all over the place, and you'll have a big mess on your hands.

REUSABLE CAULK TUBE

How often do you have dry caulk stuck in the tip of the tube but know that there's a lot of fresh stuff behind it? Get to the unused bit by first cutting two slits along the tube, on opposite sides, with a sharp utility knife. Pry out the dried plug of caulk. Then wrap the tip with duct tape, put the tube back in the gun and use up that caulk.

DISGUISING CAULK ON CONCRETE

If you're caulking concrete, either to fill a crack or to seal it around the edge, you can make the caulk almost invisible. Simply dust the caulk with dry concrete mix while it's still wet. When the caulk is finally dry, brush away the excess, and the caulk will virtually disappear.

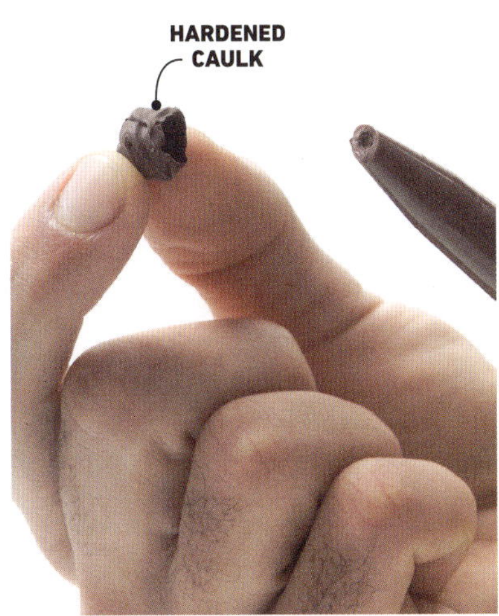

SEAL CAULK SPOUT

With a little ingenuity, every tube of caulk contains its own spout sealer. Force enough caulk out of the tube to form a peanut-sized ball. Then wet your finger and shape the ball to form a cap. The cap will slowly harden and keep the caulk inside soft for weeks.

RIDE THE TIP ON THE SMOOTH SURFACE

When one of the surfaces you are caulking is rougher than the other, try to ride the tip on your smoother surface (the brick mold in this case). If you ride the middle or the rough surface (siding), the caulking duplicates the bumps, sometimes in an exaggerated way.

CAULK WITH A STRAW

When you need to caulk in a spot that's too tight for a caulk gun, try this: Cut a sharp angle on the end of a plastic straw, just as you'd cut the spout of a caulk tube. Then, fill the straw with caulk using a caulk gun. Fold over one end of the straw and squeeze caulk out the other end. You can lay a bead of caulk in cramped quarters this way, but it's hard to squeeze out a consistent, even bead. So keep a damp rag handy and plan to smooth the bead with your finger.

SKILLS IN PRACTICE

A New Window in One Day

It can be intimidating, but replacing a window may be easier and faster than you think

By Mike Berner

The kitchen in our new house featured a garden window that was stealing useful cabinet and countertop space. We didn't like its exterior look either, and ultimately my wife, Steph, decided to take the lead on replacing it. Doing it herself saved us about $1,200, and with my help she got it done in a day. At first she thought she was biting off more than she could chew, but she quickly realized that—like many other carpentry jobs—window replacement is just a matter of following simple steps. Here's how to do it:

WHERE TO START

Before you can go shopping for a new window, you need to know the size of the "rough opening," which is the framed opening the window jamb sits inside. So your first step is to remove the window's trim on the inside of the house and measure.

You could certainly take those measurements and order a new custom window that perfectly fits inside the existing window jamb. But we went with a simple stock window, one that was available on a shelf at the home center.

With a stock window, we were limited by size and style options, but for us, that wasn't a problem. We wanted a smaller window for space to install more countertops and cabinets when we remodel the kitchen. There's some extra work involved in adjusting the opening, but we took this path for a few reasons.

- **Save Money:** We found a quality window for a few hundred dollars. A similar custom-sized window would have cost us twice as much.
- **Save Time:** The last time I ordered custom-sized windows, it took six weeks to get my hands on them. We chose our window, took it home and got to work, all on the same day.

What It Takes

TIME	COST	SKILL LEVEL
1 day	$350	Intermediate

TOOLS
Standard carpentry tools, circular saw, miter saw, drill/driver, J-roller

MATERIALS
Window, sheathing, Z-flashing, nails, caulk, cedar lap siding, flashing tape, flexible flashing tape, shims, tar paper, 2x4s, coated construction screws, roofing nails

1 REMOVE THE TRIM

Cut the caulk around the trim and the window. Pry the existing trim away from the window and siding. Remove the trim from the inside of the house as well.

2 PULL OUT THE OLD WINDOW

Remove the screws or nails that are holding the window in the opening. If the window still doesn't budge, there may be foam, more caulk or hidden screws keeping it in place. If you need to, work a reciprocating saw blade between the window and the framing and cut around the window, then wiggle the it out of the opening.

3 FRAME THE NEW ROUGH OPENING

The new rough opening needs to be 1 in. wider and 1 in. taller than the new window. That allows space for leveling the window and insulating around it. We first raised and leveled the sill and added cripple studs. Then we added trimmer studs to make the rough opening the size we needed. Make sure the trimmers are plumb and there's enough blocking for sheathing.

4 PATCH IN THE SHEATHING

Cover the framing with exterior-rated plywood or OSB. Our job required only a 2 x 4-ft.

sheet of ¾-in. CDX plywood. Steph cut it to size and screwed it into the framing with 2-in. coated screws. Then she capped the sill by nailing on a piece of cedar siding **(Photo 5)**, giving it an outward slope. If any water gets in, the slope will send it back out.

5 TUCK IN TAR PAPER

We used tar paper as the water-resistant barrier (WRB). Newer houses might have house wrap material, which will work the same way. Start at the bottom and overlap the existing WRB. Then cover the sides, followed by the top, always overlapping the previous layer and tucking extra WRB underneath the siding as best you can.

6 FORM THE WINDOW PAN

The window pan is there to protect wood from any water that might enter around the window. Cut flexible flashing tape 12 in. wider than the window opening, peel off the backing and lay the tape on the sill without stretching it. Starting from the middle, press the tape into all corners then up the sides. Fold it over the sill and stretch the tape around the corner. Many window installers don't cover the side or top corners with flashing tape, but I always add the extra layer of protection. I wrap 4-in.-wide flashing tape over the side corners, then the top. When all the tape is on, roll over it with a J-roller.

7 APPLY SEALANT TO THE WINDOW

To make the connection watertight, apply a continuous bead of sealant along the side and top flanges. Be sure the bead goes right over the nail holes; penetrations through the tape must be sealed well. Don't seal the bottom flange; if water gets in, it must have a way out.

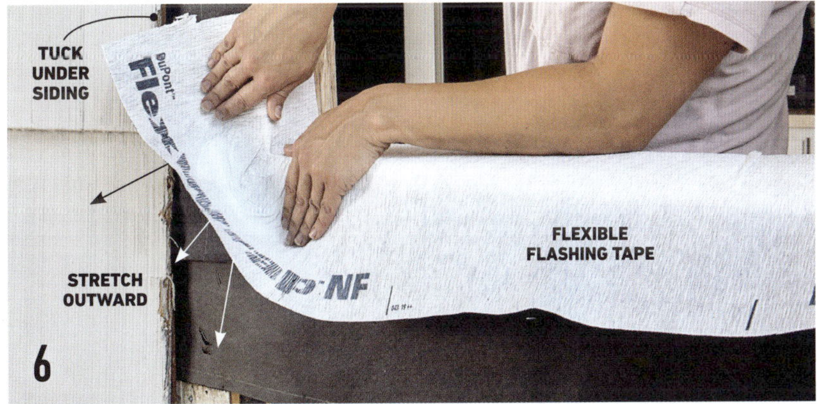

8 PLACE THE WINDOW

Rest the bottom of the window on the sill, then tilt it up and into place. You'll need a helper waiting inside to center the window. Next, the helper will raise the window with a few shims and adjust them to make sure the bottom of the window is completely level. When it's level and centered, drive a nail in the very bottom hole on each side flange.

9 PLUMB AND SQUARE THE WINDOW

Hold the window in place with a few sets of shims on both sides of the window, a pair that holds the top and one toward the bottom. Adjust the shims so the sides of the window are plumb. Once the bottom is level and the sides are plumb, drive a nail into the top hole of each side flange. The real test is how the window operates; don't nail it off until you're sure it operates smoothly.

10 NAIL THE FLANGE

When you've centered the window and it's level and plumb and operates smoothly, drive nails in all the holes on the top and sides. Don't nail the bottom flange. Then install the drip cap that came with the window.

11 COVER NAIL PENETRATIONS

As an added measure against water intrusion, cover nails in the flange with flashing tape. Start with the sides and extend the tape a few inches past the bottom nail flange. Then cover the top flange, making sure it overlaps the tape covering the sides.

12 INSTALL Z-FLASHING AND TRIM

Install Z-flashing above the top piece of trim. It should be cut to the same length and tucked under the water-resistant barrier (tar paper or house wrap) and will shed water over the trim. Then install the trim using coated trim screws.

13 REPLACE THE SIDING

Our siding is double-course cedar shakes, which we matched easily. Caulk around the window and trim using a quality exterior sealant. Then paint the siding.

CHAPTER 3

Flooring

TOOL SPOTLIGHT
TILE SETTER'S TOOLKIT
KNEEPADS
These kneepads from SuperiorBilt allow you to work all day on your knees without fatigue.
LASER-WELDED CORING BIT
Use laser-welded diamond coring bits to drill holes in tile. A laser-welded diamond coating is more durable than a coating made from braze-welded diamonds and can cut wet or dry.
SUPERIORBILT
SILICONE FLOATS
We prefer soft silicone grout floats to hard ones. They conform to rough surfaces without having to be pressed down as much. You can find them at home centers.
SUPERIORBILT
LEVELING WEDGES AND SHIMS
These wedges and shims help you set tiles evenly and avoid uneven tile edges, called lippage. They are available at most home centers and all tile stores.
TILE WEDGES
TROWELS WITH ROUNDED NOTCHES
Rounded ridges in thin-set collapse more uniformly for better coverage and fewer air pockets. That makes for a better bond.
PHANO CHINA MARKER
PHANO CHINA MARKER
CHINA PENCIL
Uses china pencils to mark tile cuts. The marks are easy to see, and they won't rinse off if you're using a wet saw.

GRINDING STONE
A grinding stone is used to ease the edge of cut tile. We really like to use one when we're working with natural stone. It helps us dress the cut edge to make it appear more like a natural break.
VARIABLE-SPEED GRINDER
Only use a grinder that has variable speed when you work with tile. Slowing down allows you to work safely, handle details and avoid overheating the expensive diamond blades.
FLUSH-CUTTING DIAMOND BLADE
Most blades for angle grinders don't cut flush. These do. Uses them when you have to cut close to a tub or under a tile that needs to come up in one piece.
MARGIN TROWEL
Most trowels are triangular, but a rectangular shape is better for mixing, scraping and scooping from a bucket. We prefer a long margin trowel.
SUCTION CUPS
Suction cups help you move large tile around or pull it back up after laying it. Be careful with textured tiles; the uneven surface may not hold suction well.
DOUBLE BOX MIXING PADDLE
This style mixing paddle minimizes air buildup in the thin-set, and saves a lot of manual work.
TILE NIPPERS
Nippers can make the small detail cuts that a tile cutter just can't. They are available in the tile section of your home center.
SCRUBBER SPONGES
Start grout cleanup with the plain side of the sponge. When the joints are nicely shaped, switch to the scrubber side. The scrubber side can be used to clean tools too.

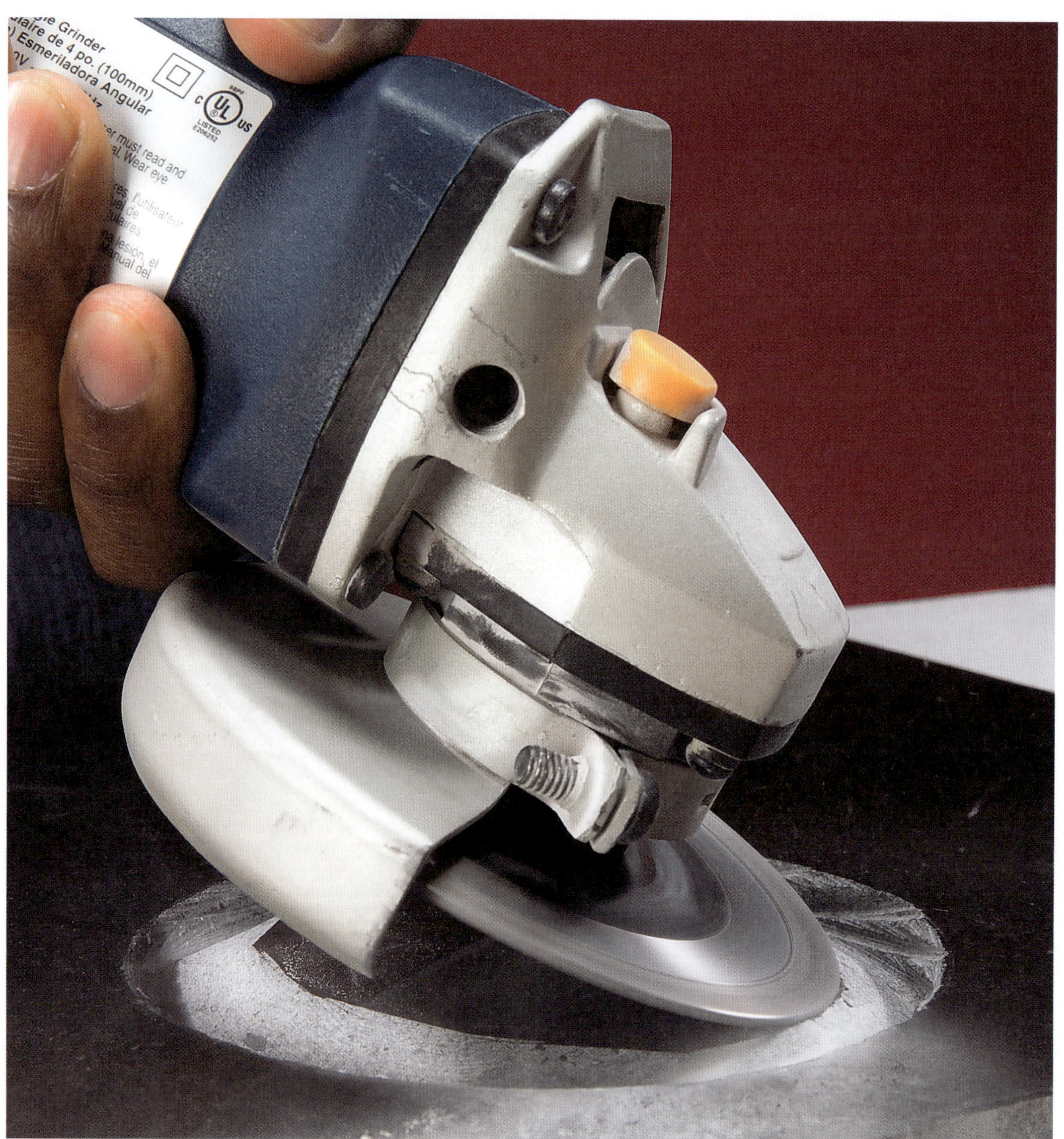

Tough Tile Cuts Made Easy

An angle grinder does what other tools can't

By Jeff Corton

Some tile jobs require only straight, simple cuts. But most require some tricky ones, such as holes for plumbing or curves. That's when an angle grinder comes in handy. This article shows you how to use an inexpensive angle grinder with a diamond blade to cut perfect circles and squares in even the toughest tile, such as porcelain. Look for a 4- or 4½-in. grinder and dry-cut diamond blade to finish these tricky cuts.

When you are picking out a diamond blade, look for one with a continuous, rather than segmented, rim for the smoothest cut. Just be aware, though, that cutting with a dry-cut diamond blade creates a lot of dust and noise. So make sure you cut in a well-ventilated area (or better yet, outside!) and always wear hearing protection, a good-quality two-strap dust mask and sturdy safety glasses.

TILT THE BLADE FOR CIRCLES

Many tile jobs require you to cut one or more large round holes for floor drains or toilet flanges. **Photos 1-3** explain how to cut a hole for a drain. We're showing how to cut a hole that's entirely within a single tile, one of the most difficult cuts. In the next section, we'll show you an easier method for cutting curves in the edge of a tile. Even with this method, try to avoid a tile layout that places the edge of the circular cutout less than ½ in. from the edge of the tile. It is better to shift the entire layout instead. Otherwise, chances are good that you'll break the tile at the narrow point while cutting.

The method shown for cutting a full circle with a grinder and diamond blade requires you to cut around the circle a couple of times, making a deeper cut with each revolution. The key is to keep the same angle and shave off progressive layers, slowly moving the cut closer to the center of the circle **(Photo 2)**.

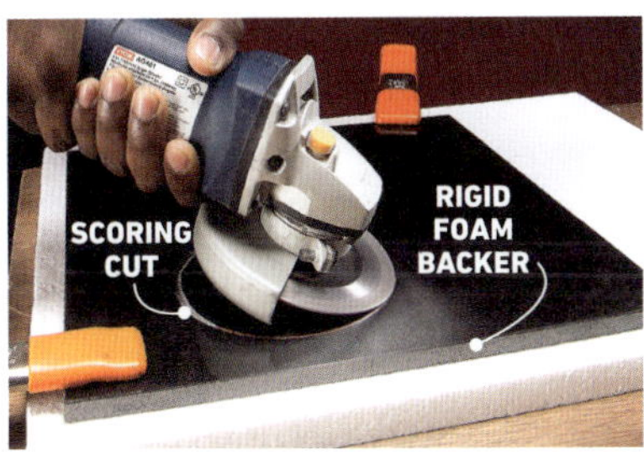

1 SCORE THE FACE
Make a shallow cut on the front of the tile along the circle guideline. Tilt the grinder about 30 degrees and cut about $^{1}/_{16}$ in. deep.

2 GRIND DEEPER
Move the blade ⅛ in. to the inside of the line and make a deeper cut. Move the blade away from the line and cutting deeper until you cut completely through.

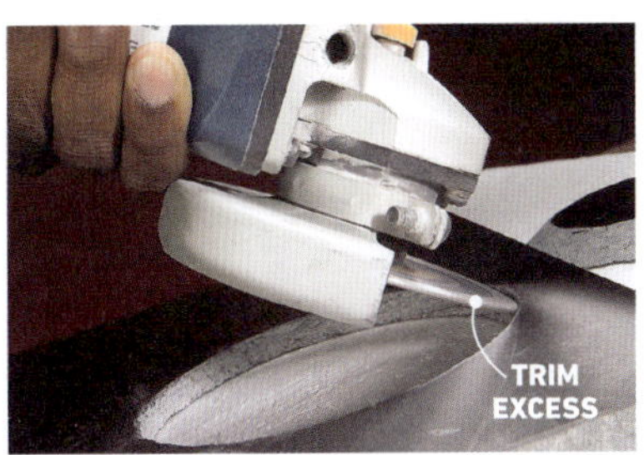

3 SMOOTH THE CUT
Grind off rough edges and trim back to the line for a perfect curve.

ROUGH OUT SEMICIRCULAR CUTS BEFORE TRIMMING TO THE LINE

The process to cut a semicircle from the edge of tiles is similar to the technique shown on p. 89 for full circles. You can start by marking the cut and scoring the face of the tile on the line. Then, rather than deepen the scoring cut, simply remove the excess tile with straight cuts **(Photo 1)**.

Before you remove the excess tile **(Photo 1)**, be sure to make short cuts on both sides of the semicircle **(cuts 1 and 2)**. Then connect the cuts as shown **(cut 3)**. Rather than make this connecting cut in one pass, make a series of progressively deeper shallow cuts until you've gone completely through the tile.

Now complete the semicircle with a series of radial cuts—like the spokes of a wheel **(Photo 2)**.

Finish by cleaning up the rough edges with the diamond blade. Or remove the leftover "tabs" with a tile nipper (a biting tool like a plier). Then grind the edges smooth for a round finish.

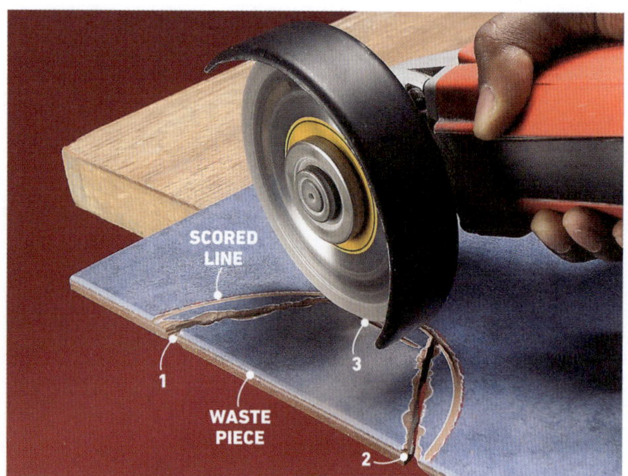

1 SCORE, THEN ROUGH-CUT

Score the profile with the blade, then cut in from the edge of the tile to remove as much waste as possible.

2 SLICE AND SNAP

Make a series of closely spaced cuts up to your scored line. Snap off the waste. Then grind the edges smooth.

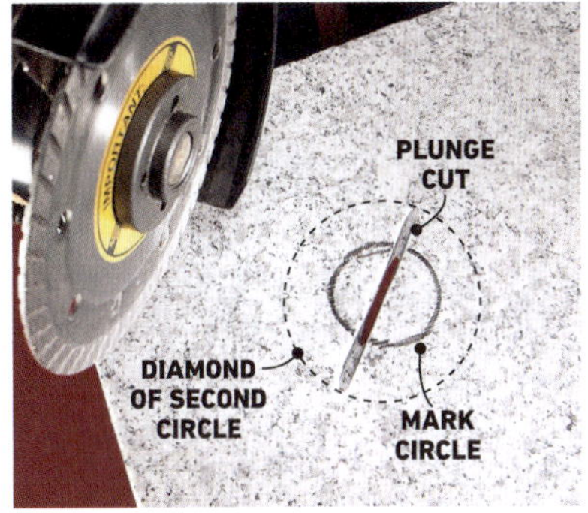

1 CUT A CENTERED SLOT
Center the cut on the hole and plunge slowly from the back. Stop when the slot through the face of the tile lines up with the edges of the desired cutout.

MAKE A DISH-SHAPED CUTOUT FOR SMALL, ROUGH HOLES

Most plumbing pipe holes will be covered up by a vanity, cupboard or appliance so a precise round hole is not usually necessary. Use the technique shown here to make rough, round holes for these occasions.

Start by marking the circular cutout on the back of the tile. Then plunge the diamond blade down through the tile, keeping it centered on the hole so the slot made by the blade extends equally on both sides of the circle marks **(Photo 1)**. Check often to see when the slot through the front of the tile reaches the edges of the desired cutout. Use the length of that plunge to gauge the diameter of a second, larger circle. Draw that larger circle on the back of the tile **(Photo 2)** and use it as a guide to make the rest of the plunge cuts. Rotate the grinder about a blade's width and make another plunge cut, stopping at the outer circle. Continue this process until you finish the hole.

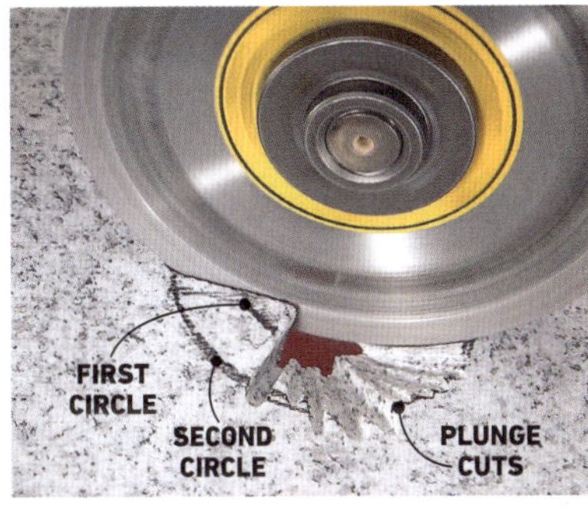

2 CUT AGAIN AND AGAIN
Draw another larger circle to guide the depth of the remaining cuts. Make repeated plunge cuts until the circle is complete.

PLUNGE-CUT FROM THE BACK TO MAKE RECTANGULAR CUTOUTS

Cutting rectangular or square holes is simple with this method. The key is to avoid cutting beyond the corners of your square where the cut might be visible. Plunge-cut slowly from the back and check often to avoid going too far.

1. **Start on the front.** Mark the cutout on the front and back of the tile precisely. Then score the front of the tile about 1/16 in. deep along the line.
2. **Overcut from the back.** Flip the tile over and plunge the cut from the back. Stop and check often as you go. Stop when the cut lines up with the corners of the marked square on the front. Plunge-cut the remaining three sides.

Replace a Damaged Tile

With a little know-how, a few days and some leftover materials, you can fix any cracked floor tile

By Jeff Gorton

When a tile chips or breaks, the only way to fix it is to replace it. The total repair time will be around two hours, spread over a couple of days. Most of your time will be spent on the first day removing the damaged tile, the grout and the old adhesive and then installing the new tile. The final step (done a day or two later) will be regrouting around the new tile.

MATCHING THE TILE AND GROUT

If you are lucky, you will have some extra tiles. If you don't have any extras, go to a few tile stores. You might be able to find a close match. If you can't find anything close, you can get creative and replace a few more tiles to make a new pattern.

Matching the grout can be a bit tricky, even though tile stores carry a wide range of colors. For the closest possible match, chip a piece of the old grout off and take it with you to the tile store.

ADHESIVES AND GROUT

Whether the damaged tile is on the floor or on the wall, the steps to repair it are similar. The main difference is the type of adhesive and grout used.

For floor tiles, use thin-set mortar as the adhesive. It comes in a powder that you mix with water. Follow the directions on the package for the right mixture consistency. To regrout floor tile, use sanded grout. For a tiled wall repair, use premixed mastic adhesive and nonsanded grout for best results.

Always check the adhesive package for the required drying time before applying the new grout. If you rush the regrouting step and the tile shifts, you will need to start over. Lastly, seal the grout with grout sealer, which you can buy from the tile dealer.

All of the specialized products, including the grout saw **(Photo 2)**, grout float **(Photo 6)** and adhesive trowel are sold at tile stores.

PRO TIP Mix some grout before you start the project to make sure the color matches. Grout changes color as it dries, and you may find you'll need to do some color adjusting by mixing two colors.

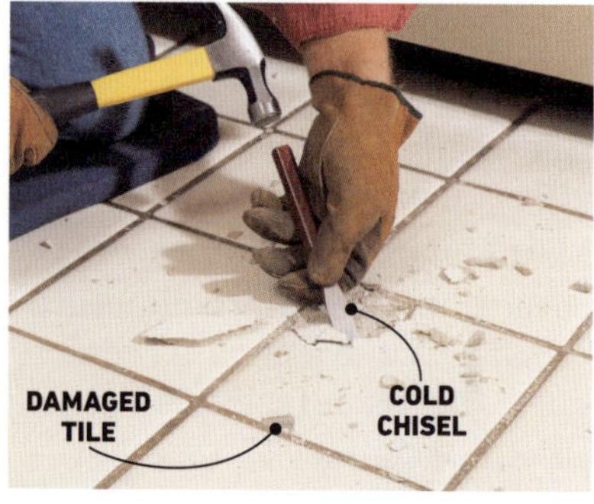

1 CHIP OFF THE TILE

Remove the damaged tile with a cold chisel and hammer. Start at the edge of the tile, in the grout. Ceramic tile is brittle so small pieces will fly! Wear safety glasses and gloves. Be careful not to chip the surrounding tiles.

2 GET RID OF GROUT

Remove the old grout with a grout saw. Some of the grout can be chipped out with the chisel; however, you'll need to saw away all of the old grout to ensure a proper fit for the new tile.

3 PREP THE FLOOR

Scrape off the old adhesive with a cold chisel. Get rid of as much as possible so the new tile will adhere properly and lie flat. Scraping is always the best way to remove old adhesive. Don't use a solvent or heat gun unless you want a big mess.

4 LAY DOWN THE ADHESIVE

Apply the adhesive (thin-set mortar for a floor tile) with a notched trowel on the back of the tile. Be sure to spread the adhesive out to the edges. Don't skimp: Too little and the tile will sit lower than the others. Any excess can be removed after the next step.

5 SET THE TILE

Place the tile, making sure that the grout lines are even with the adjacent tiles. To set the tile firmly into the adhesive, use a short length of wood and gently tap it with a hammer. If the tile is lower than the surrounding tiles, simply remove it, apply additional adhesive and then reset the tile. Scrape out any excess adhesive from between the tiles with a screwdriver. Once the tile is set, stay off it until the adhesive is dry, usually 24 hours.

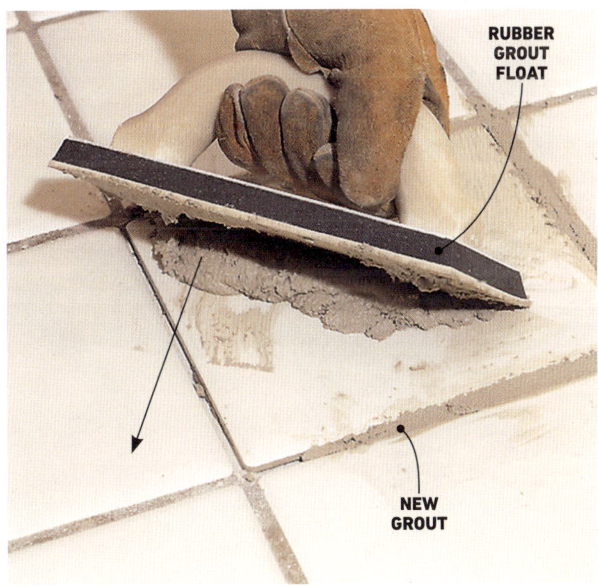

6 FILL GAPS WITH GROUT

Spread the grout using a rubber grout float. Hold the float at a 45-degree angle to the tile. Move the grout in both directions at an angle to the grout lines to make sure it fills the gaps between the tiles. Let the grout set for about 10 minutes and then wipe the area with a damp grout sponge. A grout sponge has rounded corners and is the best way to shape the grout lines. Once the grout has dried, usually overnight, wipe off any residue with a soft cloth.

Tearing Out Old Carpet

Having new carpet installed? Removing the old stuff yourself is a smart move—here's how to do it quickly and efficiently.

By Eric Smith and Ehren Babb

BEFORE THE TEAR-OUT

Talk with your installer to find out exactly how much you'll save by tearing the carpet out yourself. Your installer can also give you advice on handling any unusual situations in your home and what to do with the old carpet. Many trash haulers will accept short rolls of carpet along with the regular trash, and some cities have carpet recycling programs.

Before you begin tearing up your carpet, remove any doors that swing into the room, including bifold closet doors. Doors that swing into adjoining rooms can stay in place. Then clear the floor completely, removing all the furniture from the room. Slip on a pair of gloves to protect your knuckles from the abrasive carpet backing and needle-sharp tack strip. There's a lot of dust and dander trapped inside old carpet. So it's smart to strap on a dust mask too.

1 CUT INTO SECTIONS
Fold the carpet over for easy cutting and slice it into narrow strips. Roll up the strips and tape them for easy handling.

2 AVOID TRANSITIONS
Leave transitions alone. Cut the carpet a few inches from where it meets other flooring and let the installer tackle the transition work.

PULL, CUT AND ROLL

To detach the carpet from the tack strip that holds the carpet in place along walls, start in a corner; just grab the carpet with pliers and pull. Then grab the carpet by hand and continue to pull it up along an entire wall. Fold back about 3 ft. of carpet and cut it into easy-to-handle strips **(Photo 1)**. Carpet is much easier to cut from the back than from the front. Use a sharp new blade in your utility knife and be careful not to slice into the walls or baseboard.

Keep pulling back the carpet and slicing it into strips. When you come to a "transition" where the carpet meets another section of carpet or other flooring, cut along the carpet and leave the transition in place **(Photo 2)**. If you have a metal transition that's in good condition, the installer may decide to leave it in place. That can save you a few bucks per transition. If the carpet is seamed to another section of carpet, the installer can separate the seam without damage to the carpet that's staying in place.

3 SCRAPE AWAY PADS AND STAPLES
Get rid of carpet pad staples fast with a floor scraper. If the blade digs into the wood, scrape from a low angle.

To remove carpet from stairs, start at the top. If there's a metal nosing at the top of the stairs, try to pry it up to remove it. If not, cut the carpet near the top of the top riser, grab the cut end and pull the carpet off the stairs by hand. Always wear gloves to protect your hands from the staples that hold the carpet in place. Some stairs are covered with short sections of carpet that wrap over just one tread and riser. If you find yourself pulling up one long piece, slice off sections as you go to make pulling easier. When you have torn off all the carpet and pad, pull out the staples with pliers.

Cut the pad into strips and roll it up just as you did with the carpet. On a concrete floor, pads are often glued in place, so big chunks of pad will remain stuck to the floor. To remove them, use a floor scraper. You can find a long-handled scraper or a shorter version for tight spaces at most home centers. Some scrapers have razor-sharp blades; others feature blunt blades. Either type works fine on concrete.

On a plywood or particleboard subfloor, you'll have hundreds of staples to deal with. You can pull them with pliers, of course, but that can take hours. The job takes a few minutes with a sharp-bladed floor scraper **(Photo 3)**. The blade will shear off some staples and yank out others. Be sure to go over the whole floor so you don't leave any behind. If the scraper digs into the floor, flip it over so that the blade's beveled side faces down. If it still digs, try working at a lower angle.

TRASH THE TACK STRIP?

In most cases, you should leave the old tack strip in place, but there are a couple of exceptions: Remove any sections that are rotten, delaminating or badly rusted. Rust can "bleed" through the carpet, creating stains on the surface. You should also remove the tack strip if it's less than ¼ in. from the baseboard. The installer needs a gap at least ¼ in. wide to tuck the edge of the carpet down against the baseboard. To remove tack strip, just pop it up with a flat pry bar. Tack strips are available at home centers, but you'll save very little money, if any, by installing it yourself.

Flawless Floor Sanding

A refinishing expert offers his best tips

By David Radtke

Sanding hardwood floors might seem as if it's a pros-only project. It's a big job that creates big disruptions in your household. And then there is that big, scary sanding machine ...

But it's really not that difficult or scary. I've helped hundreds of homeowners, some of them DIY novices, successfully prep their floors for a new finish. Here are some of my most important tips for smooth sanding.

GOOD-BYE, BASE SHOE

If a room has quarter-round molding (aka base shoe) at the bottom of baseboards, I usually pry it off and reinstall it later in the process. Here's why: Edge sanding slightly lowers the floor and leaves the baseboard standing on a little plateau. You think you won't notice this, but you will. Edge sanding also scuffs up base shoe, which means more touch-up work later.

Removing the base shoe can sidesteps both of those problems. Label the base shoe as you remove it to avoid confusion when you reinstall it. Exception: If the base shoe is bonded to the baseboard by decades of paint buildup, I'll leave it in place. If you have newer baseboards and no quarter-round, leave it in place, but expect lots of the aforementioned touch-ups.

PET STAINS ARE FOREVER

Water stains usually disappear after a couple of passes of the sander. But stains caused by pet urine often penetrate so deep into the wood that you just can't sand them out. Bleach formulated for wood floors may be worth a try, but in my experience the results are usually mediocre at best, and at worst, the wood can be left pitted and blotched.

Often, the only solution is to replace the affected wood—or finish over the stain and think of it as a permanent memorial to a beloved pet.

How do you tell water from pee? Pet stains tend to be darker (deep gray, almost black around the edges) and often look like a map with big and small islands covering a large area.

DETECT NAILS
Drag a metal snow shovel across the floor (upside down). When it hits a nail, you'll hear it.

PREP THE ROOM

Some of the floor prep work is obvious, like removing all the furniture and covering doorways with plastic. Here are some steps DIYers often don't think of:

- Cover or plug air grilles to keep dust out of ducts. Turn off the HVAC system at the thermostat. Less blowing air movement means less dust traveling around your house.
- Remove all window coverings and any art on the walls. If you don't, you will need to clean and dust them later.
- Remove doors that open into the room. You can't reach and completely sand under doors, even by opening and closing them.
- Raise low-hanging light fixtures; just tie two links of the chain together with wire. Otherwise, you're guaranteed to bump your head. Repeatedly.
- Nail down any loose boards with finish nails.
- When you're sanding, nail heads will rip the sanding belt (which costs you money) or gouge the sanding drum (which can cost you more money). So countersink all nails by at least ⅛ in.

SCRAPE OUT CORNERS

When the sanding is done, use a paint scraper to attack spots that the machines can't reach. A sharp scraper would leave a super-smooth glazed surface that won't take finish the same as the surrounding wood. So rough up scraped areas with a coarse 80- or 100-grit paper.

RENTAL TIPS

You'll need two rental machines: a drum sander to sand most of the floor and an edger to sand along baseboards. Here are some tips:

- Rent from a flooring specialty shop rather than a general rental store. You'll get more expertise at no extra expense.
- Measure the room. Knowing your square footage will help the crew at the rental store estimate how many sanding belts and discs you'll need.
- Prep before you rent. The work will take longer than you think. Don't waste money by picking up the sanders before you're ready to use them.
- Get a drum sander that uses a continuous belt or sleeve, not one that requires you to wrap a strip of abrasive around the drum. That's tedious and often leads to chatter marks on the floor.
- Think twice before you rent a flat-pad sander (aka orbital or square-buff sander). Sure, they are easier to use, but they are not aggressive enough to bite into finishes or hardwoods.

ONE CRITICAL FEATURE
Choose a sander that has a lever to raise and lower the sanding drum. That makes graceful stops and starts easier—and reduces gouging.

PICK A STARTING GRIT

It takes a very coarse abrasive to cut through a finish and into the hardwood. But determining the coarseness isn't easy for a DIYer. So I recommend a trial-and-error process: Start with 36-grit. If that doesn't completely remove the finish in one pass, step down to 24-grit. If 24-grit doesn't remove at least three-quarters of the finish in one pass, go to 16-grit. Regardless of which grit you start with, all the finish must be gone before proceeding to the next step.

NIX THE STRIPPER
DIYers often think that paint stripper is a good way to get rid of the finish before sanding. But don't waste your time. Sanding is faster. And much cheaper.

EDGER EDUCATION

The edger is basically a sanding disc mounted on a big, powerful motor. A simple tool, but not so simple to use. Here are some tips to help you master the edger and minimize the inevitable swirls left by the spinning disc:

- Follow up each phase of drum sanding with edging. After you've drum-sanded at 36-grit, for example, edge with 36-grit.
- Place a nylon pad under the sand-paper. This cushion minimizes gouges and deep swirls. You can get pads at the rental store.

- Replace the sandpaper when it's dull. Dull paper won't remove swirls left by the previous grit.
- At the end of the job, lay a flashlight on the floor to highlight any leftover swirls. Then hand-sand them out with 80- or 100-grit paper.
- A warning to woodworkers: You'll be tempted to edge with your belt sander, but even the biggest belt sander can't cut half as fast as an edger. You'll also be tempted to polish out swirls with a random orbit sander. But beware: That can overpolish the wood so it won't take finish the same as the surrounding belt-sanded wood. Hand-sanding is safer.

CHANGE BELTS OFTEN

I sell sanding belts, so this might sound self-serving. But trust me. Using dull belts is a strategy you'll regret. Here's the problem: After the floor finish is gone, you can't see whether the sander is doing its job. So you just keep sanding. The machine is raising dust and everything seems fine. But the dull paper isn't cutting deep enough to remove any of the scratches left by the previous grit. And you may not discover this until you put a finish on the floor. A dull edging disc is even worse, since it won't remove the ugly cross grain scratches left by the previous disc.

Even if paper feels sharp, it may be beyond its prime. So the best way to judge is by square footage covered. The belts I sell cover about 250 sq. ft., and edger discs are spent after 20 sq. ft. Those numbers vary, so ask at the rental store.

DON'T SKIP GRITS

The initial coarse grits removes finishes and flattens the wood. But that's not enough. You need

to progress through each grit to polish off the scratches left by the previous grit. On most of my jobs, the sequence is 24-36-60-80 for coarse-grained wood such as oak. Scratches are more visible on fine-grained wood like birch or maple, so I go to 100-grit.

CLEAN UP BETWEEN GRITS

Sweep or vacuum the floor before you move up to the next grit. Even the best abrasives throw off a few granules while sanding. And a 36-grit granule caught under a 60-grit belt will leave an ugly gash in the floor. Wrap the vacuum nozzle with tape to avoid marring the floor.

DOES DIY MAKE CENTS?

On average, especially on jobs that are larger than 500 sq. ft., my DIY customers can save hundreds by doing it themselves. Not bad for a weekend of work. Keep in mind that pro costs vary a lot, so it's worth making a few calls to check on pro rates in your area.

SCREEN THE FLOOR

After you've finished with the sanders, the floor will look so amazing that you'll be tempted to skip this step—but don't. "Screening" blends the perimeter, which is edge-sanded with the drum-sanded field and polishes away sanding scratches. You can do it with a rented buffing machine or with a sanding pole (just as the one used for sanding drywall). Either way, the abrasive to use is 120- or 150-grit sanding screen (again, just as the stuff used on drywall).

Refinish a Wood Floor

Renew a floor without the hassle of sanding

By Mac Wentz

When a wood floor loses its luster, the usual solution is to fully sand it down to the raw wood and completely refinish it. But often, that's the wrong solution.

All wood floors are protected by a clear coating that eventually becomes scratched, scuffed and dull over time. But as long as the damage is shallow—in the coating, and not deep in the wood itself—you can renew the floor by adding a new coat of polyurethane right over the old finish.

TEST FOR ADHESION

Pick at least two test areas on the floor: one in a high-traffic zone, the other along a wall or in a closet. Clean each area with a wood floor cleaner and roughen a 6 x 6-in. area with sanding screen. Then wipe away the sanding residue, mask around the test area, and give it a coat of polyurethane **(Photo 1)**.

After 24 hours, take a look at the polyurethane. Aside from a few tiny "whiskers" caused by tiny dust particles, it should be smooth. Then scrape the test polyurethane with a coin. Press down firmly, but not too hard. Even a sound finish scrapes off if you press too hard **(Photo 2)**.

If the polyurethane is smooth and it does not scrape off with moderate pressure, your test is a success. You can move forward and recoat the floor.

But if the polyurethane flakes off as you scrape with the coin, or if the surface has a crackled or orange-peel texture **(Photo 3)**, there's something on or in the old finish preventing the new finish from adhering properly. That "something" could be furniture polish, residue from window cleaner or a hundred other things. But whatever it is, there's only one solution: You have to sand down all the way to bare wood and completely refinish the floor.

4 SCRUB THE FLOOR
Clean the floor using a wood flooring cleaner. A dull putty knife is handy for scraping up petrified chewing gum and other gunk. For tough marks, use a scouring pad dampened with mineral spirits. If that fails, try sanding screen. As you clean, use pieces of masking tape to mark any deep scratches, ridges or areas where the finish has worn away.

5 HAND SAND THE EDGES
Roughen the existing finish along walls and in corners where the buffer can't reach. The purpose is only to scratch up the finish, not to wear it down—or worse, sand right through it. Three or four passes with the sanding screen are usually enough. Wear gloves to protect your hands from the abrasive screen.

As with any wood-finishing project, 90 percent of this job is preparation. Thoroughly clean the floor, touching up any deep scratches and roughening the existing finish so the new finish will adhere well. Expect to spend at least one full day on this prep work. The recoating itself usually takes less than an hour.

Recoating takes a lot less time, skill and money than full-scale sanding and refinishing. And while roughing up the existing finish creates plenty of dust, it is still much less messy than sanding down to the bare wood. There's another advantage: Every time you sand a floor down to bare wood, you remove some of the wood. A solid wood floor can be sanded several times before that's a problem. But laminated floors, such as glue-down or floating floors, have only a very thin layer of good-looking wood veneer over a base like plywood. The veneer can be sanded once or twice. But after that, sanding will expose the plywood core beneath.

WHERE RECOATING WON'T WORK

The type of flooring you have doesn't matter. Recoating works on solid wood, laminated wood and parquet floors alike. But a new coat of polyurethane may not stick to your existing finish.

If the floor's finish was applied before the 1970s, then it was most likely wax, old-fashioned varnish or shellac. No new finish will stick to a wax finish or any other finish that has ever had a wax applied to it. Polyurethane might adhere to an older, unwaxed varnish or shellac finish. But these finishes do wear out, and since they're probably almost 50 years old, it's best to sand them off and start over.

In fact, if your finish is from the days before polyurethane, your only alternative to sanding is wax. If the floor is still in fair condition, wax can restore the shine. A wood flooring dealer can recommend a suitable product. Wax is easy to use, but not very durable. You'll probably have to rewax every six months or so.

Even if the existing finish is polyurethane, good adhesion is not a sure thing. Residue from all kinds of household chemicals, such as furniture polish, glass

6 START BUFFING

Set the buffer on the sanding screen. The screen isn't attached to the buffer at all, but stays put under the weight of the machine. The screen will wear out after 10 to 15 minutes of use. When it does, flip it over or start with a new screen. Check the screen for grit every few minutes and wipe away any large particles that might scratch the floor.

Note: Be sure to lock the buffer's adjustable handle in place before you begin buffing.

cleaner, insecticide and wallpaper paste, can all interfere with the adhesion. Since you can't know for certain all the potions that have landed on your floor, you must test for adhesion before you recoat your floor.

MONEY AND MATERIALS

Recoating a typical floor (200 sq. ft. or so) is a relatively cheap project. Most of that goes for tools and renting the buffer, so recoating floors in two rooms costs only a few bucks more.

PROBLEM AREAS

- As you're cleaning, you may find deep scratches that go through the finish and into the wood. You usually can't make these scratches disappear completely, but you can make them a lot less noticeable. If your floor is as light or lighter than the floor shown here, first wet the scratch with mineral spirits. A wet coat of mineral spirits produces about the same look as a coat of polyurethane. And on a light-colored floor, it might darken the scratch just enough to hide it.
- If that doesn't work, apply some wood stain to the scratch using a cotton swab. Because the scratch is rough and porous, it will absorb a lot of stain. So begin experimenting with a stain that's much lighter than the tone of your floor and wipe away the excess stain right after you apply it. For best results, use two stain colors to match the light and dark patterns in the wood grain **(Photo 7)**.
- If the floor has a high-traffic area where the clear finish is completely worn away, wet the area with mineral spirits to see what it will look like with a coat of polyurethane. If it looks good, clean the area fully, apply a coat of polyurethane and give it at least two days to cure. Then you can buff and recoat the new layer of polyurethane along with the rest of the floor.
- Look out for ridges. The buffer will eat right through the finish down to bare wood at high spots. And if your floor is colored with wood stain, you'll be left with light-colored strips where the stain has been rubbed off. **Photo 8** shows how a solid-wood floor can buckle in high humidity. But smaller ridges, where the wood strips cup slightly or one plank sits a bit higher than the next, can cause just as much trouble.
- If you can flatten a ridge by standing on it, fasten it down with a finishing nail or two. If you can't flatten the ridge, you'll have to roughen the area by hand using sanding screen. Remember to avoid that area with the buffer later on.
- Stains that have penetrated through the finish as well as the wood can only be removed by sanding. But there's no harm in recoating over them—if you can live with them.

7

9 GENTLY BUFF

Buff the floor starting at one wall and moving backward across the room. Slowly swing the buffer left and right as you go. Pass over each area only once or twice so you don't cut through the finish. To make the buffer swing to your right, gently lift the handle. To swing left, lower the handle. To control dust, place fans in open windows, close ducts, seal off the work area and wear a dust mask.

All the tools and materials for this project are available at home centers. Wood flooring dealers also carry most of the products. Here's what you'll need:

- A liquid floor cleaner that's formulated specifically for wood floors.
- Scouring pads (also called "synthetic steel wool") to remove marks on the floor. Scotchbrite is one common brand. Regular steel wool will also work, but don't use steel wool if you plan to use a water-based finish; the tiny particles of steel left behind will cause rust stains.
- A 2- or 3-in. natural bristle brush made specifically for applying varnish and other clear coatings.
- A finish applicator pad that's designed for applying floor finishes **(Photo 12)**. You could buy a long handle that screws into the applicator, but any push broom handle will work. Some applicators are made just for oil-based finishes; others are made for water-based products. Just check the label.
- A respirator that has organic vapor cartridges to filter out harmful fumes **(Photo 10)** while you're using the intense mineral spirits and oil-based polyurethane. Respirators are pricey, but also absolutely necessary for your health.
- A gallon of mineral spirits, 100-grit sanding screen and a dust mask.
- A buffer **(Photo 9)**, which are available by day at a rental center or flooring store. You will also need a buffing pad (made from synthetic mesh) and sanding screen discs (which are the same material used to roughen the floor by hand). These screens are available in several grits. Use 150- or 120-grit if available. They're less likely to cut through the finish into the wood than 100-grit. Get at least three screens for a typical room. You can always return any you don't use.

Tip: The buffer is a heavy and powerful machine. Try practicing with it first on a smooth concrete floor, using only the pad.

CHOOSING A FINISH

The best floor finish for any DIYer is polyurethane. Other floor finishes are either less durable or much more difficult to work with. You'll find two types of polyurethane at home centers:

The oil-based polyurethanes (or "oil-modified urethanes") are easier to apply because they dry slowly, giving you more time to spread and smooth the finish. They have a yellowish hue and slowly darken with time, which may be good or bad depending on the look you want. The biggest drawback to oil-based products is the nasty vapor they give off. You must open any windows in the room and wear a respirator.

Water-based polyurethanes (or "water-borne urethanes") are generally a bit more durable than oil-based versions. They have a milky color when wet, but they dry crystal clear and stay clear. The milky color makes them fairly easy to see, so you're less likely to miss spots. Still, the water-based products are harder to apply because they dry fast.

Note: With either type of polyurethane, double check to be sure it's recommended for wood floors before you buy.

10 REMOVE ANY AND ALL DUST

Clean the room thoroughly, beginning with windowsills, moldings and any other surface where dust might gather. Vacuum the floor, then wipe it with a rag dampened with mineral spirits. The rag should be free of lint and should not have been washed with a fabric softener, which can interfere with the polyurethane's adhesion.

Important: Dust that settles on the wet polyurethane will create tiny craters or bumps.

11 COVER ALONG THE WALLS

Brush polyurethane along a wall that runs parallel to the wood strips. Then brush about 3 ft. along adjoining walls. This will give you a 3-ft. wide working area that runs the entire length of the room. Finish that area using the applicator pad **(as in Photo 12)**, then brush along walls to prepare the next 3-ft. wide section. Even with oil-based polyurethane, you have to move fast so you can begin each section before the previous one starts to dry.

12 MOP ON THE POLYURETHANE

Apply polyurethane using an applicator pad attached to a long handle. When spreading the finish, you can dip the applicator into a paint tray filled with polyurethane, but a cardboard box lined with a plastic bag is less likely to tip over. To smooth the finish, first "unload" the pad by pressing it hard against a dry part of the floor. Then drag the applicator lightly across the floor from one end of the room to the other.

Replace a Laminate Floor Plank

Don't hide that damaged plank under a rug, repair your floor in just a few hours

You can fix minor chips and scratches in a laminate floor with filler products from the home center. But if the damage is severe, you have to replace the plank (you did save a few from the installation, right?). It's a job you can do yourself in about two hours. In addition to a spare plank, you'll need a circular saw, hammer, chisel, router or table saw, drill and wood glue.

While some flooring experts recommend removing the base molding and unsnapping and numbering every plank until you get to the damaged portion. That works if the damaged plank is close to the wall. But trust us: If the damaged section is more than a few rows out from the wall, it's actually faster to just cut it out. And if your laminate floor is glued together, the unsnapping routine won't work at all.

Start by drawing a cutting line 1½ in. in from all four edges of the plank. Drill a ⅜-in. relief hole at each corner of the cutting line and again ¼ in. in from each corner of the plank.

Cut out the center section with a circular saw, cutting from hole to hole **(Photo 1)**. Next, cut from the center section of the plank into each corner, stopping at the drilled hole **(Photo 2)**. Finally, make a relief cut from the center section out toward the seam of each plank. Tap a chisel into each relief cut to break out the uncut portion. Then remove all the cut pieces from the floor.

The new plank has a groove at one end and one side, as well as a tongue at the opposite end and side. But you can't install it until you cut off the bottom lip of both grooves and the side tongue. Use a utility knife to remove them **(Photo 3)**. Here's a tip for cutting off the groove. Stick the blade inside the groove and cut off the bottom from the inside (or use a table saw).

Apply a bead of wood glue to all four edges of the new plank. Insert the glued tongue of the new plank into the groove of the existing flooring and drop your new plank into place. Wipe off any excess glue and load up books on the plank until it's dry.

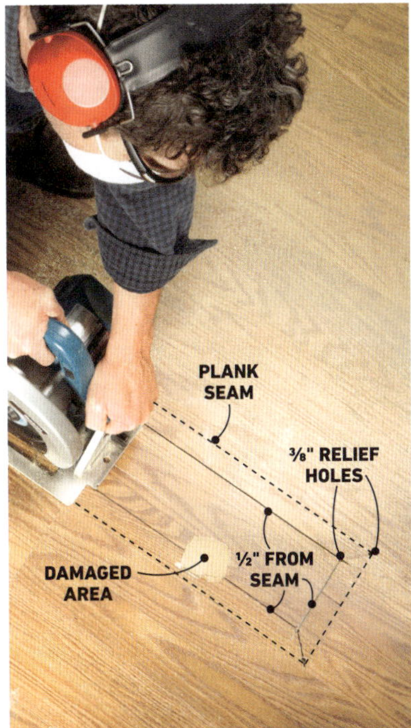

1 REMOVE THE CENTER SECTION

Set the depth of your circular saw a tad deeper than the floor thickness. Lift the blade guard and cut along the line.

2 CUT TO THE CORNERS

Cut from the center section to the drilled hole in each corner. But don't go farther! Break out the remainder with a chisel.

3 REMOVE THE BOTTOM LIP

Score the tongue several times with a utility knife. Then snap it off with pliers. Shave off any remaining scraps with your knife.

REMOVING GLUED PLANKS

Most of the early laminate floors were fastened with glue. But that doesn't mean you can't do an "in-place" patch on those floors too. Follow all the cutting directions for a snap-together floor. Then use your pliers to break the glue bond **(Photo 1)**. Clean off the old glue **(Photo 2)** and lay in the new plank.

1. **Raise the floor to gain leverage.** Slip a dowel or scrap piece of flooring under the seam. Grab the section with pliers and tilt it down until the glued seam cracks apart. Then snap it upward to break any of the remaining glue.
2. **The old glue has to go.** Use a flat-blade screwdriver or small chisel to chip out the old glue. Get the surfaces as smooth as possible for a flush fit and a good bond with the new glue.

Two Solutions for a Bouncy Floor

A reader asks how to reduce the spring in their step as they cross room

By Brett Martin

Q: The floors in the kitchen and living room in our ranch house have a springy feel as you walk across them. Engineered I-joists were used throughout the house. Can I brace these joists?

Virgil Kupfer, Old Monroe, MO

A: Assuming you have access to the underside of the joists, you can install either bridging or a layer of plywood to reduce the bounce in your floor. First try the bridging method. Simply nail short I-joist sections between your existing joists **(Photo 2)**. To prevent squeaks, apply construction adhesive to the top side of the bridging where it contacts your floor.

If the joist span is shorter than 14 ft., install one row of bridging at the midpoint. If the span is longer than 14 ft., install two rows of bridging, the first one at about one-third of the span and the other around two-thirds of your joist span.

If the floor is still too bouncy, glue and screw ½-in. plywood to the bottom of the joists **(Photo 1)**. Start the first row at a corner, then stagger subsequent rows so the seams don't fall on the same joists. The drawback is that you have to leave ceiling access to all of the plumbing and gas valves, electrical boxes or other fixtures. Of course, the best method is to install a beam and few posts near the midspan, but they would be obstacles in the room below.

1 STIFFEN WITH PLYWOOD
Fasten 4 x 8-ft. sheets of ½-in. plywood to the underside of the I-joists with 1½-in. screws.

2 ADD BRIDGING
Toenail a line of I-joist blocks between the joists across the full length of the room.

SKILLS IN PRACTICE

Ceramic Tile Floor

Simplify the instillation process by building over existing vinyl flooring

Whether you're replacing an old shabby floor or installing a new one, you can't beat ceramic or stone tile for durability and appearance. When laid properly, it's virtually a forever floor that requires almost no care and maintenance. And you can select materials from a vast array of colors and textures.

What's equally attractive is that you can lay a first-class tile floor yourself, often in one weekend, and save cost of hiring a pro.

The key to keeping the job simple is to cover the old vinyl or other flooring with a new thin underlayment that gives you a fresh, clean start. No messy tearout and repair. On the following pages, expert tile installer Edward Read-Morgan of Straight Line Tile and Stone explains how to install a floor.

This is a two-day project for most bathrooms, even if you don't have any previous tile experience. If you are pretty comfortable using basic hand tools and have the patience to align tiles just right, you can handle this job. The entire cost of this project for a typical bath is a few hundred dollars.

ASSESS YOUR FLOOR

The success of any tile job depends on a solid base, that is, a floor that flexes very little as you walk across it. If you have a concrete subfloor, this isn't an issue. You can lay tile directly over the existing vinyl as long as it's well adhered.

If possible, avoid tearing out vinyl flooring. Leaving it in place saves time, of course, but it also reduces asbestos hazard concerns. Asbestos was used in sheet vinyl and vinyl tile until the mid-1980s. By leaving the vinyl undisturbed, you won't risk sending asbestos fibers into the air.

If you have a wood subfloor, there's a good chance that you'll have to install backer board over your existing vinyl to make the floor thicker and stiff enough for tile. The easiest way to see the flooring thickness is to pull off a floor register. Otherwise look for plumbing passageways through the floor. As a last resort, drill through the floor with a 1 in. or larger spade bit (your new floor will cover the hole later). To prevent asbestos dust from becoming airborne, mist the bit with a spray bottle as you drill. In addition to floor thickness, you will need to determine joist spacing. If there's an unfinished basement or crawlspace below the floor, simply measure the spacing. If there's a ceiling, probe for joists with a drill bit.

If the joists are spaced 16 in. apart, the layers of structural flooring under the vinyl should add up to at least 1⅛ in. With joists every 24 in., you need at least 1½ in. If your floor is too thin for tile, add a thicker layer of tile backer board. If your floor is already thick enough, you can simply prep your old vinyl floor **(Photos 1-4)** and skip the backer installation **(Photos 5-8)**. Then tile directly over the vinyl. Just follow the same steps used over backer board.

Regardless of the subfloor type, there are two situations where you can't leave vinyl in place: First, if large areas of the vinyl are loose, don't set tile or backer over it. Small loose spots are acceptable and easy to deal with **(Photo 4)**. Second, "cushioned" sheet vinyl must be removed before you can set tile. Cushioned vinyl has a foam backing that makes it noticeably thicker and softer than most standard vinyl flooring. It's far too spongy to support tile or backer board, and can cause tile or grout to crack. Before removing it, be sure to call your local health department for specific instructions on how to check for asbestos. They will be able to provide the proper procedures if you find that asbestos is present.

Materials

- Backer board
- 1¼" backer board screws
- Alkali-resistant mesh tape
- Thin-set
- Grout
- Acrylic additive
- Scouring pad
- Toilet extension ring
- Wax ring
- Silicone caulk
- No. 12 x 2" stainless steel screws
- 2½" galvanized screws
- Transition threshold
- Construction adhesive
- ⅜" backer rod
- Sanded caulk
- Masking tape
- Duct tape
- 1x4 guide boards
- Chalk line
- T-square or other straightedge
- Drywall saw
- Scoring knife
- Kneepads
- Notched trowels
- Grout float
- Margin trowel
- Sponges
- Tile spacers
- Wedge spacers
- Tile cutter
- 4-in. diamond blade
- Angle grinder
- Drill mixer
- Buckets

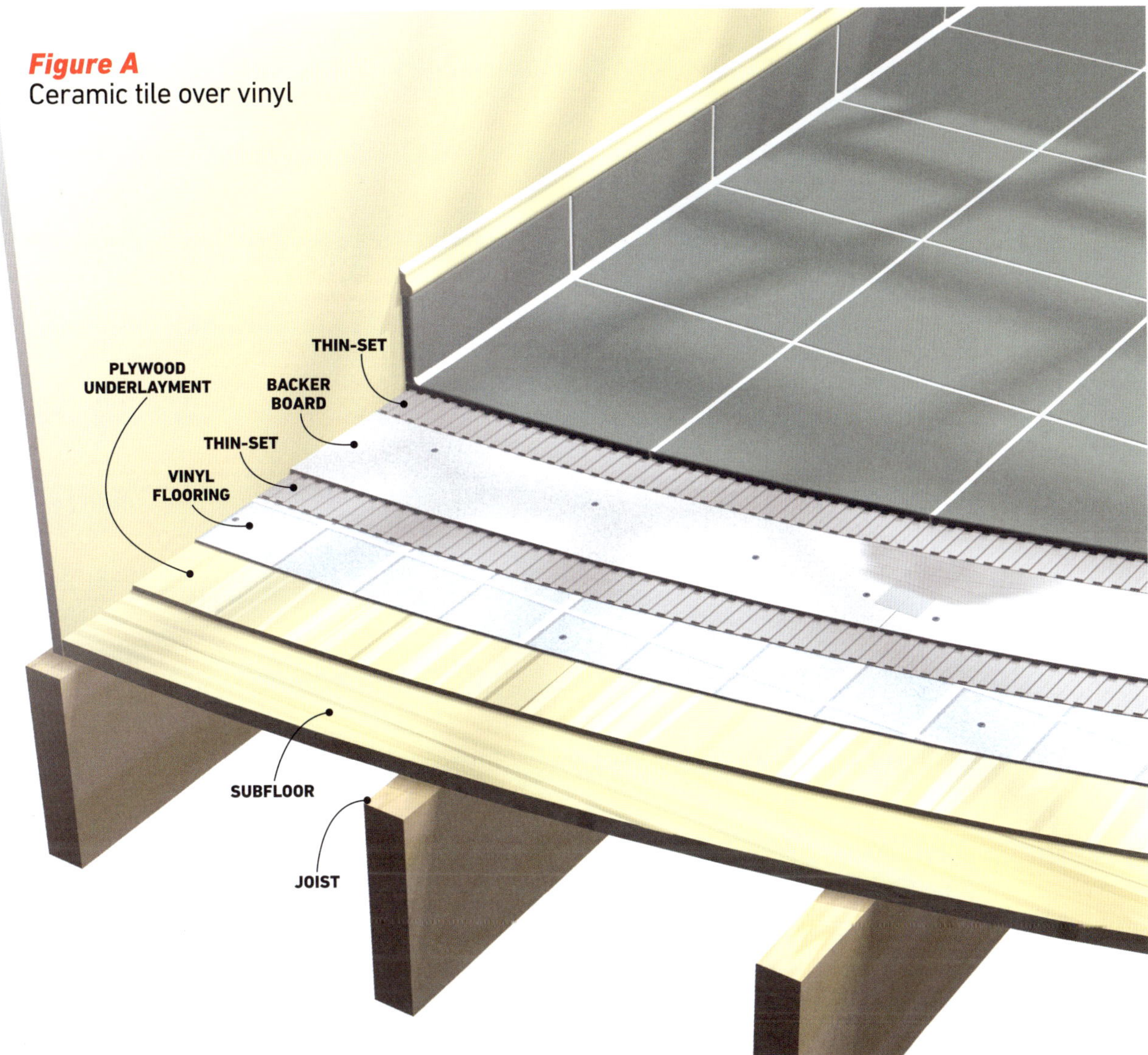

ESTIMATING THE COST OF A TILE PROJECT

The tile itself will be your biggest cost, so start by measuring the square footage of the floor. Then add 10 percent for cutting waste. If you choose a more complex layout than the simple grid pattern shown here, your waste will be greater. Most tile sells for $5 to $15 per square foot, but you can spend as little as $3 or more than $50. If you have to install backer board, add about $2 per square foot to the cost of the tile. Other materials will cost around $90, regardless of bathroom size. The tile tools (including a tile cutter) will total near $60 to $80.

GATHER ADVICE WHILE YOU SHOP

Home centers carry everything you need for this project, but begin shopping at a tile store, where you're more likely to get expert advice. Snap a photo of your floor plan and jot down all the dimensions. Also take a photo of the floor at the doorway. This will help the tile store staff recommend a "transition" to neatly join the new tile to the hallway flooring. Transitions come in different styles to suit any situation. When you choose the tile itself, ask if it requires any special installation steps. Some tile, for example, should be coated with grout release before you grout the cracks. Also ask about cutting techniques for the tile. You'll use sanded grout for the floor. Ask if sanded caulk is available in a color that matches your grout for the floor/tub and floor/wall tile joints.

PREPARE THE ROOM

First, get the toilet out of your way. Stuff a rag in the hole to block sewer gases. If your home only has one toilet, you can leave it in place until you install backer board. Keep a supply of wax rings on hand if you plan to reinstall the toilet at the end of each day.

If you expect to keep your vanity for many years to come, leave it in place and tile around it.

ILLUSTRATION: FAMILY HANDYMAN

1 CLEAR AND CLEAN THE FLOOR

Remove the baseboard and toilet. Using an abrasive pad, scrub the floor hard with water mixed with vinyl floor stripper.

2 DRIVE SCREWS

Mark the floor joists with chalk lines and drive 2½-in. screws every 8 in. Don't leave any screw heads protruding.

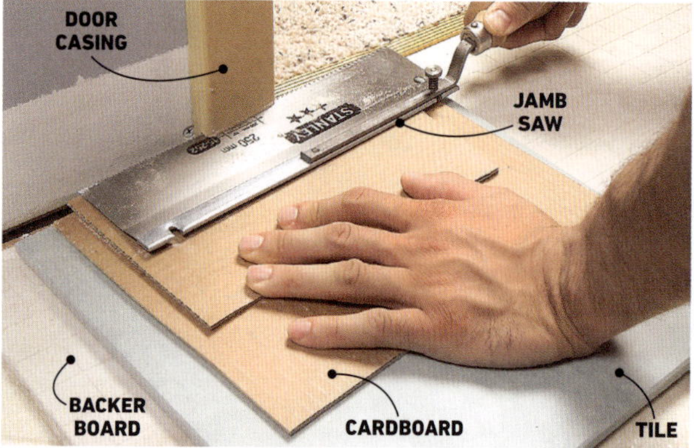

3 CUT THE DOOR TRIM

Undercut door trim using a handsaw or jamb saw. A piece of backer board, tile and two layers of cardboard raise the saw to the correct height.

4 REMOVE LOOSE VINYL

Cut out any loose sections of vinyl with a utility knife. Fill the void with thin-set using the flat edge of a notched trowel.

But if you think you might replace it, remove it now. When the job's done, you can reinstall your old vanity or put in a new one. Having the vanity out of the way gives you more workspace, and you won't have to cut backer board and tiles to fit around it. This also eliminates the floor repair problem if you install a smaller vanity or pedestal sink in the future.

Pull off the baseboard or plan to add base shoe molding. This leads to a neater-looking job because the edges of the tile will be covered later—jagged cuts and slight measuring mistakes are hidden. If your baseboard has base shoe molding, remove only the base shoe.

Backer board and tile will raise your floor ¾ in. or more. So you will have to remove and undercut the door. To mark the door for cutting, stack backer board, tile and two layers of cardboard on the floor **(Photo 3)**. Mark the door ½ in. above the stack's height, remove the door and cut off the bottom so it clears the new floor.

SCRUB, SCREW AND PATCH THE FLOOR

Scrub the floor with a vinyl floor stripper following the manufacturer's instructions. The stripper will dissolve wax and other residue. Scrub hard with an abrasive scouring pad **(Photo 1)**. The tiny scratches left by scrubbing help the thin-set bond much better.

Next, drive screws through the floor into the joists **(Photo 2)**. This ensures that the subfloor

CAUTION Cement products such as thin-set and grout draw moisture from skin and can even cause burns that require medical attention. While most pros work bare-handed, wear gloves if you have any skin sensitivity. Also wear eye protection while mixing thin-set and grout.

and underlayment are securely fastened. If there's an unfinished basement below the floor, finding the joists is easy: Go downstairs to the basement and drill a few ¼-in. holes up through the floor next to a joist. If you can't locate the joists from below, pick a spot near one wall and drill a hole. If the bit breaks through to hollow space, move over 1 in. and drill another hole. Keep going until you hit a joist. Then go to the opposite wall and find the other end of the joist. Measure at intervals of 16 or 24 in. from the first joist to locate the others.

While you're driving screws, look for any spots where vinyl has loosened from the floor. Cut out loose spots and fill them in **(Photo 4)**. If there are any copper pipes that pass through the floor, wrap them with duct tape at the floor level. Cement-based thin-set and grout can corrode copper.

INSTALL BACKER BOARD

The backer board is fastened with a combination of screws and thin-set adhesive. Cut and lay out all the pieces before you mix the thin-set **(Photos 5 and 6)**. You can run the sheets in any direction, but be sure to stagger the joints so you never have four corners meeting at one point. Leave a ⅛-in. space between the sheets and along the vanity, tub or shower. The gap along walls must be at least ⅛ in. wide, but a wider gap (about ½ in.) makes the panels easier to set in place. After cutting and fitting, label the location of each one and set them all aside.

Vacuum the floor and have your drill and screws ready to go before you mix the thin-set. Read the thin-set's label. Spread the thin-set with a ¼-in. notched trowel. Comb in one direction so air can escape when you embed the backer **(Photo 7)**. Drive screws every 6 in. around the

5 CUT BACKER BOARD DETAILS Cover the floor with backer board. Cut inside corners, circles and curves with a drywall saw. Space pieces ⅛ in. apart and hold each one in place with two temporary screws.

6 COMPLETE BACKER BOARD CUTS Make straight cuts with a scoring knife. Make three or four scoring passes, then snap the backer over a 2×4. When all the pieces have been laid out, label them and set them aside.

7 LAY THIN-SET AND BACKER BOARD Comb out a bed of thin-set just large enough for each piece of backer board using a ¼-in. notched trowel held at a 45-degree angle. Screw the backer down before spreading thin-set for the next piece.

8 TAPE JOINTS

Press adhesive-backed mesh tape over the joints and skim over the tape with thin-set. When the thin-set is firm but not fully hardened, scrape away any ridges with a putty knife.

perimeter of each piece and every 8 in. "in the field" (across the face of the panel). If the leftover thin-set is still workable, you can immediately embed mesh tape over joints **(Photo 8)**. If the thin-set is too stiff or chunky, mix a new batch. Only use "alkali-resistant" tape that's meant for backer board. While the tape coat of thin-set hardens, run a putty knife over all the screw heads to scrape off the "mushroom" bulges around all the screws. Drive in any screw heads that may be protruding that you come across.

9 LAY OUT TILES

Dry-lay tile to determine the best layout. Start with centered rows, leaving equal spaces at walls. Then reposition rows until you find the optimal layout.

10 MAP TILE GUIDES

Screw guide boards to the floor following your chosen layout. Position the guides so you can lay all the field tiles without moving the guides. Set the guides at a right angle by measuring a 3-4-5 triangle.

CAREFUL LAYOUT PAYS OFF

Too often, tile novices simply start setting tile in a corner and continue along two walls until the floor is covered. Sometimes they get lucky and the floor looks good. But more often this method leads to trouble: They end up with awkward-looking, thin slivers of tile along a prominent wall or at the doorway. And the tile looks even worse when walls are badly out of square or crooked. A straight grout line running too close to a wall emphasizes the wall's imperfections.

Whether you're laying a simple grid pattern as shown here, or a diagonal pattern with a border, the best tile layout usually calls for centering full tiles between walls so the partial tiles along the edges will end up all the same size. Don't rely on your tape measure and mental arithmetic. Rip open a carton of tile, grab a handful of spacers and start to experiment with your layout on the floor.

To begin, center rows of tile between walls so you have equal spaces along walls that face each other **(Photo 9)**. Set the two rows parallel to the room's two most prominent walls. Then make adjustments, trying to achieve these three goals:

- Use full tiles at doorways and along the bathtub or shower. These are usually the only places where the edges of the floor aren't covered by baseboard. If you use full tiles in these exposed spots, you don't have to worry about making smooth, perfect cuts.
- Minimize cutting and try to avoid difficult cuts. For example: Cutting tile to an L-shape to fit around an outside corner is especially difficult when one arm of the "L" is less than 2 in. wide. The arm tends to break off as you cut.

- Avoid narrow tiles along walls. Ideally, you'll end up with tiles cut to half size or larger. Avoid cutting tile to widths less than 2 in.

Chances are, your layout won't meet all these goals. Because the shower stall was the focal point in this bathroom, it is the No. 1 layout priority. Full tiles are used in front of the shower, leaving 3-in.-wide tiles along the opposite wall, which is less prominent.

Once you determine a layout, establish lines to guide your tile positioning. The usual method is to snap chalk lines on the floor. But chalk lines are hard to see after you've spread thin-set, and one row of tile may slip as you set the next row. Pros use a more reliable guide: Choose straight boards a foot shorter than the length and width of the room. Tape one edge of each board so thin-set won't stick to them. Then screw the boards to the floor at a right angle to form a guide that eliminates guesswork and shifting **(Photo 10)**.

SET THE TILE (FINALLY!)

It's usually easiest—and most efficient—to set tile in two phases: First set all the full "field" tiles **(Photo 11)**. Then, when all the thin-set has hardened for several hours, cut all the perimeter tiles and set them **(Photo 12)**. Here are some tips for both phases:

- The trowel you use for setting tile may be different from the one you used to embed the backer. The thin-set label tells you which notch size to use relative to tile size.
- Dampen the backer board with a sponge just before applying thin-set. This keeps the thin-set from drying out too quickly.
- Comb the thin-set in one single direction so pockets of air won't be trapped under the new tile.
- Open three or four cartons and mix the tiles as you set them. Pattern and color vary slightly from one carton to the next.
- Don't just set each tile into place; press down and wiggle the tile to embed it firmly in your thin-set. Use spacers between tiles.
- Watch for "tipped" corners. When you press a tile in place, it's easy to tilt it slightly so that one corner stands higher or lower.
- When you complete a section of tile, inspect it before moving on. Make sure the tiles line up correctly and spacers are in place. Wipe any thin-set off the face of tiles with a damp sponge to avoid a mess later.
- When the thin-set becomes chunky or too stiff, throw it away and mix more. Never try to extend thin-set or grout by adding water.
- Cut perimeter tile so that caulked joints (at tub or shower) are the same width as grouted joints.

11 SET DOWN CENTER TILES

Comb out a few square feet of thin-set and set tile against the guides. Continue until all the full tiles are in place. **Tip:** Watch for squeeze-out between tiles and get it out with tile spacers.

12 PLACE PERIMETER TILES

Cut and set the perimeter tiles after the thin-set beneath the full tiles has hardened. In spaces too narrow for your trowel, comb thin-set onto the backs of tiles.

13 ADD AN EXTENSION RING
Remove the old screws from the toilet flange and apply a heavy bead of silicone caulk. Fasten the extension ring over the old flange with stainless steel or brass screws.

14 WORK ON THE TRANSITION
Glue the transition into place with construction adhesive. If carpet meets the transition, you may have to add a new tack strip.

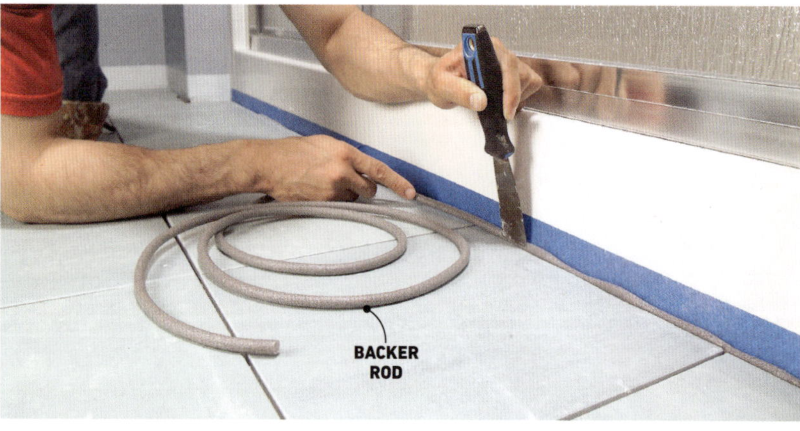

15 SQUEEZE IN BACKER ROD
Push the backer rod into joints that will be caulked later. The foam rod keeps grout out of joints. After grouting, pull out the rod and caulk the joints.

PREPARE THE FLOOR FOR GROUT

When all the tiles are in place and the thin-set has hardened, remove all the spacers. Next, raise the toilet flange by adding an extension ring or two **(Photo 13)**. The extended flange should be flush with or higher than the surrounding tile. When you grout, fill in between the flange and tile. That way, any future leak around the flange will show up on the bathroom floor instead of on the ceiling below.

If you plan to use a glue-down transition, install it now. Remove the old metal strip, then cut your transition strip to fit between the door jambs using a miter saw. Next, add a tack strip to hold adjacent carpet in place. Before gluing the transition to the floor **(Photo 14)**, you may have to remove a thin strip of the old vinyl floor.

Grout is too brittle to handle the slight shifting movements that are normal in any room. Keep grout out of joints wherever the floor meets the tub, shower, vanity or walls **(Photo 15)**.

PACK THE JOINTS WITH GROUT

The thin-set directions will tell you how soon you can grout the floor—usually 24 hours. Grouting isn't complex. Just plop a couple of scoops of grout onto the floor in a corner, work the grout into joints **(Photo 16)** and scrape off the excess grout before moving to the next section. In addition:

- Mix the grout to a mashed potatoes consistency. Adding extra liquid makes grout easier to work with but weakens it.
- Don't just spread the grout over the joints; press hard to pack it into the joints. If you're doing it right, you'll feel your forearm will get a good workout.
- Whether you're filling joints or scraping off excess grout,

16 SPREAD GROUT Work the grout across the floor, diagonal to the joints. Hold the float at a 45-degree angle. Scrape off the excess grout, holding the float almost upright.

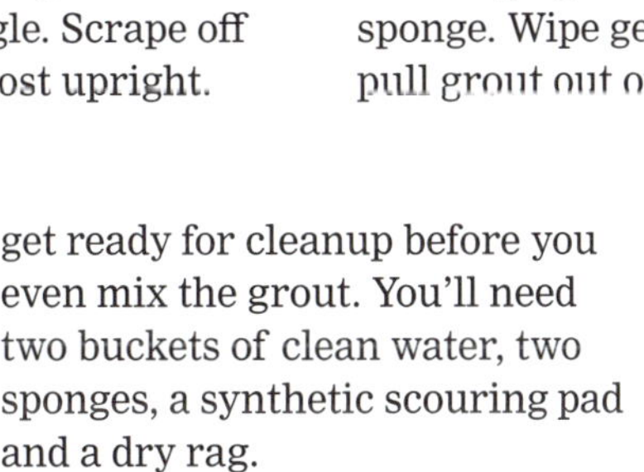

17 CLEAN THE EXCESS Wipe grout off the tile surface with a damp sponge. Wipe gently on the first pass so you don't pull grout out of the joints. Rise the sponge often.

always push the float diagonally across the tiles.

- Scrape off the excess to leave tile as clean as you can. The less grout you leave on the tiles, the easier cleanup will be later.
- When you're done, cover the grout bucket with a plastic bag and set it in a cool place to slow down the hardening process. During cleanup, you may find spots that need a little extra.

GROUT CLEANUP

Clean the surface of the tile when the grout is stiff enough to stay put in the joints but still soft enough to wipe off the tile surface. During hot, dry weather, grout can become difficult to wipe away in just 10 minutes, so get ready for cleanup before you even mix the grout. You'll need two buckets of clean water, two sponges, a synthetic scouring pad and a dry rag.

As soon as you're done with grouting, go to the first section you grouted and wipe across a joint with a damp sponge. If your sponge pulls grout out of the joint, wait five minutes and try again. In cool, damp weather, the grout may stay too soft for an hour. When the grout is hard enough, gently wipe the tile with a damp sponge. Rinse the sponge frequently as you wipe the entire floor **(Photo 17)**. If you come across tough spots, scrub them with the scouring pad. Be careful where you put your feet and knees—don't mar your perfect grout joints.

Immediately after the first pass, grab the second bucket of clean water and the fresh sponge and make a second, more thorough pass. Then, as the tile surface dries, wipe it with a microfiber cloth. The dry haze should buff off easily. If not, go for fresh water and sponge the floor again.

FINISHING UP

Let the grout cure overnight before you caulk joints, set the toilet or reinstall baseboard. Grout sealer is a good precaution against staining: Some products can be applied 24 hours after grouting; others require a two-to-three-week wait. If you have leftover tile or grout, keep them in case you have to make repairs in the future. Be sure to write down the brand, color and retailer of the tile.

CHAPTER 4

Electrical

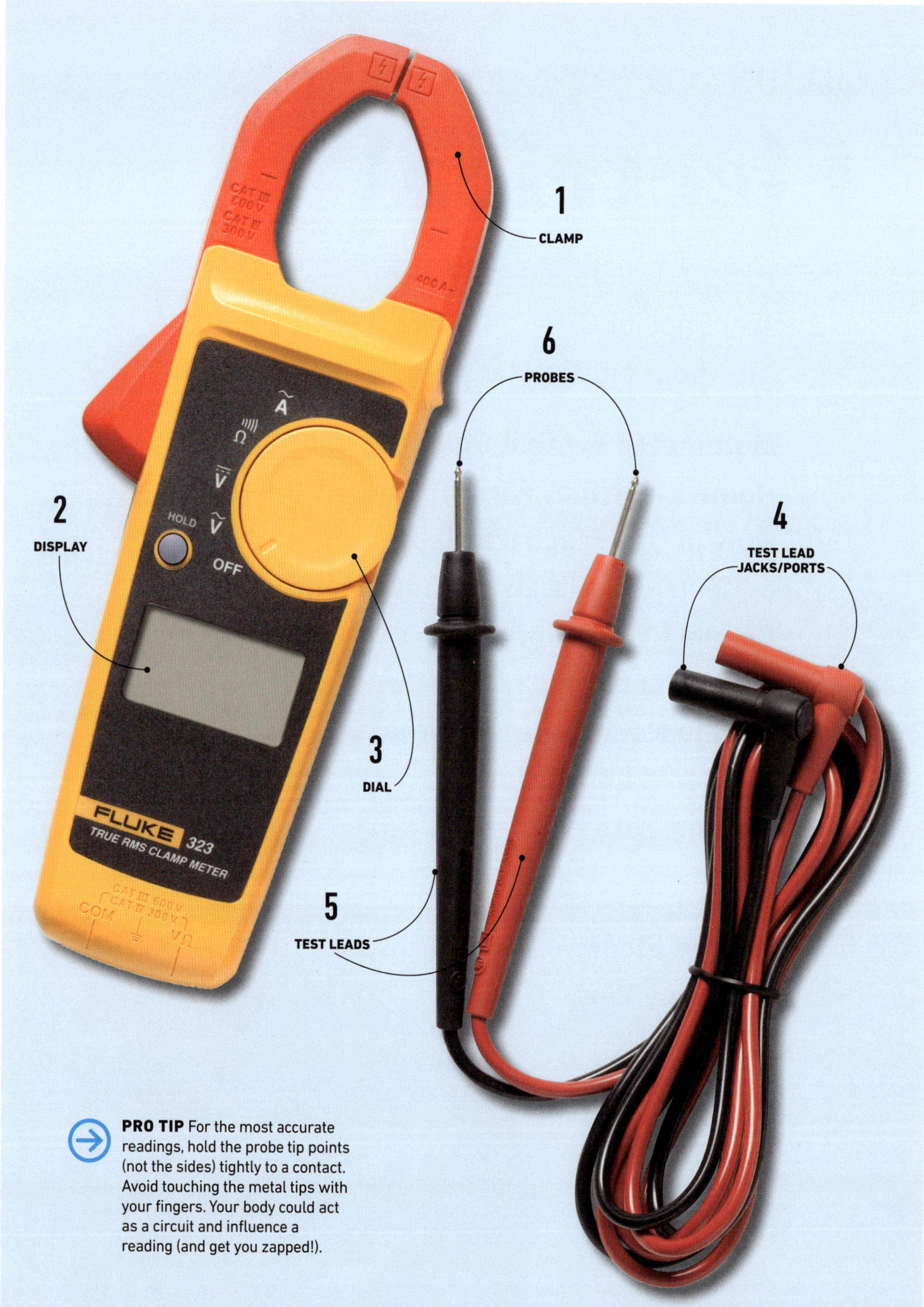

1
CLAMP

6
PROBES

2
DISPLAY

4
TEST LEAD JACKS/PORTS

3
DIAL

5
TEST LEADS

PRO TIP For the most accurate readings, hold the probe tip points (not the sides) tightly to a contact. Avoid touching the metal tips with your fingers. Your body could act as a circuit and influence a reading (and get you zapped!).

FLUKE CORPORATION

TOOL SPOTLIGHT

All About Multimeters

What to look for when you need to measure amps, voltage and more

By Harrison Kral

WHAT IS A MULTIMETER?

A multimeter, also known as a volt-ohm-milliammeter (or VOM), is a device that measures voltage, current (amps), resistance and continuity. Multimeters are used by electricians, auto mechanics, HVAC professionals and other technicians who troubleshoot electrical and electronic equipment. The tool was invented by a British post office engineer named Donald Macadie who was tired of carrying around several instruments while trying to troubleshoot telecommunication circuits. These are the common parts of a multimeter:

1. Clamp
2. Display
3. Dial
4. Test lead jacks/ports
5. Test leads
6. Probes

HOW IS A MULTIMETER USED?

The black test lead always stays in the common port, which is often abbreviated as COM. The red test lead will get moved from one jack to another depending on they type of meter you have and what you are testing, such as voltage, current (amps), resistance or continuity. The dial is set to the type of current you are testing for (AC or DC) and the range of the volts or amps you will be working with. Electricity is inherently very dangerous, so always refer to the manual for instructions/warnings for your specific multimeter.

WHAT ARE THE DIFFERENT TYPES OF MULTIMETERS?

In addition to digital multimeters, there are analog multimeters that have a physical scale and a needle or pointer. Only a small number of analog multimeters are still being made compared to digital meters. Clamp multimeters are common and can be distinguished by the clamp on the top that resembles a pincer. The other differences will mainly be found in the range of voltage and amps that can be measured and accuracy. A less expensive multimeter can be bought for around $10, while a super-accurate laboratory version will cost thousands. The bells and whistle also vary widely from one multimeter to another. Some meters are even combined with infrared imaging cameras.

WHAT MAKES A GOOD MULTIMETER?

- Durable
- Easy-to-read display and labels
- Large buttons and dials that can be operated while wearing gloves
- Compact
- Backlit screen
- Quality carrying case
- Clamp for easy current measurements
- Auto shut-off
- Hold button to record the highest and lowest readings

Multimeter Symbol Guide

When testing electrical equipment around the home, it's vital to know what all those symbols on your multimeter mean

By Chris Deziel

Back in the early days of electricity, lab workers measured electric current using an ammeter (galvanometer) and voltage using a voltmeter. From there, they calculated resistance in ohms.

In 1920, The AVOmeter was invented, which measured all three quantities: A = amps, V = volts and O = ohms. Soon after, electricians working in the field got their hands on somewhat portable versions of this influential invention.

Today's multimeters do the same jobs as the AVOmeter, but they're more sophisticated and can do multiple other tests as well. Depending on the model, a multimeter can tell you whether a diode or capacitor is working, distinguish between alternating and direct current and measure wire temperature. Functions are denoted by symbols arranged around a dial.

Homeowners doing their own electrical work don't need the same functionality as electronics technicians, so multimeters sold in hardware stores are generally less complicated than those sold at electronics supply outlets. Even so, the symbols can be difficult to decipher for first-timers. Here's a rundown of the electrical terms and symbols you'll find on a basic multimeter for home use and what they mean.

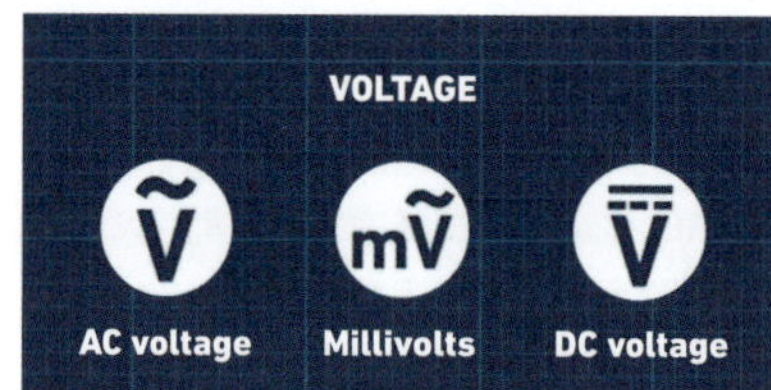

VOLTAGE

Multimeters measure direct current (DC) voltage as well as alternating current (AC) voltage, so they need to display more than one symbol. On some older models, the designation for AC voltage is **VAC**. These days, it's more common for manufacturers to place a wavy line over the V to signify AC voltage.

To signify DC voltage, the convention is to place a dotted line with a solid line above it over the V. To get voltage readings in millivolts (one-thousandth of a volt), set the dial to mV.

- **"V" with a wavy line over it** is AC voltage.
- **"V" with one dotted and one solid over it** is DC voltage.
- **"mV" with one wavy line or a pair of lines, one dotted and one solid, over it** is AC or DC millivolts.

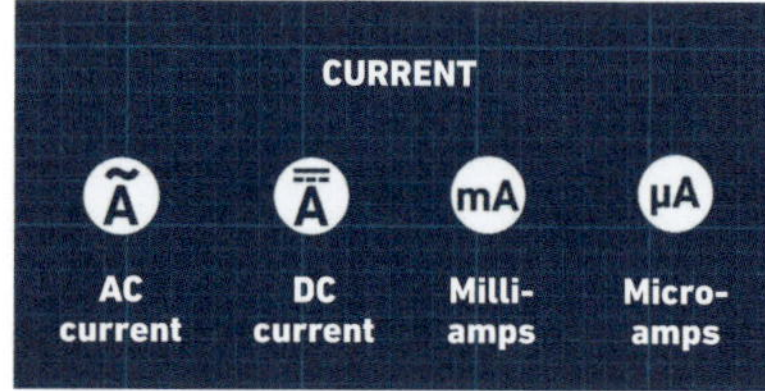

CURRENT

Like voltage, current can be AC or DC. Because the unit for current is amperes, or amps, the symbol for it is A.

- **"A" with a wavy line over it** is AC current.
- **"A" with two lines, one dotted and one solid, over it** is DC current.
- **mA** is milliamps.
- **µA** (µ is the Greek letter mu) is microamps (millionths of an amp).

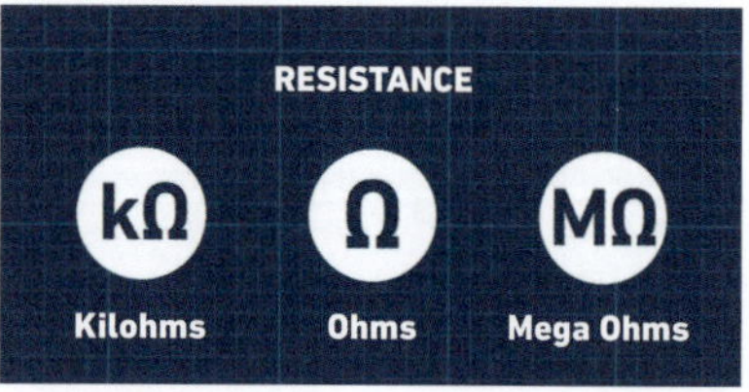

RESISTANCE

A multimeter measures resistance by sending a small electric current through the circuit. The symbol for the unit of resistance, the ohm, is the Greek letter omega (Ω). But meters don't distinguish between AC and DC resistance, so there are no lines above this symbol.

On meters with range selection options, you can select either the kilohm (1,000 ohms) scale or pick the mega ohm (one million ohms) scale, which are kΩ and MΩ.

- **Ω** is Ohms.
- **kΩ** is Kilohms.
- **MΩ** is Mega ohms.

CONTINUITY

Use a multimeter to test for a break in an electrical circuit. The meter measures resistance, and there are only two outcomes. Either the circuit is broken (open), in which case the meter reads infinite resistance, or the circuit is intact (closed), in which case the meter reads 0 (or very close to it).

Because there are only two possibilities, some meters beep when they detect continuity. This function is denoted on the dial settings by a series of left-facing brackets of increasing size, like a sideways version of the wireless reception symbol on a laptop.

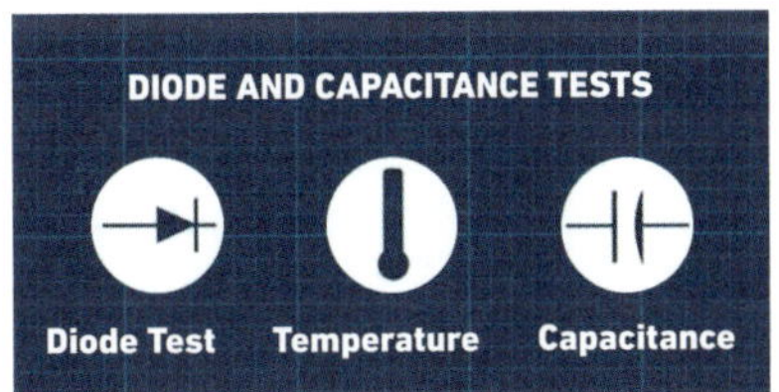

DIODE AND CAPACITANCE TESTS

Electronics technicians are far more likely to use the diode and capacitance testing features than electricians or homeowners. But if you have a meter with these functions, it helps to know what the symbols mean.

The **diode test function** looks like an arrow pointing toward the center of a plus sign. When this function is selected, the meter will tell you whether a diode (a common electronics component that changes AC current into DC current) is working or not.

The **capacitance function** resembles a right-facing bracket to the right of a vertical line. Both are crossed by a horizontal line. Capacitors are electronic devices that store charge, and the meter can measure the charge.

The **temperature function** measures the temperature of the circuit wires. It's denoted by a thermometer.

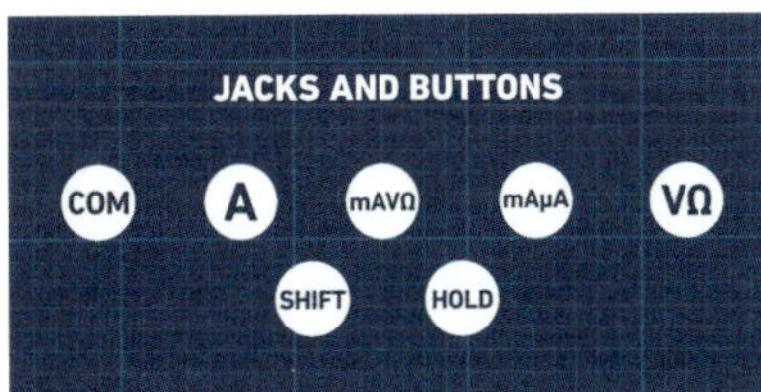

JACKS AND BUTTONS

Two leads are supplied with every multimeter, one black and one red. Some meters have three jacks and some four. The jacks into which you plug the leads depend on what you're testing.

- **COM** is the common jack, and it's the only black one. You always plug the black lead into this jack.
- **A** is the jack where the red lead goes if you're measuring high current up to 10 amps.
- **mAVΩ** is the jack for every other type of measurement, including sensitive current measurements, voltage, resistance and temperature, if the meter has only three other jacks.
- **mAμA** is the jack for sensitive current measurements (less than 1 amp) if the meter has four jacks.
- **VΩ** is the jack to use for all other measurements except current.

At the top of the meter display, above the dial, you usually find two buttons, one to the left and one to the right.

- **Shift.** To save some space, manufacturers may assign two functions to some dial positions. You access the function marked in yellow by pressing the shift button, which is usually also yellow and may or may not be labeled "shift."
- **Hold.** Pressing this button freezes the current reading for later reference.

MANUAL VS. AUTO RANGE

An older analog multimeter with a needle needs to have more than one range setting. Because if the meter had only a large range, it couldn't be used for sensitive measurements because the needle would hardly deflect. But on the other hand, if the meter had only a small range, any measurement exceeding that range, no matter what it was, would deflect the needle to its maximum.

Digital multimeters with LED displays were introduced in the 1970s, and today the majority of multimeters are digital. Some still have range settings that you select with a dial. But increasingly, the meter selects the range automatically.

Because these multimeters don't have range settings (which can occupy up to 18 positions on the dial), the newer auto-range multimeters tend to have more functionality than those with manual range settings.

Note: Read the multimeter's owner's manual thoroughly before use and save it for reference. Follow all safety precautions. Improper use of the multimeter can result in severe damage to equipment or personal injury. Keep the manual, test leads and multimeter together in a zip-top freezer storage bag.

ILLUSTRATIONS: FAMILY HANDYMAN (5)

Home Electrical Wiring Tips and Safety

Wire better, faster and neater with these pro tips

By Ally Childress

Do-it-yourself electrical projects are very rewarding. You're taking care of your own home, learning new skills and saving money on tasks that are often very doable for a smart, diligent and careful person. However, working with electricity is dangerous, and that's why the world needs licensed electricians like me.

If you have a few projects around the house, don't be afraid to dig in. Swapping out a light fixture, adding a USB-charging receptacle or replacing a switch with a new dimmer are perfect starter tasks. Below, I will walk you through some common wiring tips and safety issues so you can be a more confident DIYer.

If you ever feel the task is too complex, especially regarding your electrical service panel, that's a good time to call a pro.

ELECTRICAL SAFETY

The first rule of electricity club is: Turn off the breaker! Never start a project without double-checking that the power is off. Old-timers talk of when "working hot" was the norm, and I've had to do it a few times myself when turning off the power would cause a major disruption. It is scary as heck and dangerous. There is no need for you to do it in your home.

Carry a noncontact voltage detector in your tool bag and use it whenever you do electrical work for peace of mind.

READ THE INSTRUCTIONS

"Instructions? Who needs 'em?" some may think. Well, you do. I do too, and that's why I read the paperwork, especially when you're doing something new. Manufacturers are very detailed when it comes to explaining how to put in their devices, and the National Electrical Code (NEC) actually requires that you follow their advice. I know electricians who immediately throw away the instructions, and believe me, those are the people who screw things up.

UNCOIL CABLE WITHOUT KINKS

Nonmetallic sheathed cable, better known as Romex, is often solid copper, and it's tough to pull through your walls or framing if you don't fully uncoil it first. Electricians have a few tricks for this, but one easy way is to grab a handful of coils from the roll and just give it a toss. Then, walk along the length and straighten it out (you can even step on it as you go). Leave the rest of the wire contained in the packaging.

TAKE PICTURES

This tip will save you tons of time if you're replacing a fixture or you have to take apart multiple splices. Snap a few pics with your phone before you undo anything so you can refer back to them when it's time to put in the new fixture. Labeling your wires with electrical tape and a Sharpie will help too.

CHECK THE WALL VOID

Cutting a hole in the wall for a switch or receptacle outlet? Find the studs first, then run your stud finder over the entire section to find any other obstructions. There may be wires, pipes or blocking that could screw up the placement

of your new device or your ability to pull wire through.

When you cut the hole, make the horizontal cuts first. If you run into an obstruction, make that spot the new outside edge of your outlet. Then, simply turn your saw around and go back the other way.

FISHING BASICS

Fishing wire through walls is an exercise in patience and perseverance. There's nothing more depressing than hearing the "thunk" of your fish stick (aka glow rod or fish rod) hitting a header you didn't realize was there. If you plan on renovating a lot, invest in a set of quality fish sticks and a long flex bit for drilling in hard-to-reach spaces.

If you're just adding a single receptacle, and you have access to the top of the wall, use your tape measure as an impromptu fish stick. Just drop it down to your new outlet, tape a string

or your Romex right to it, and pull it up through the cavity.

MAKE NO-SNAG CONNECTIONS

Fish tape, a thin, flexible metal or nylon wire-pulling tool, is often used to snake wire through pipes. It also works well through walls, floors and studs, as long as the hooked end doesn't get snagged on something. To make a smooth transition on the end of your fish tape, strip off 6 to 8 in. of the sheathing from your NM-B cable.

Cut off all but one wire and trim the cable at a steep angle to avoid leaving a "shoulder." Slide the single long wire through the end of the fish tape, fold it over and wrap the electrical tape tightly around the entire head (including the cut-off edge of the Romex). As you wrap the tape, smooth out any bumps to make the head as smooth as you can. It should make a huge difference.

PACK BOXES NEATLY

I just replaced a receptacle with one I can use to charge my phone, and the box was so messy that I spent an hour straightening up the wires. Jammed boxes with lots of extra nonsense call you out as an amateur, so take the time to neatly fold and push bundles of wires to the back of the box, using pigtails or short pieces of wire to attach to the device (when you have room).

Speaking of room, stuffing too many wires in an electrical box is a code violation. The NEC will periodically update "box fill" requirements, so find out which code cycle your jurisdiction is following to ensure you're keeping things safe and legal.

LABEL YOUR BREAKERS

This is a fantastic entry-level project that makes your life easier and your house safer. When I moved into my current house, I needed to turn off the dishwasher circuit to replace a drain pump. Was it the breaker labeled "dishwasher"? Nope! That one controlled the countertop receptacles. For some reason, electrical panels are very rarely properly labeled.

Enlist a friend, and start flipping breakers. If you don't have a willing pal, buy a circuit tracer (which is very affordable nowadays), a receptacle tester or just use a loud radio. Plug it in, turn it up, and flip the breakers until the radio goes off. Once you have the breakers worked out, label them somewhere inside or near the electrical panel.

How to Use Electrical Tape

It takes a bit of finesse, but once you get it, you get it

By Ally Childress

One of my first jobs as an electrical apprentice was to pull wire. No, not the 12- or 14-gauge nonmetallic sheathed cable (NM-B, aka Romex) you see in your home, but massive, inch-thick wires used to bring power to U.S. Bank Stadium. When a wire gets this big, they don't bother color-coding it like the black, red, white and green you buy at the store. It comes out to the job on giant reels, and it has one color: black.

Enter electrical tape. I was given a stack of brown, orange, yellow, and gray tape—the colors are different on a 277V service than in your home's 120V service—and was told to get busy. The one problem? There is definitely a bit of a learned technique to taping. A technique I definitely didn't have yet. My foreman saw me awkwardly handling the tape and came over to give me a lesson.

I know it sounds ridiculous. Who doesn't know how to use tape? But electrical tape differs from Scotch tape, painter's tape and duct tape. Below, I'll walk you through some helpful tips and tricks you can use in your own home. You might just be surprised at what electrical tape can do.

USES FOR ELECTRICAL TAPE

Here are all the most common official uses (and one nonofficial use) for electrical tape.

Identification. Electrical tape is fantastic for wrapping around wires to identify them by color (called phasing) or for making flags to write on with a permanent marker. You could also ID your breaker switches and label electrical boxes.

Wire pulling. Wrap electrical tape around bundles of wire to organize them, then tape the head of your bundle and fish tape to effortlessly (well, sometimes) slide the wires through walls and conduit.

Protecting terminal screws. This is slightly controversial, but many electricians (including me) were taught to wrap the electrical tape around the terminal screws of receptacles and switches before shoving them into the box. The idea is to prevent shock if the device is handled while energized, but it's not required by either the NEC or manufacturers. Ironically, following manufacturer labeling is required by the NEC, hence the controversy.

Splice insulation. Electrical tape comes in various materials and insulation ratings to protect splices in high or medium-voltage connections (such as utility transmission lines). This usage requires extensive training to ensure the splice is secure and protected. Never use electrical tape instead of wire nuts or other connectors.

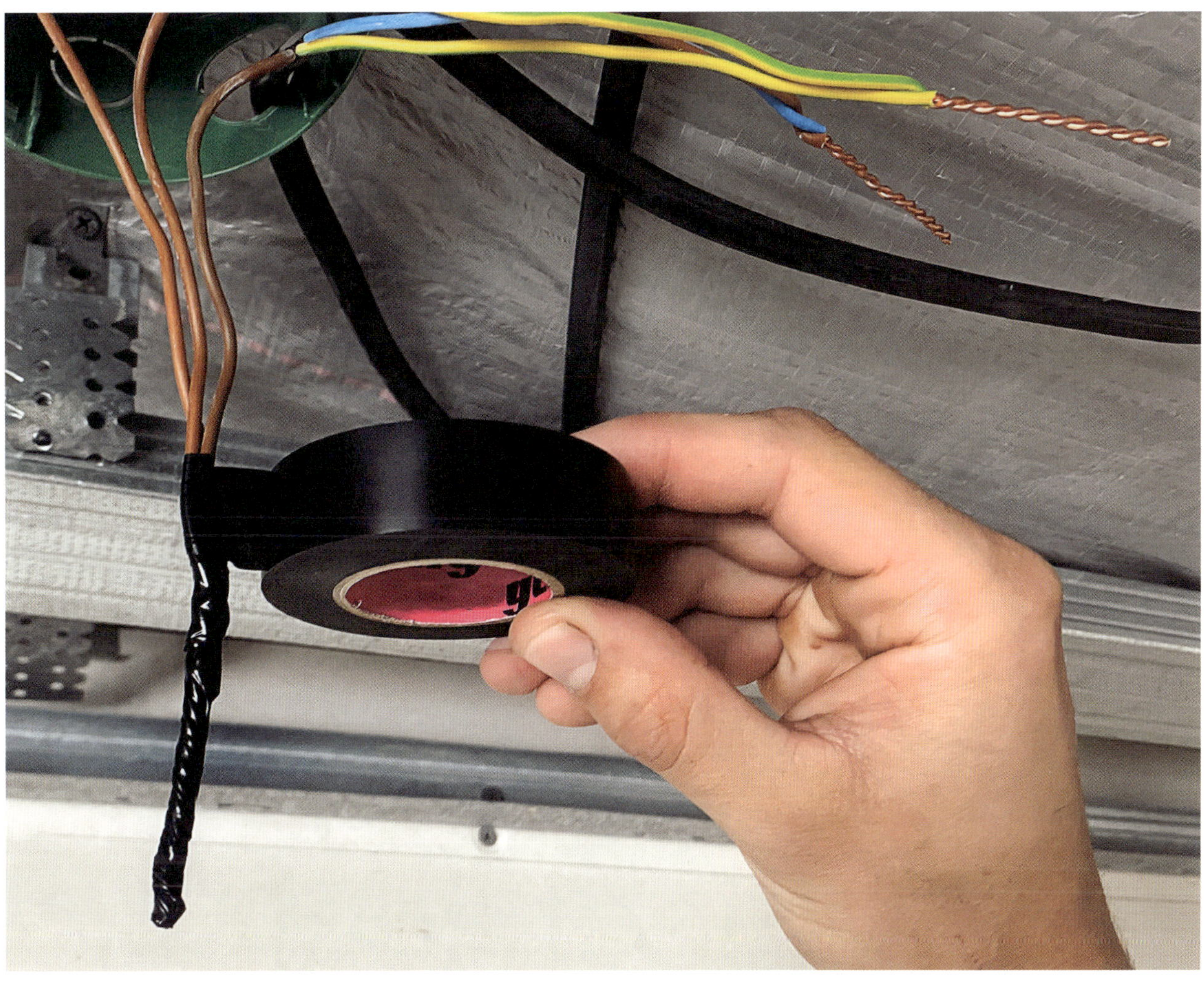

Connecting motor leads to feeders. Motors often run 24 hours a day in dirty, greasy environments. Electrical tape protects all of the electrical connections against chemicals, corrosion, temperature changes and moisture. Kits are sold for this purpose nowadays, but using tape this way is a time-tested skill that many electricians learn.

Minor or temporary repairs. We've all wrapped electrical tape around small scrapes and nicks in wire insulation, but if you can see the wire itself, do not use electrical tape to fix it.

Keeping paint scuff-free. This is my favorite nonstandard use. Using a metal torpedo level on a painted wall (to level a device or faceplate, for example) leaves marks that do not come off. Wrap the edges of your level with electrical tape to keep your paint scuff-free.

HOW TO USE ELECTRICAL TAPE

To wrap electrical tape around a cable, a bundle of wires, a pipe, a fish tape or another cylindrical object, hold the tape loosely in your dominant hand, with your thumb on top of the tape. Unstick the flap on the tape. Hold the object in your opposite hand. Stick the flap to the object, hold it down and begin your wrap. Grip the tape between your index finger and thumb, stretching it as you pull the tape toward you and down. Don't pull off too much tape, or the roll will flop around and get twisted. You want just enough free tape to encircle the object once. Keep pressure on the tape so that it stays taut as you stick it to the object at a slight angle.

When you get underneath and to the backside of the object, flip the roll over the top with your fingers. Grab it, pull it taut and start another wrap, overlapping by half the width of the tape as you move down the length of the object. Play around with your technique. For example, you might like wrapping away from you and behind the object first.

When you reach the end of the taping job, grip the tape with your thumb and finger right next to the object and give it a quick jerk. This will rip the tape roll cleanly away, leaving a short flap. Fold or twist into a "buddy flag," which makes it easy for the next guy or gal to unwrap the tape.

6 Electrical Mistakes DIYers Make

Here's what to look for, and how to fix what you find

By Ally Childress

Working on your own home is empowering, and it saves you money. Even before I became an electrician, I tackled DIY projects from plumbing to painting to carpentry. Electrical projects require a special level of precaution, though, because just a few milliamps of current can be deadly. You can do this, though. To help, I talked to two experienced electricians to walk through these top six electrical mistakes to avoid.

MISTAKE Misusing your tester. On job sites, electricians always carry noncontact voltage testers with them, and you should have one too. They are inexpensive and easy to use, and they help keep you safe when doing DIY electrical work.

SOLUTION Test. Use. Verify. First, test the tester by holding it to a known live circuit, such as a powered appliance or lamp cord. Or insert it into a receptacle (use the smaller slot, which is the hot side). The tester should light up, beep or both. Locate the circuit you'll be working on and turn off the breaker. Use the tester to verify the circuit's off, then check the tester on the same live circuit as before to confirm it functioned correctly.

MISTAKE Not using an electrical box. "Electrical boxes, sometimes referred to as junction boxes, protect connections from accidental damage, and help contain sparks and heat from a loose connection or short circuit," says Gerald Talbot, licensed electrician with Mister Sparky. "Failing to make connections inside the electrical box is arguably the biggest mistake a homeowner can make, as this can result in major hazards."

SOLUTION Add a box. If you start a project and find a jumble of taped-together wires stuffed in the wall cavity instead of neatly contained in a junction box, don't ignore it. (This happened to me, with a century-old knob and tube wiring.) Ensure the power is off, add a box and reconnect the conductors. If you're not near a stud, use "old-work" remodel boxes (sometimes they're called drywall brackets) that grip right to the drywall.

MISTAKE Too short wires. Trying to join, aka splice, tiny little wires in an electrical box is tough. "Short wires can cause a host of potential hazards and make connections difficult," Talbot says. Bad splices can cause electrical arcs and fires, so the NEC requires 6 in. of free conductor at every electrical box. Over time, though, conductors tend to get shorter as people swap out devices over the life of a home.

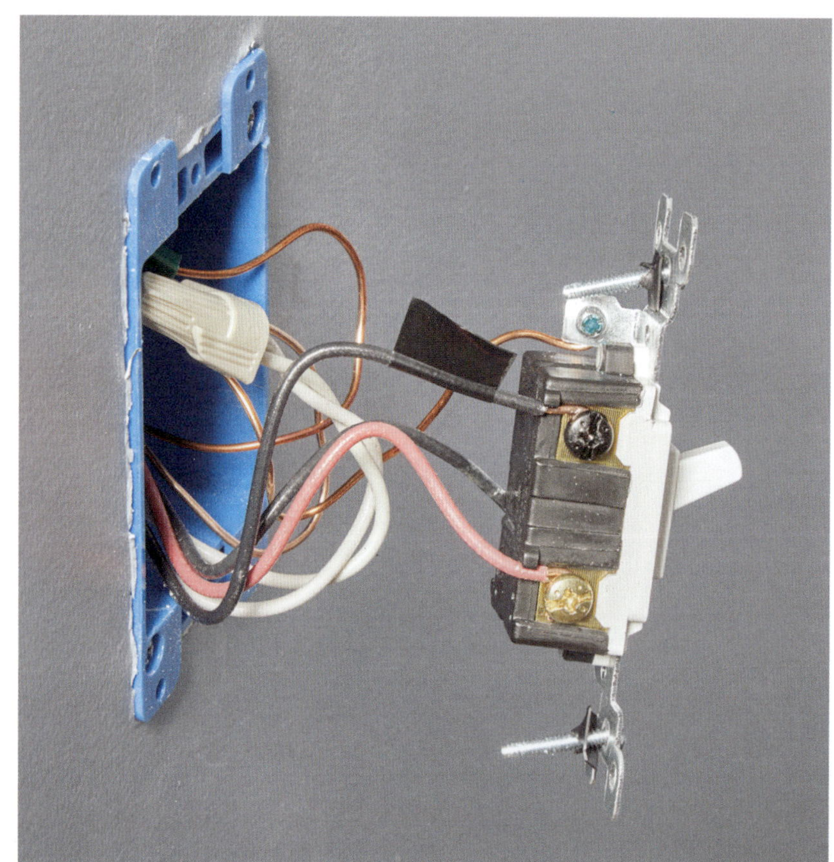

SOLUTION Add pigtails. If you open up an electrical box to find stubby conductors, add pigtails, which are short pieces of wire used to extend electrical connections. Of course, you still have the problem of splicing the pigtails onto the tiny conductors. To make things easier, use a push-in connector or lever nut, aka Wago, rather than trying to spin on a traditional wire nut.

MISTAKE Backstabbing electrical connections. Receptacles and light switches have holes where you could insert the conductors instead of attaching them to the terminal screws. While "backstabbing" is technically acceptable (after all, the holes are right there), but your connections tend to loosen over time, potentially causing electrical arcs and fires.

SOLUTION Use the screw terminals. Every electrician I've ever met (including me) prefers using the terminal screws, or pigtailing to them, instead of backstabbing. Make a hook on the end of the conductor and wrap clockwise around the terminal screw. Tighten with a screwdriver.

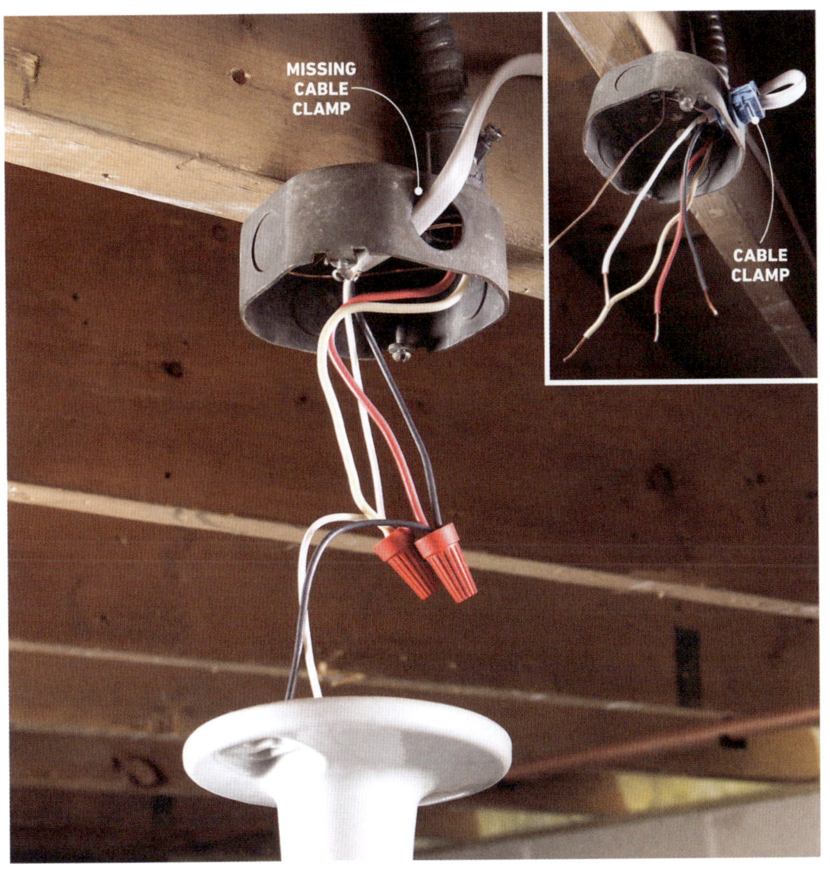

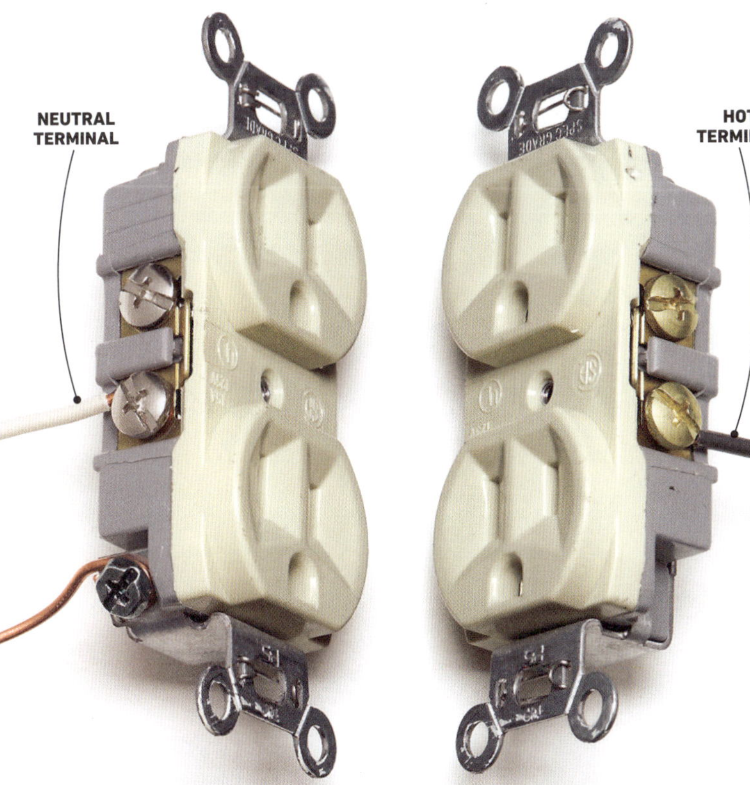

MISTAKE Missing cable clamp. I can't tell you how often I've found NM-B (Romex) cable resting, or pulled taut, against the sharp edges of a metal electrical box. Over time, this friction point wears down the wire's insulation and is a major fire hazard.

SOLUTION Use a cable clamp. "When using metal junction boxes, it is important to use a cable clamp to ensure the cable is securely fastened within the box and conductors will not get exposed outside of the box," says Chris Lozano, master electrician and virtual electrical expert at Frontdoor. Make sure the clamp is secure around the cable, Lozano says, but don't crank down too much to avoid constricting the wires.

MISTAKE Reversing hot and neutral. This creates a shock hazard, and because the light or device will likely still work, you won't even know it until it's too late.

SOLUTION Identify wires and terminals. In a standard NM-B cable, the black wire is the hot, the white is the neutral and the bare copper wire is the equipment grounding conductor (EGC). When wiring receptacles and light switches, attach the black wire to the brass screw (labeled "HOT"), and the white wire to the silver screw (labeled "WHITE"). The bare ECG goes to the green ground screw.

For wires that aren't clearly marked by color, like on a lamp cord, the hot is the smooth wire, and the neutral has ribs, grooves or other markings.

Connect Wire Right

Simple tools and techniques for faster, safer connections

By Mac Wentz

CAUTION Always turn power off at the main electrical panel before doing any electrical work.

Done right, electrical connections will provide safe, trouble-free service forever. Done wrong, they can loosen as wires expand and contract with changes in temperature. At best, these loose connections are annoying: They interrupt power to lights or outlets and can cost you hours of troubleshooting. But at worst, they could overheat and burn down your house. Making good connections does not take any more time or effort than making bad ones. But it does take know-how ...

STRIPPING WIRE

The first step in connecting any wire is to remove insulation. The cable used to wire most homes has two layers of plastic: You have to slit and cut away the sheath that contains the bundle of wires **(see Photos 1 and 2)**. Then you strip off the insulation that covers individual wires **(Photo 3)**.

For slicing the sheath, use the cheap and simple "cable ripper" (a few bucks at home centers and hardware stores). The ripper's tooth is dull enough so it cuts sheathing without damaging wire insulation. But to make that dull tooth cut, you have to squeeze and pull hard.

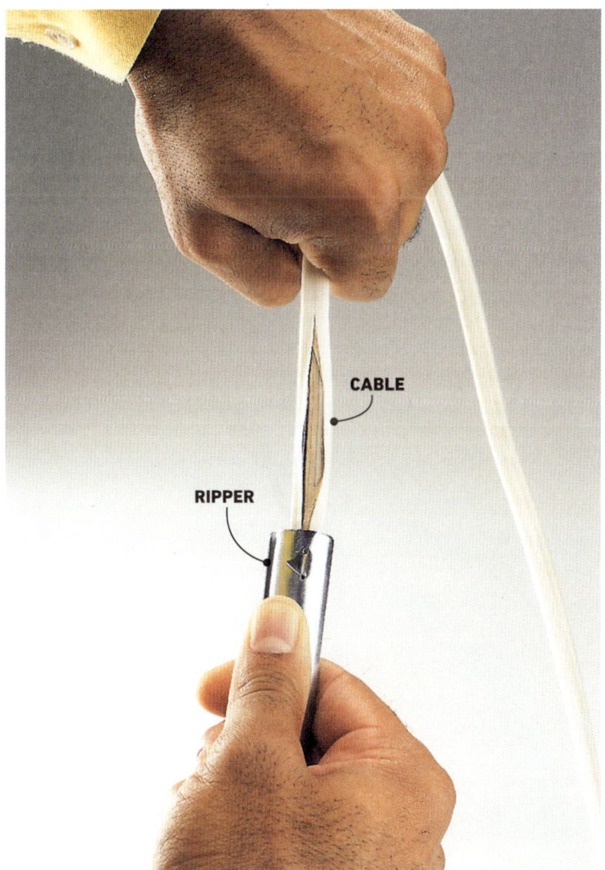

1 SLICE THROUGH
Cut a slit in the cable's plastic sheath with a cable ripper. Just place the ripper about 10 in. from the end of the cable, squeeze the jaws together and pull hard; the tooth inside the ripper slices the sheath.

2 SNIP AND REMOVE THE SHEATH
Pull the cable's sheath and paper insulation to one side and cut them off. You can use wire strippers, wire cutters or a knife to cut away the sheath—just don't damage the plastic insulation on the individual wires.

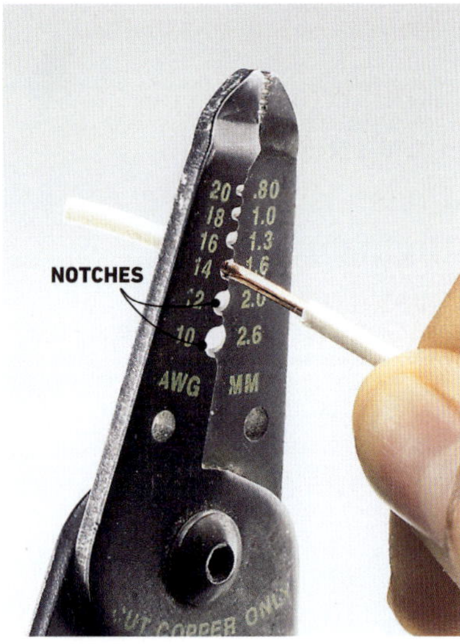

3 STRIP THE ENDS
Remove about ⅝ in. of insulation off the end of each wire. Be sure to match the gauge of the wire (it's stamped on the cable's sheath) with the right pair of notches; if you use a smaller pair, you'll damage the wire.

The best tool for stripping the insulation is a wire stripper. There are a few types available, but I like the one shown here because it works well for other wiring tasks too **(see Photos 2, 7 and 8)**. Strippers have several pairs of notches that are marked according to the wire size or gauge they're intended for. Remember, the smaller the number, the thicker the wire.

Note: "Stranded" wire, which consists of dozens of tiny wires, is slightly thicker than a solid wire of the same gauge. To avoid cutting into stranded wire, jump up one notch on the stripper. (To strip 18-gauge stranded wire, for example, use the 16-gauge notch.)

People will often use utility or pocketknives for both slicing the sheath and stripping the wire. But a knife is hard to control; it's easy to slice into the insulation when cutting a sheath, or damage the underlying wire when you're stripping insulation.

TWIST-ON CONNECTORS

Wire connectors, usually referred to by the brand name Wire-Nut, come in several color coded sizes. You can tackle just about any household wiring job with the yellow and red sizes. Connector packages list the connectors' capacities. You can connect up to three 14-gauge wires with a yellow connector, for example, but if you want to connect four 14-gauge wires, you'll need the larger red connector.

A pack of 50 connectors sells for about $6. Make sure the ones you buy are UL listed. There's not much difference between one brand of connector and the next, but you'll find that connectors with wings are easier to grip.

4 ADD A CONNECTOR
Hold the wires tightly with the ends even and insert them into the connector. If you're connecting more than two wires, hold them in a tight bundle, not all side by side. You don't have to twist the wires together before inserting them.

5 TURN THE CONNECTOR
Twist the connector clockwise until you've screwed the wires as far into the connector as they can go (you'll feel them hit a dead end). Then give the connector a few more turns to twist the wires together outside the connector.

SCREW TERMINALS

The screw terminals found on light switches and outlets are nearly foolproof. Just be sure to hook the wire around the screw clockwise; if you run the wire counterclockwise, the hook will open as you tighten the screw.

To prevent contact with the bare ground wire inside the electrical box, it's a good idea to cover the screws by wrapping electrical tape around the body of the switch or outlet a few times.

Warning: Many outlets and switches have screw terminals and holes in the back. These "stab-in" holes make for quick, easy connections: Just push the wire into the hole. But since they don't lock onto the wire the way screw terminals do, stab-ins can be unreliable, even dangerous. So always use the screw terminals.

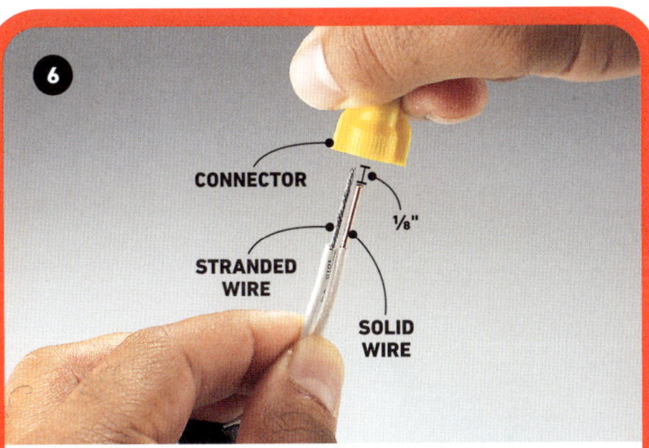

CONNECTING STRANDED WIRE TO SOLID WIRE

If you've ever installed a light fixture, then you've probably experienced this: You hold the stranded wire coming from the fixture against the solid wire coming out of the wall or ceiling and twist on the connector. But something doesn't feel right. So you give the wires a gentle tug and—just as you suspected—the stranded wire pulls right out of the connector.

This happens for two reasons: First, the stranded wire, made up of individual wires, is flexible and gets pushed out of place as you twist the connector. Second, most of the connectors that come with light fixtures have soft plastic threads; they just don't bite into the wire like the metal-threaded connectors that you buy separately.

Here's how to make the connection work:

1. Twist the tiny wires of the stranded wire tightly together.
2. Toss the light-manufacturer's connectors in the trash.
3. Hold the wires so that the tip of the stranded wire is about ⅛ in. beyond the tip of the solid wire.
4. Twist on a yellow connector.

7 CREATE A HOOK
Bend the exposed wire into a U-shaped hook using wire strippers or needle-nose pliers. Then loop the wire over the screw so that it runs clockwise around the screw.

8 SECURE THE HOOK
Pinch the hook tightly around the screw. The hook doesn't have to completely encircle the screw, but it must run at least two-thirds of the way around.

Troubleshooting a Dead Outlet

It's inconvenient to plug something in and it doesn't work, but take these steps before you call an electrician

When an outlet goes dead, it's easy to jump to conclusions and assume the worst. But more often than not, the problem is something simple, and you can save the cost of a service call just by taking a few steps to trace the cause. Don't worry if you're not comfortable doing electrical work. Better than half the time you'll solve the problem without even lifting a tool. We'll show you how to start your search for the problem by checking in the most likely places. If that doesn't work, we'll show you where to look for loose connections that may be to blame and how to fix them. Of course, there will always be problems that are best left to an electrician. But if you take these steps first, there's a good chance you'll find the solution.

FIRST, SEE IF OTHER OUTLETS ARE DEAD

Before you head for the circuit breakers, take a few minutes to check if other outlets, lights or appliances are affected. Switch lights on and off and test nearby outlets for power (use a voltage tester or plug in a lamp to test the outlets). Unplug lamps and appliances from dead outlets to eliminate the possibility that a short or overload from one of them is causing the problem. Note the location of dead outlets or mark them with a piece of masking tape so you'll be able to find them again after you've turned off the power.

REPLACE BURNED-OUT FUSES

Look inside the fuse for charred glass or a broken filament—evidence of a blown fuse. Just unscrew the suspect fuse and replace it with one of the same type and amperage.

1 FIND THE BREAKER

Locate the circuit breaker box and open the door to search for tripped circuit breakers.

2 LOOK FOR TRIPPED BREAKERS

Locate tripped breakers by looking for breaker handles that aren't lined up with the rest. Last, push the breaker handles toward the "on" position. Tripped breakers will "give" a little rather than feel solid.

3 TURN IT OFF

Reset a tripped breaker by switching it off first. Press the handle firmly to the "off" position. You should hear a click.

4 FLIP IT BACK ON

Finally, reset the breaker by pushing the handle firmly to the "on" position. It should line up with all the rest. If it "pops" back to the tripped position, there's a problem in the wiring or in something that's plugged into the circuit.

CHECK THE CIRCUIT BREAKERS

After you unplug all the devices from the dead outlets, the next step is to check for a tripped circuit breaker or blown fuse. You'll find the circuit breakers or fuses in the main electrical panel, which is usually located near where the electrical wires enter the house. Garages, basements and laundry rooms are common locations. Locate the panel and open the metal door to reveal the fuses or circuit breakers. **Photos 1-4** show a typical main panel and the process for resetting a tripped circuit breaker. Always remember to power down your computer before you switch the circuit breakers on and off.

Tripped circuit breakers aren't always apparent. If you don't see a tripped breaker, firmly press every breaker fully into the "off" position **(Photo 3)**. Then switch them back on. If the tripped breaker will not reset without tripping again, there could be a potentially dangerous short circuit or ground fault condition. Switch the circuit breaker off until you've located the problem. In most cases, a tripped circuit breaker is caused by a temporary overload on the circuit or a short circuit in some device plugged into the circuit. But in rare cases, a loose wire in an electrical box could be causing the problem. Follow **Photos 1 and 2, p. 144**, to look for and repair any loose electrical connections.

CHECK THE GFCIS

GFCI (short for ground fault circuit interrupter) outlets, those unusual outlets with the test and reset buttons, are required in areas of the house where shock hazards are greatest. They can protect against deadly electrical shocks by sensing leaks in the electrical current and immediately tripping, shutting off the power. But it's easy to overlook a tripped GFCI as the source of a dead outlet problem. That's because in areas where GFCI-protected outlets are a requirement, electricians often save money by connecting additional standard outlets to one GFCI outlet. A current leak at any one of the outlets will trip the GFCI and cause all connected ones to go dead. GFCI-protected outlets should be labeled **(Photo 1)**, but the label often falls off.

Look for GFCIs in bathrooms, kitchens, basements or garages, or on the home's exterior. Test and reset every GFCI you find **(Photo 2)**. If the GFCI "reset" button doesn't pop out when you press the "test" button, there may be no power to the GFCI or you may have a bad GFCI. On the other hand, if the "reset" button trips again every time you press it, there could be a dangerous current leak somewhere in the circuit. In either case, solving the problem requires additional electrical testing that we won't cover here. You can refer to other electrical repair manuals or call an electrician for help. If you reset all of the GFCIs and it did not power up your dead outlet, then the last resort is to look for loose connections.

STILL NO POWER? LOOK FOR A BAD CONNECTION

If checking your breakers and resetting the GFCIs still haven't restored power to the outlet, the next step, without getting into circuit testing, is to remove the outlet from the box and look for loose connections behind the outlet plate.

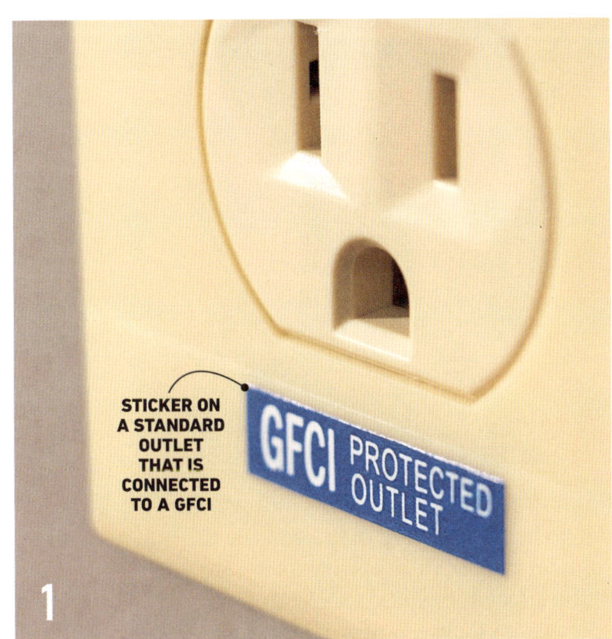

LOOSE WIRES AT THE STAB-IN CONNECTIONS

As a quick time-saver for electricians, some outlets can be wired by pressing stripped wires into holes on the back of the outlet. This wiring method is allowed by the electrical code, but it isn't good practice since these stab-in connections can loosen over time and cause problems. Look for stab-in connections as you troubleshoot your dead outlet. Tug each wire to check for loose connections. If you find a stab-in connection that's loose, don't just reinsert the wire. Instead, cut and strip the end of the wire and then try to connect it to the screw terminal on the side of the outlet. Or better yet, cut and strip all of the wires and connect them to a new outlet (**Photo 3**).

1 SWITCH OFF First make sure all computers are turned off and everyone in the house knows you'll be turning off the power. Then switch off the main circuit breaker. Keep a flashlight handy because all the lights will go out.

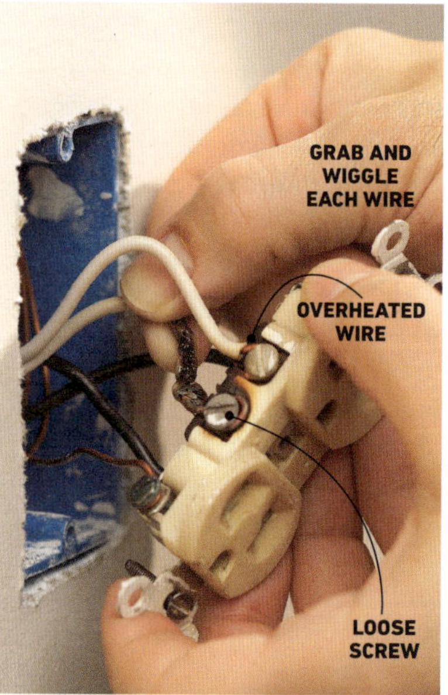

2 INSPECT SCREWS Inspect the screw terminals for broken or loose wires. Bend the wire at each screw terminal to see if it's loose (it will turn under the screw or the screw will move). Look for broken, burned or corroded wires or screws.

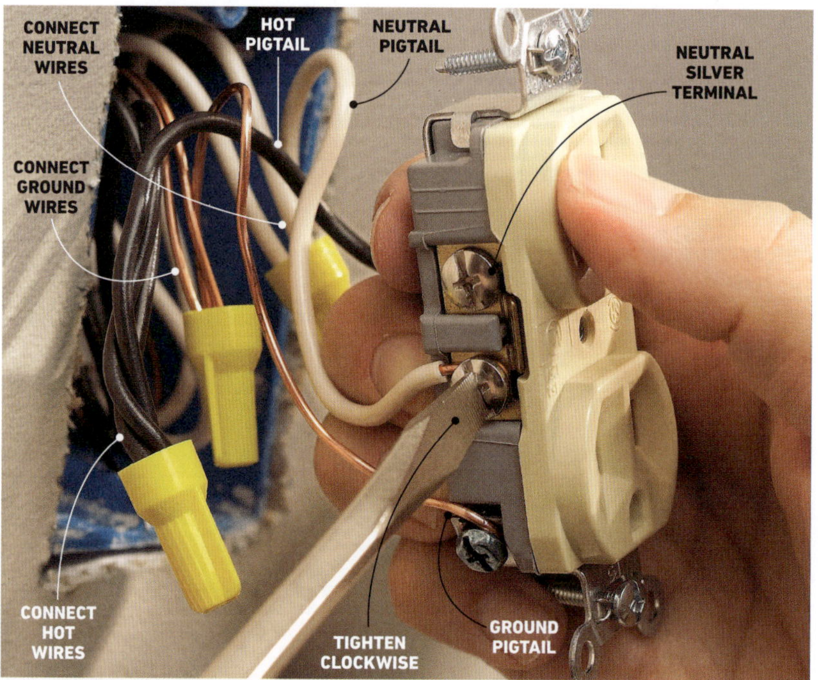

3 ATTACH WIRES TO SCREWS Install a new outlet by bending a loop in the ends of the hot, neutral and ground wires. Connect the hot (black) wire to the brass screw, the neutral white wire to the silver screw and the ground wire to the green ground screw. Loop the wires clockwise around the screws and tighten.

We'll show you three common types of loose connections: loose terminal screws, loose stab-in connections and loose wires at wire connectors. You may find one or more of these after you remove your outlet and take a look in the electrical box.

LOOSE OR BROKEN WIRES

The first problem we show is a loose connection under the outlet's terminal screw. In **Photo 2, p. 144**, you can see the charred outlet and melted wire insulation that are a result of heat generated by the loose connection. These telltale signs aren't always very present, though, which is why you should double-check the connections by gently bending each wire to see if it moves under the screw.

CAUTION If you have aluminum wiring, don't mess with it! Call in a licensed pro who's certified to work with it. This wiring is dull gray, not the dull orange that's characteristic of copper.

If you do discover a loose connection at an outlet, whether it's at the screw terminal or a stab-in connection, we strongly recommend replacing the outlet with a new one. That's because loose connections almost always create excess heat that could damage the outlet and lead to future problems. **Photo 3, p. 144**, shows how to install a new outlet.

If the outlet you're replacing is wired like the one shown in **Photo 2**, with pairs of hot and neutral wires (wires under all four screws), connect the pairs of like-colored wires along with a third 6-in. length of wire, which is called a pigtail, under one of the wire connectors **(Photo 2)**. Then you can connect the loose end of each pigtail to its appropriate outlet screw.

This method reduces the chance that a loose connection under a screw will cause a problem with other outlets on the circuit.

CHECK WIRES FOR LOOSE ENDS

A wire that's come loose from a wire connector is another problem that can cause a dead outlet. Just follow the steps in **Photos 1 and 2, p. 144**, to find and fix this type of loose connection. If you don't find any loose connections in this box and are still anxious to pursue the problem, expand your search to other outlets in the vicinity (start with the ones you marked with masking tape earlier). Always make sure to turn off the main circuit breaker **(Photo 1, p. 142)** when you're checking in an outlet for loose connections.

When you're done looking for loose connections, reinstall the outlets and switch the main circuit breaker back on. Test the outlets again to see if you solved the problem. If you still have dead outlets, call an electrician.

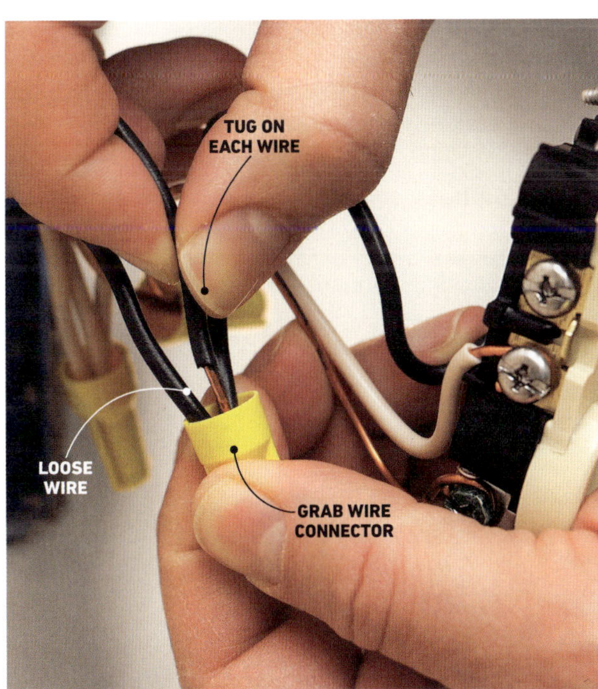

1 CHECK THE CONNECTOR

Tug on each wire attached to the connector. If you find a loose wire, remove the connector. Cut and strip the wires to expose ½ to ¾ in. of fresh copper wire, depending on the connector instructions.

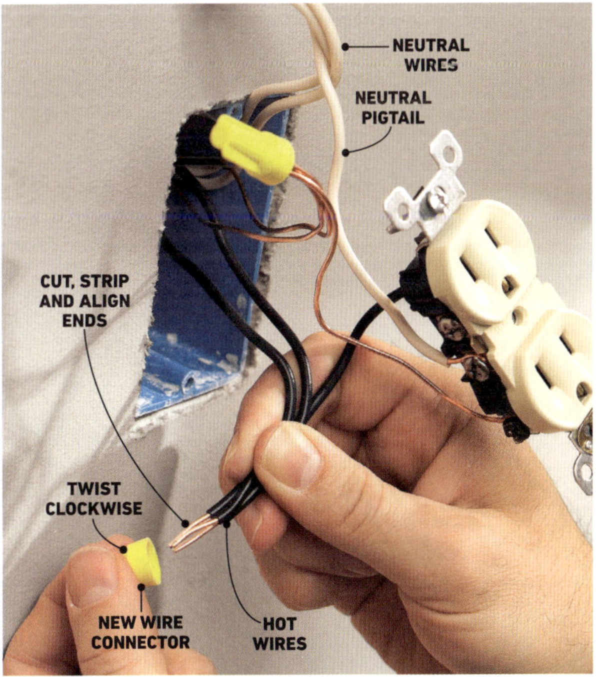

2 ADD PIGTAIL WIRES

Gather the wires, making sure their ends are lined up, and twist a new wire connector on clockwise. Match the connector to the number of wires based on the connector packaging.

How to Reset a Circuit Breaker

You may already know how to reset a circuit breaker, but you're not always around. Show this guide to everyone in your household to be extra prepared.

1 DON'T WORRY!

All the dangerous parts are behind the breaker switches. You can't get a shock by flipping breaker switches.

2 FIND THE TRIPPED BREAKER

Open the panel's door and look for the breaker switch that's out of line with the others. It will be about midway between the "off" and "on" positions. You may have to look closely to spot it.

3 RESET THE BREAKER

To reset a breaker, move the switch all the way to its "off" position, then back to "on." You might hear a few beeps from smoke detectors and appliances when you turn the power back on, but that's normal.

4 IT TRIPS AGAIN

If that happens, the circuit is probably overloaded. To reduce the load, unplug or switch off items that are using the circuit. If that doesn't work, there may be a problem with your electrical system. If you lack the know-how to troubleshoot your wiring, call an electrician.

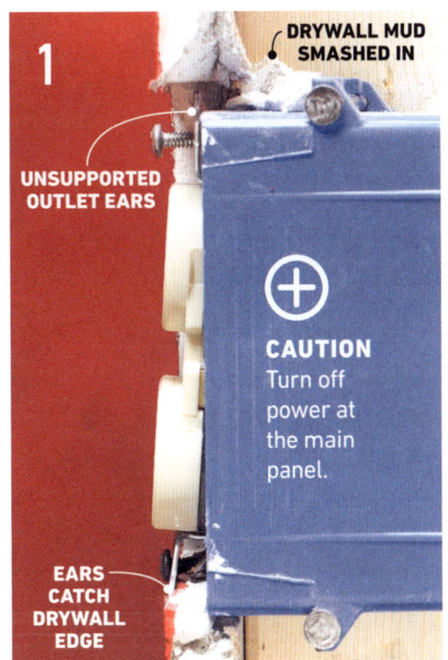

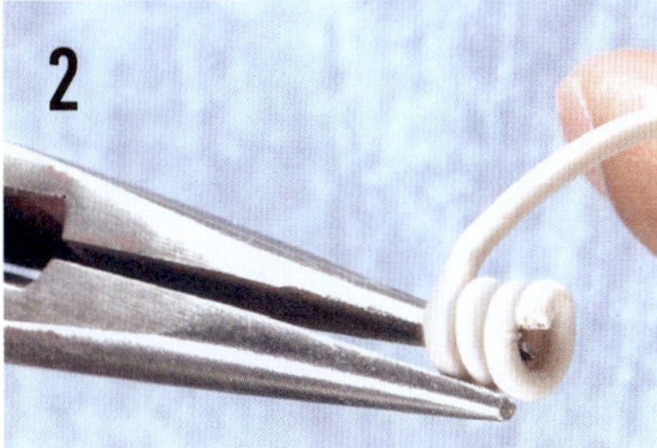

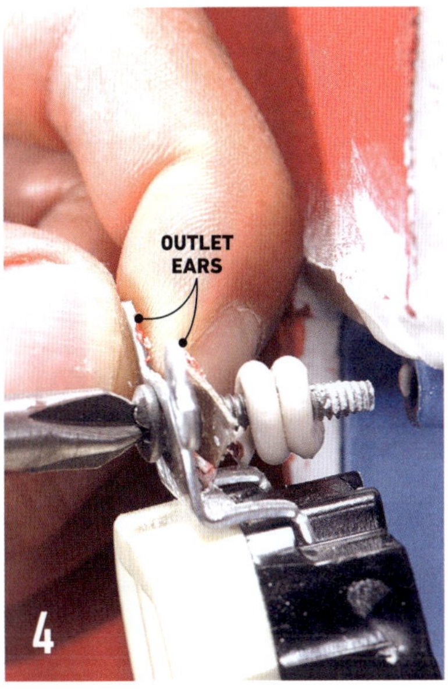

Tighten a Loose Outlet

A loose outlet pushes in every time you insert a plug. Often it happens because the cutout around the outlet box is too big. When the drywall is taped, gaps around the electrical boxes are filled with mud, which supports the outlet ears. In a heavily used outlet, this mud can break loose, leaving the outlet ears unsupported. Eventually the cover plate cracks. A scrap of 12- or 14-gauge electrical wire and a few common tools are all you'll need to lock that outlet down tight.

Always start by shutting off the power to the outlet **(Photo 1)**. **Photos 2** and **3** show how to convert scrap electrical wire into a coiled spacer, which will bridge your gap between the outlet and the electrical box. Once the spacer is completed, install it between the outlet and electrical box as shown in **Photo 4**. Note: If the face of the box isn't flush with a wood or another combustible material, or the box is more than ¼ in. behind a drywall wall, you must add a box extender.

1 POWER OFF
Turn off the power at the main panel and remove the broken cover plate. The drywall is often broken behind the outlet ears, leaving them unsupported.

2 TWIST WIRE INTO A COIL
Strip the exterior sheathing off a 12-in. scrap of 12- or 14-gauge electrical cable and remove one of the individual wires. Twist the wire into a tight coil with a pair of needle-nose pliers.

3 SNIP THE COIL
Snip the coil so it extends just past the wall; the insulation will compress slightly when tightened.

4 SCREW THE OUTLET DOWN
Slide the coil spacer over the outlet-mounting screw. Screw your outlet down until the outlet ears are flush to the wall.

Fishing Wire

Fishing wires and cables through finished walls can be tricky. You might be tempted to cut in a bunch of access holes, but you don't have to if you play it smart. With a few simple tools and these tips you can avoid a lot of drywall patching.

By Mark Petersen

1 CHECK THE WHOLE WALL CAVITY WITH A STUD FINDER

A decent stud finder is a total must-have for every wire-fishing job, but don't throw it back in your pouch after you've located the studs. Use your stud finder to check the whole wall cavity for obstacles. You don't want to find out the hard way that you should have fished your wire one stud cavity to the left or right.

2 THE TOOLS YOU NEED

Flex bits and glow rods are the go-to tools. Flex bits are great for drilling holes in hard-to-reach spaces. Buy a bit that has a hole on the end of it so you can use the bit itself to pull wires (more on that later).

Once your hole is drilled, you can shove a glow rod through the hole, attach your wire to the eyelet at the end and pull it back through. Glow rods can also be used to hook wires to pull them out. As their name suggests, glow rods glow in the dark. This makes them easier to spot when you're working in dark areas (which is most of the time).

Glow rods come in various lengths and thicknesses, and you can combine as many sections as the job requires. Thinner rods flex more and work better when you have to make sharp turns. A thicker rod can span longer distances and can be better for hooking wires that are more than a few feet away.

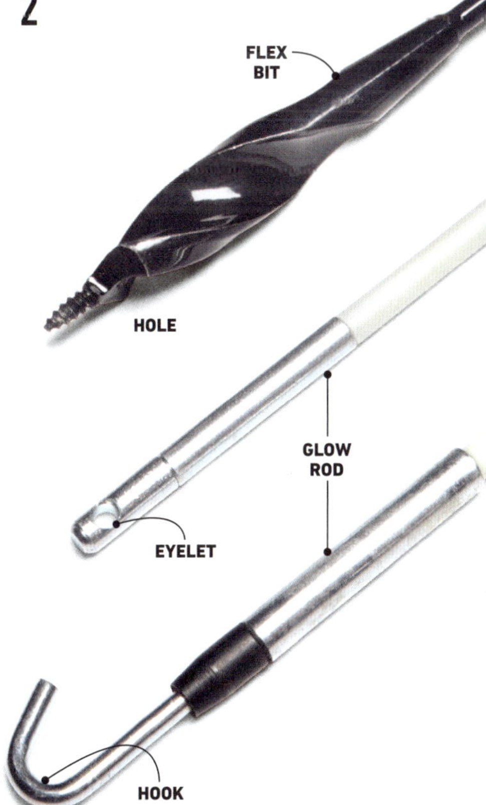

PRO TIP Seal the holes. If you're drilling holes through top and bottom plates or running wires through a fire wall in the garage, you must seal those holes with a fire-resistant caulk or foam sealant to comply with fire and energy codes. Fire-blocking insulated foam sealant is sold in cans at home centers and hardware stores.

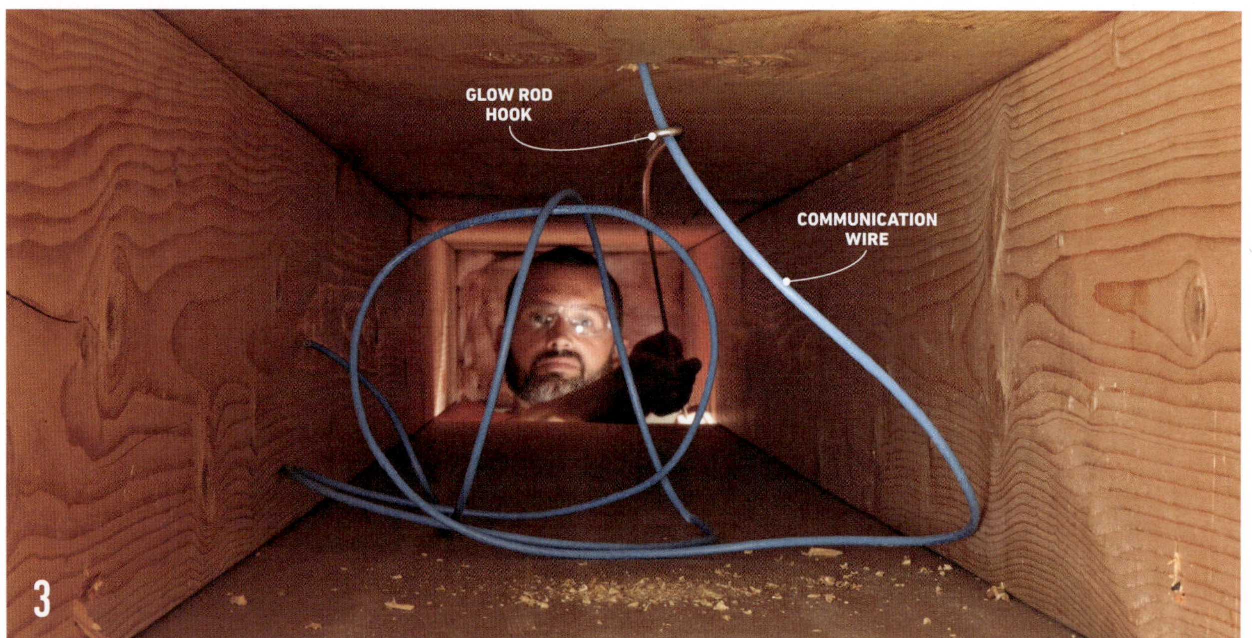

3 PUSH THROUGH MORE THAN YOU NEED

When hooking a wire to pull it toward you, make sure there's more than enough wire to hook on to. Sometimes it can be a real challenge to grab hold of a wire, and once you have it hooked, you don't want to lose it.

4 HOOK ON TO A FLEX BIT

Sometimes you don't need to use glow rods at all. Most flex bits have holes in the ends of them. If you have access to where the flex bit pops out, attach your wire directly to the bit and try to fish your wire through that way. Twist the wire and tape it up to make sure it doesn't come off when you're pulling it back through. Remove your bit from your drill before pulling so you don't accidentally spin the bit and twist up your wire.

PRO TIP Buy extra wire. Have plenty of extra wire or cable on hand, because it's not likely that you'll be able to fish a wire in a straight line from Point A to Point B. There's also the possibility that your wire might get hung up on something, and you'd have to abandon it and start over.

5 FISH WIRES THROUGH THE HOLES FOR RECESSED LIGHTS

When you're installing new recessed can lighting, fishing wires from one light to another is easy because you have a great big hole to pull the wires through. But even if you're not installing new lighting, you can use the existing openings. Many cans can be easily popped out of the opening by removing a few screws.

6 PROTECT DRYWALL WITH A MUD RING

Mud rings, which are also called drywall brackets or low-voltage "old-work" brackets, are great for protecting the drywall when you're drilling with a flex bit or cranking on a glow rod. They're easy to install (just tighten two screws) and inexpensive. Once the wires are connected, you can screw the wall plate to the mud ring. Mud rings are approved only for low-voltage wires such as coaxial cables. If you need to install a box for an electrical receptacle or wall switch, install the mud ring temporarily just to protect the drywall while you fish the wire, then remove it.

7 INSTALL CONDUIT INSIDE CABINETS

Additional outlets above the counter space is one of the most popular electrical retrofits. In this case, you can simply fish the wire through a flexible conduit installed right through the base cabinets. If you drill the holes for the conduit as far back and as high as you can, no one will ever notice.

8 GET A BETTER VIEW WITH AN INSPECTION MIRROR

You know your wire is in there somewhere, but you just can't seem to find it. It's probably hung up on another wire or pipe, but guessing isn't going to solve the problem. Shine a flashlight onto an inspection mirror to find out exactly what's going on. This is a simple, inexpensive tip that can save you a lot of time and frustration. Pick up an inspection mirror at an auto parts store.

9 DON'T SPIN THE BIT IN INSULATION

The best advice for fishing wires through insulation? Avoid it if you can. The potential is always there to damage the vapor barrier or bunch up insulation, leaving cold spots in the wall. If you must fish wires through exterior walls, the best tip is to avoid spinning your flex bit until you make solid contact with the wood you plan to drill through. If you drill too early, you'll end up creating a large insulation cotton candy cone, which will make retrieving your bit difficult, if not impossible.

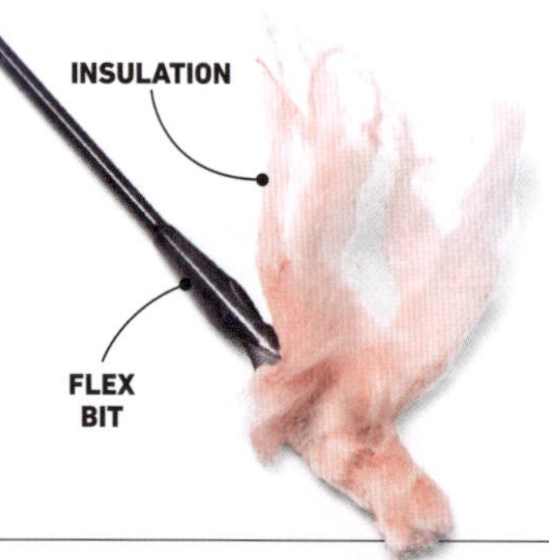

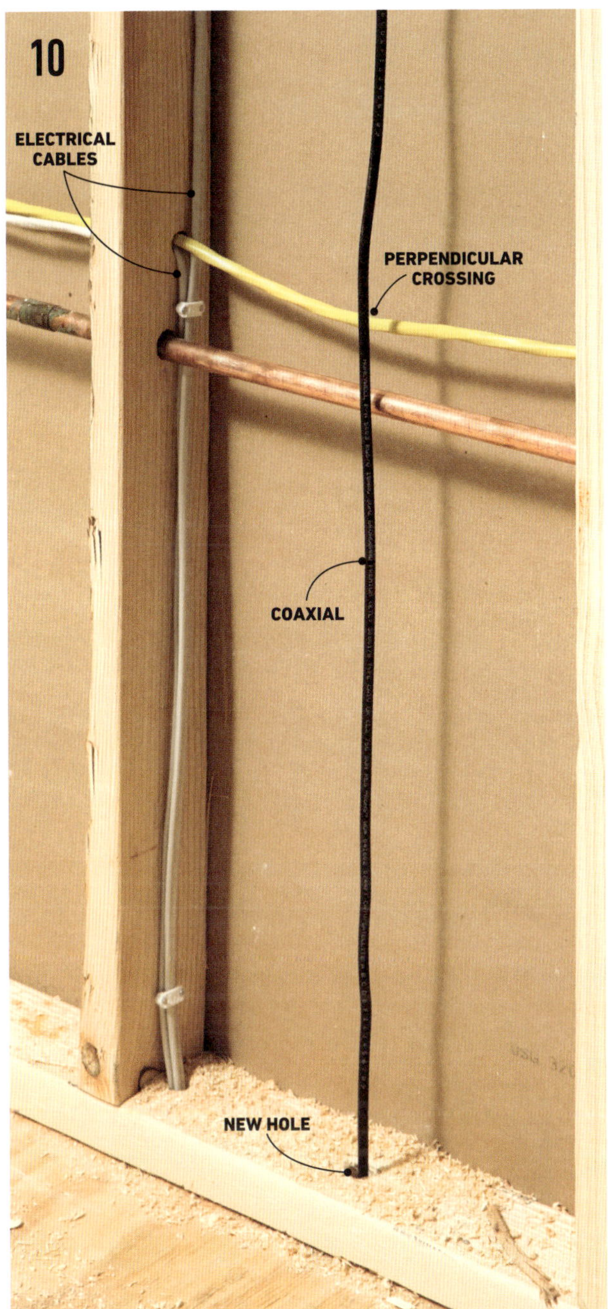

10 KEEP LOW-VOLTAGE WIRES AWAY FROM ELECTRICAL CABLES

Although it's really tempting to fish low-voltage wires (such as coaxial cable) through existing holes occupied by electrical cables, don't do it! Even though cables are insulated, the high-voltage current can interfere with the signal in the low-voltage wires. This could result in bad TV reception or unreliable Internet service. Drill a new hole, and keep the new low-voltage wire several inches away from electrical cables. It's OK to run low-voltage wires perpendicular to cables, and it's also OK to run low-voltage wires next to electrical wires that are completely encased in conduit or metal sheathing.

11 INVEST IN A BUMPER BALL

Wires aren't supposed to be installed any closer than 1¼ in. from a penetrable surface (the outside of the drywall). That means you shouldn't be drilling holes right next to the drywall. But it's not always easy to control where a flex bit goes. A Bumper Ball flexible drill bit guide installed on the end of your flex bit will help maintain the proper space between the bit and the outside of the wall cavity. You can buy a set of two Bumper Balls at electrical suppliers or online for relatively cheap.

REDPIXEL.PL/SHUTTERSTOCK

SKILLS IN PRACTICE

Heated Floor: The Easy Way

Heat film has big advantages over other options

By Jay Cork

Who wouldn't want to step onto a toasty warm kitchen floor when they fetch their morning coffee? I recently found out how easy in-floor heat can be. With a film-type heating system, you don't have to deal with thin-set or glue. You basically just unroll the mats, run the wiring and install your floor. I was able to install it under my floating floor in a weekend. Here's what you need to know.

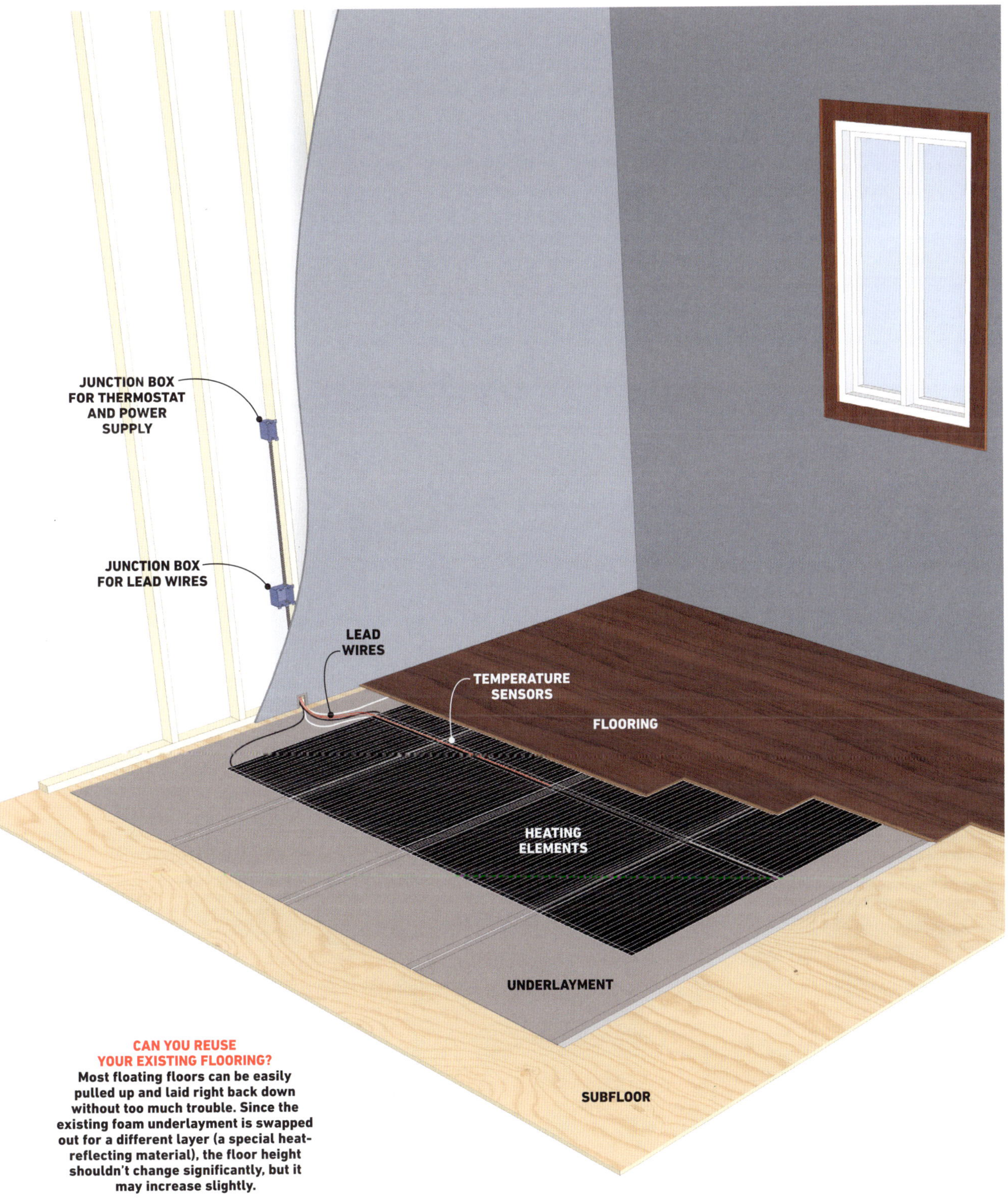

CAN YOU REUSE YOUR EXISTING FLOORING?
Most floating floors can be easily pulled up and laid right back down without too much trouble. Since the existing foam underlayment is swapped out for a different layer (a special heat-reflecting material), the floor height shouldn't change significantly, but it may increase slightly.

FLOOR HEAT SIMPLIFIED

To install a film-type system, you first lay down foam underlayment, securing it with duct tape. Then you tape down the plastic film, which contains the electric heating elements. The power supply to the film is controlled by a thermostat connected to temp sensors in the floor. When the wiring is done, you're ready to install the flooring.

COST OF OPERATION
The typical electricity cost is about 30 cents a day. QuietWarmth provides a handy energy cost calculator at *mpglobalproducts.com*.

SELECTING A SYSTEM

- Film is a super-easy DIY option, but it's not cheap. The total cost for most systems is about $8 to $10 per square foot. Mine cost about $9 per square foot.
- I chose a QuietWarmth system, but several brands of film-type systems are available. To find more, search online for "in-floor heat film."
- Systems such as this are intended to keep your feet comfy. They'll add a little heat to the room, but they're no substitute for the HVAC system in your home. Just as the seat warmer in your car won't heat the whole cabin, this system won't heat an entire room.
- Most film heating elements can be cut to length so they perfectly suit the dimensions of the room. Others come in various lengths. If they don't match your room perfectly, you'll have unheated areas along the edges of the floors, but that's usually not a serious problem.
- To learn more about your floor-heating options, search for "floor heat" at *familyhandyman.com*.

WHAT FLOOR IS IT GOOD FOR?

Most film-type systems are suitable for flooring that's not nailed or glued to the subfloor. That includes carpet and wood, vinyl and laminate floating floors. You can even install the system on top of a concrete slab. But be sure to check the manufacturer's fine print for restrictions. The system I used, for example, isn't recommended for bathrooms.

POWERING THE SYSTEM

Wiring the system is not really complicated, but getting power from your main panel to the room might be. For help with that, see "Fishing Wire" on p. 148.

The system I used requires a dedicated 20-amp circuit. Since the actual dimension for the heated area is 120 sq. ft., it'll

TOP: MP GLOBAL PRODUCTS, LLC

work with a 120V circuit. Floors larger than 200 sq. ft. will need 240V circuit.

A DEDICATED THERMOSTAT IS REQUIRED

This system must be controlled by its own thermostat. Connecting it to your whole-house thermostat won't work and may damage the heating elements as well as your floor. There are many thermostat choices for this purpose, but I wanted one I could control with an app on my phone. The programmable Wi-Fi thermostat from QuietWarmth was a great choice. It doesn't talk to Alexa or Google Assistant yet, but it will in the near future.

YOU'LL NEED A MULTIMETER

It would be a disaster to finish installing brand new heating elements, only to find that one was damaged in the process. That's why it's very important to confirm the impedance reading for each roll of film with your multimeter set to "Ohms" and to double-check that reading every step of the way. QuietWarmth provided a handy spec sheet that helps me keep track of these readings. A good multimeter costs about $30 at a hardware store or home center.

INSTALL A BACKUP SENSOR

If you're already installing one temperature sensor, you might as well take the time to install a second one as a backup. It'll cost an extra $25, but it's a small price to pay for peace of mind. If the primary sensor fails, it's so much easier to swap two wires in the thermostat than to pull up your flooring to replace the bad sensor! Don't count on an extra sensor being included; you must specify that you want an extra one when you place your order.

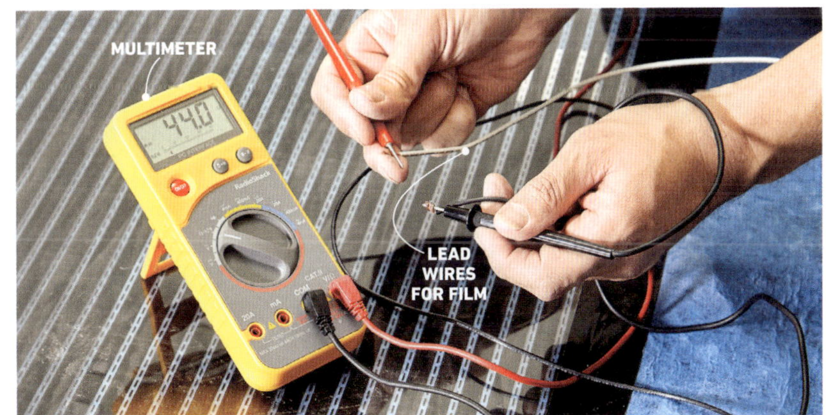

CHAPTER 5

Painting

TOOL SPOTLIGHT
PAINTER'S TOOLKIT
SMALL LED FLASHLIGHT
It will help you find those little imperfections on the wall.
WIRE BRUSH
Great for cleaning dried paint off paintbrushes.
SCRAPER
This scraper will clean roller covers, open paint cans, spread spackling paste, remove old paint and more!
ROLLER SCREEN
Hang it in a 5-gallon bucket of paint for an instant roller tray.
ROLLER COVER CANISTER
Attach a hose to this canister and clean the roller cover the easy way.

PRESS'N SEAL
Wrap this around your roller covers or brushes to keep the paint fresh for later.
MINI ROLLER PAIL
This dual-purpose pail can be used as a handheld bucket for brushing.
SANDER/MOP ATTACHMENT
A must-have tool! First use it to sand, then put the mophead on to clean the surface.
BRUSH AND ROLLER SPINNER
This tool dries your roller covers and brushes without damaging them.
SHERWIN-WILLIAMS MINI ROLLER
The mini roller is great for spot touch-ups, getting into tight spaces and painting cabinets.
PAIL HOOK
Be hands-free on the ladder! Clip this to the handle of a paint bucket, then hang it from a ladder rung.
PAINT REMOVER
Drips happen. And if they're not caught right away, a little paint remover can save the day.
REPAIR PATCHES
Self-adhesive wall patches simplify and speed up repairs to damaged walls.
SHERWIN-WILLIAMS CAULK GUN
This caulk gun is both ergonomic and rugged.
ORIGINAL FORMULA
OOPS!
REMOVES
• Graffiti & Paint
• Marker & Inks
• Tar & Sealant

Pro Tips for a Perfect Finish

It's the little tricks that make any paint job look professional

By Jay Cork

Bryan Alft is a lifelong painter. It's in his blood; the Alft family has been in the business since 1948. Bryan learned the tricks of the trade working side by side with his grandfather, his father and his uncles. Collectively, they've seen all the trends, innovations and silly ideas come and go. Now a business owner himself, Bryan shared some of his best painting tips and tricks.

1 PREP WITH SANDPAPER, NOT LIQUID

Liquid surface conditioners and deglossing products claim to "etch" the surface to improve bonding. They seem like a quick fix, but sandpaper does the job without nasty chemicals. For some hard-to-sand profiles or shapes, a liquid surface conditioner may be the best option, but use it with care; always do a small test to see how it affects the surface you're preparing.

2 SAVE TIME BY MASKING THE BASE

Even if you're really good at "cutting in" with a brush, painting along the baseboard takes more time than masking. Besides eliminating the need to cut in, 2-in.-wide tape shields against roller splatter.

3 COVER TOUGH STAINS

There are many stain blockers on the shelf, so I asked Bryan which he uses. He always has a quart of Zinsser BIN on the job, which in his experience does a great job and dries fast. He says that oil-based stain blockers do

a better job of covering stains than water-based products, but they produce more fumes. Work in a well-ventilated area when you use oil-based stain blockers.

4 BETTER TAPE FOR BETTER PAINT LINES

FrogTape and 3M Edge-Lock are formulated to seal the edge when it's exposed to the moisture in the paint. But occasionally paint still seeps in. After masking natural wood, Bryan preseals the tape with a clear water-based urethane. Even if the poly bleeds in a little, it will be invisible. The same goes for masking an area where two different colors meet: Use the paint color that's underneath the tape to preseal the edge, and you'll get a perfect paint line.

5 PAINT ALL THE TRIM FIRST

Bryan paints the trim first in most situations. He can do it faster, but it also makes it easier to sand the first coat without being concerned about hitting the walls. It also allows him to caulk the trim to the wall (see the next tip) to get a perfect line.

6 MASK AND CAULK TO HIDE GAPS

Often there are gaps between the top of the base molding and wall. Bryan suggests taping the base molding, and then running a small bead of caulk along the top of the base and the wall. Using a finger, remove as much caulk as possible, leaving only what fills the gaps. Paint the wall and remove the masking tape as you normally would. No more gaps!

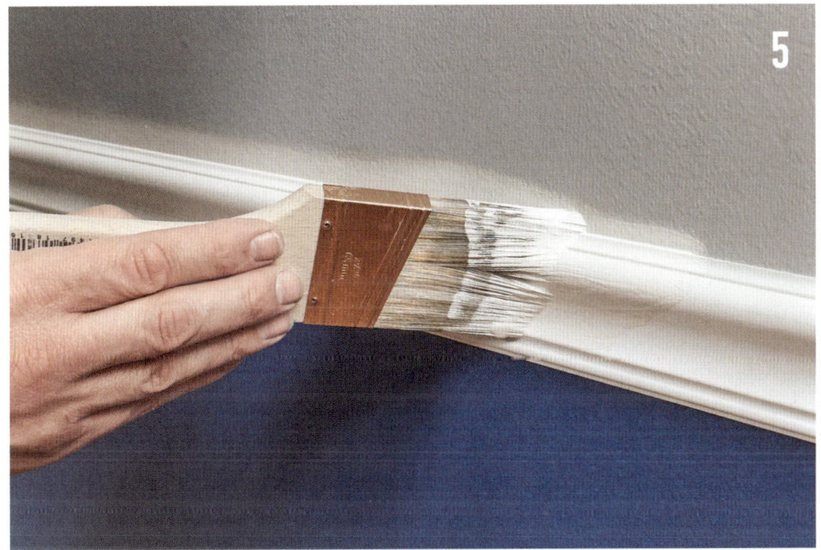

7 MAKE TOUCH-UPS DISAPPEAR

Even if you use paint from the same can, touch-ups sometimes stand out from the surrounding paint. But for walls, here's a technique to help blend them in: Dab paint in the center of the patch and move it outward in a circular motion, feathering the paint into the surrounding color. Wait until the paint dries to see if you need to go over it again. You shouldn't expect an absolute perfect match, but it's easier than repainting the entire wall! To help blend the color, thin the paint with a little water before you paint the repair.

8 WIDE PAINT BUCKET

Wider rollers need wider buckets. Bryan installed some wheels on his bucket.

9 SPOT FLAWS WITH A LITTLE LIGHT

Raking light across any surface highlights little flaws, so in addition to his movable light stand, Bryan uses a small handheld LED light. It can reveal small surface imperfections that a central light source might miss or even hide.

10 DRY PAINT FASTER WITH A FAN

Getting the air moving will help paint dry faster so you can apply the next coat sooner. Bryan has tried many different fans over the years, but Vornado fans are his favorite. They're quiet, and they move air very effectively. You can get one for about $130 online.

11 LED WORK LIGHT

Utilitech work lights are versatile, rugged and, at around $130, won't break the bank.

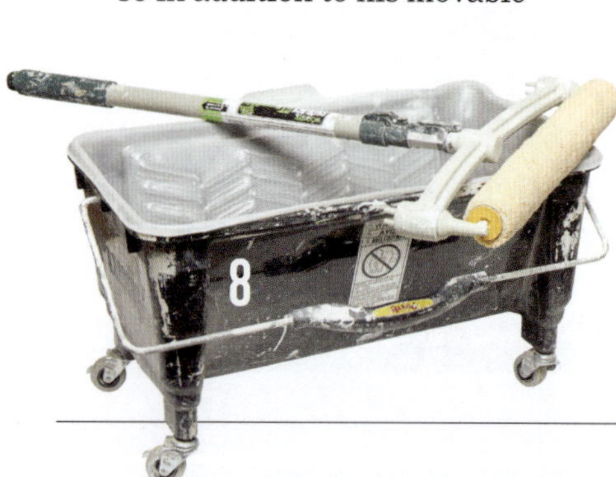

COMMON PAINTING QUESTIONS

Q: Do I always have to use primer?

A: At times, Bryan uses a full coat of primer, such as when he's working on new drywall or large repairs. For smaller areas, he'll use a trick called selfpriming—that is, spot-priming with the topcoat paint instead of a dedicated primer. I also asked Bryan about the primer/paint-in-one formulations, and he said since they always apply at least two coats of paint, there is no need to buy combination paint and primers.

Q: Should I invest in a paint sprayer for my painting project?

A: Sprayers are an essential tool for Bryan. But unless you are painting a completely empty room in a remodel or new construction, spraying is often more work than painting by hand. You have to mask absolutely everything and wear protective gear. It's also likely you'll need to back-roll (run a roller over the sprayed finish) to achieve an even texture, eliminate runs and improve adhesion. After all that, you still have to clean all of your equipment.

Master Masking Tape

Masking tape tips for clean, straight edges

By Jeff Gorton

Masking off baseboard and other trim is a fantastic way to get a professional-looking paint job. You'll get a crisp, clean paint line where the walls meet the trim. And the job will go quicker because you'll avoid time-consuming "cutting in" with the paintbrush and the cleaning up of paint spatters from your woodwork. Of course, the masking process itself requires a little patience and skill. Wavy tape will result in an uneven paint line. Poor adhesion will allow the paint to creep. And ragged tape in corners will leave blotches. Here are some techniques that will solve these problems and make your masking job go smoothly.

PULL FROM THE ROLL TO GET THE TAPE PERFECTLY STRAIGHT

One of the trickiest parts of masking is getting the tape on straight and tight against the wall. There are many techniques; here's one we know works great. Strip 8-to-10-in. of tape from the roll and use the roll itself, held tightly against the wall, to pull the tape straight **(Photos 1 and 2)**. It's a little awkward at first, and it may seem slow, but the results are nearly perfect every time. Use this technique wherever you're masking at a right angle to another surface.

1 STICK THE END

Position the end of the tape precisely and stick it down. Hold it in place while you pull about 8-to-10-in. of tape from the roll.

2 ATTACH A FEW INCHES

Lay the tape roll flat against the wall and rotate the roll to tighten and straighten it. Slide your finger across the tape to press it down.

SEAL THE EDGE TO PREVENT BLEEDING PAINT

Seal the tape to the surface by pressing it down firmly with the edge of a flexible putty knife as shown. This is the most important step in good masking, and it only takes a few moments. If you skip it, you risk a loose seal that will allow paint to seep underneath. You'll have to scrape off the seeped paint later and touch up the trim.

Keep in mind that you don't have to press down the entire width of the tape. Sealing about 1/32 in. along the edge is all that's needed. Hold the putty knife at an angle as shown. This puts pressure along the critical wall edge of the tape.

TIPS FOR REMOVING MASKING TAPE

A couple things can go wrong when you remove masking tape. If you wait too long, the adhesive will harden and remain stuck to the woodwork. Or if the paint sets but isn't completely dry, some of the wall paint may peel off along with the tape. Here are solutions to these problems.

- If you're a procrastinator, check the label and choose tape that's designed to be left on for several days.
- To avoid peeling paint, pull the tape off immediately or wait at least overnight for the paint to dry completely. Remove tape at a 45-degree angle to the painted surface. If the paint still peels with the tape, use a utility knife to cut the seal between the wall and the tape before you remove the tape.

USE EXTRA TAPE TO MAKE PERFECT INSIDE CORNERS

Getting two long pieces of tape to meet exactly in the corner is difficult, so don't even try. Instead, start the pieces of tape about ¾ in. from the corner and run them using the method shown on p. 166. Then go back and finish the corner with small lengths of tape using the technique shown in **Photos 1 and 2**.

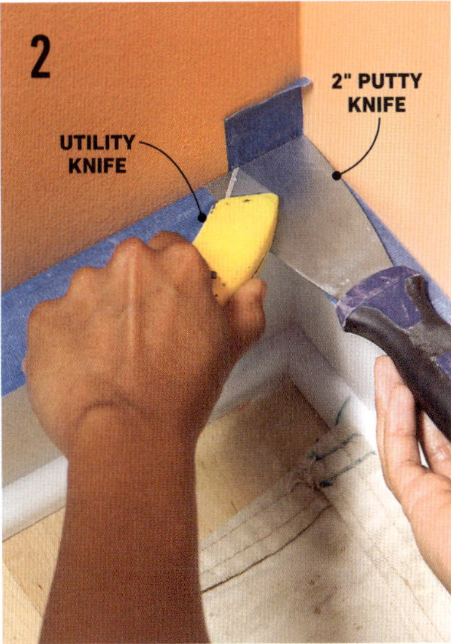

1 LAY THE TAPE

Press a short section of tape into the corner with the blade of a flexible 2-in. putty knife.

2 CUT THE EXCESS

Cut the tape using the putty knife as a guide. Peel off the extra tape to create a perfect corner.

Prep Problem Walls for Painting

Fix any wall to get a super-smooth finish

By Brett Martin

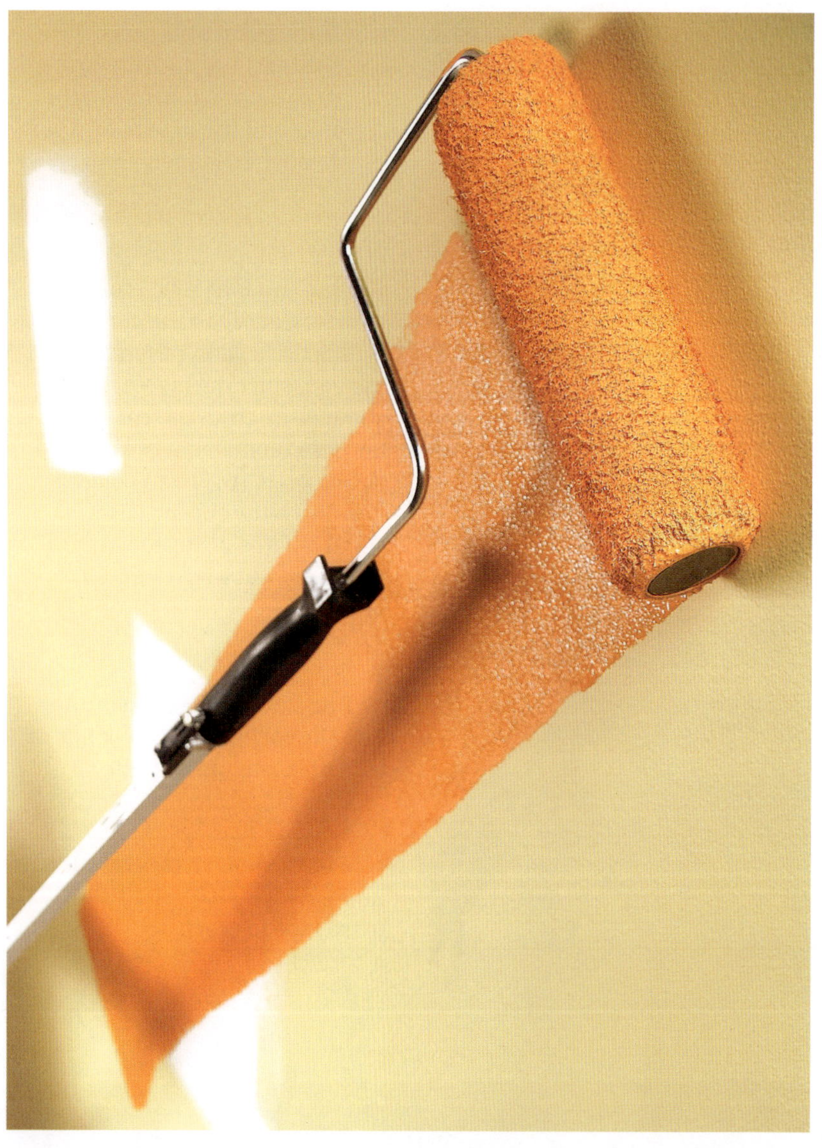

It doesn't matter how much abuse your walls have taken; you can repair them and make them perfectly smooth. Most repairs are cheap and take only a few hours. If you hired a pro to do the work, you'd pay hundreds. That's because they would have to make many trips to your house to complete the job, as most fixes require two or three coats.

We'll show you how to fix these common wall problems before you paint. Everything you need is available at home centers. For small fixes, pick up some spackling compound. For larger repairs, use all-purpose joint compound. You may also need mesh tape.

1 FIX NAIL POPS FOREVER

Seasonal expansion and contraction of studs can push nails out of the drywall. You can't just resink the nail and apply joint compound over the top—the nail will pop back out. To permanently fix the problem, drive a drywall screw about 2 in. above or below the popped nail. Use a 1¼-in. screw (screws hold better than nails). A longer screw isn't better—it's actually more likely to pop out than a shorter one.

Now pull out the nail, holding a wide putty knife under your pry bar to protect the wall. Tap the empty nail hole with the putty knife handle to knock protruding drywall fragments into the wall (or you won't get a smooth coat of filler on the wall). Finally, cover the screw head and fill the nail hole with three coats of joint compound.

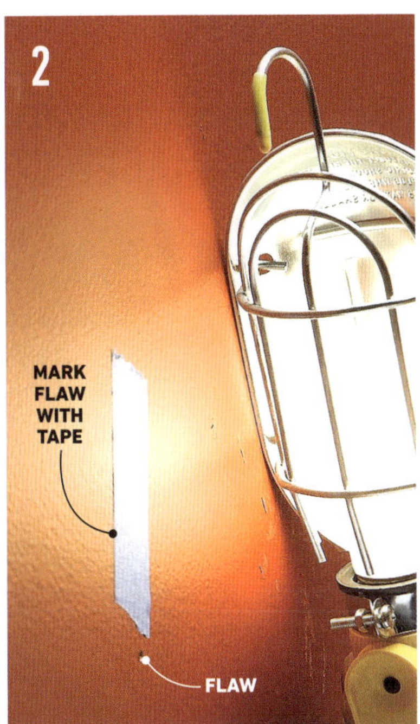

2 HIGHLIGHT HIDDEN FLAWS

Minor wall flaws are often hard to spot—until the afternoon sun hits them and makes them embarrassingly obvious. Find and mark any imperfections. Start by turning off all the lights in the room and closing the curtains. Then hold a trouble light next to the wall and move it across the surface (a process called "raking").

Wherever the light highlights a new problem, even a small one, stick a piece of tape next to it so you can easily find it when you come through with spackling or joint compound. Tape works better than circling the problems with a pencil or pen (which can bleed through the paint).

3 SEAL TORN PAPER

The back of a chair, a flying video game remote or even an aggressive kid with a toy truck can tear the drywall paper face. A coat of paint or joint compound over torn paper will create a fuzzy texture. For a smooth finish, seal the torn paper. Start by cutting away any loose paper. Then seal the exposed drywall with a stain-blocking primer. This keeps the drywall from absorbing moisture from the joint compound you will apply. Wait for the primer to dry, then sand the exposed drywall edges to remove paper nubs. Cover the gouge with a thin layer of joint compound, feathering it out along the wall. If necessary, apply a second coat, feathering it as well, then wait for it to dry and sand it smooth.

PRO TIP After applying joint compound, be sure to cover it with primer before painting to prevent "flashing." Flashing occurs when joint compound absorbs the paint, dulling the finish.

TAPE AND FILL DAMAGED CORNERS

Metal corner bead dents easily, causing cracks in the wall. Fortunately, fixing it is relatively simple. Use a hammer to knock the bead back into shape with several light taps instead of hard blows **(Photo 1)**. Use a level to make sure the bead doesn't stick out past the finished walls or you won't get a clean corner (bury the bead in the wall a little if needed). Round sharp edges with a file.

When you hit the bead with a hammer, you probably sent cracks up and down the corner, especially if the bead wasn't taped. Place mesh tape over the cracks, then apply joint compound over the tape and corner bead on one side only **(Photo 2)**. Work on one side at a time—the first side needs to be hard to square the other side. Once the first side is dry, apply joint compound to the second side. Then recoat the corner, let it dry and sand it smooth.

1. Shape the corner bead with a hammer until it's flush. Don't worry about making drywall cracks along the corner worse.
2. Cover the crack with mesh tape, then cover the tape and the corner bead with joint compound. Fill in one side, let it dry, then fill in the other side.

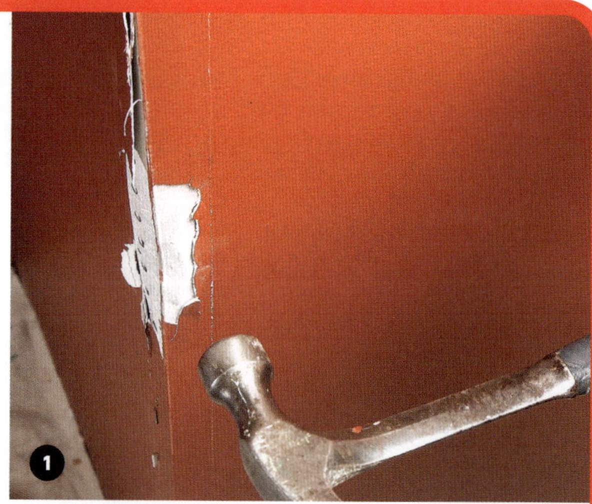

4 FILL HOLES THREE TIMES

Fill small holes and indents (less than ⅛ in.) with spackling compound. For larger holes, use joint compound instead.

Apply either compound with a putty knife, spreading it thin on the wall. You'll apply two more coats (the compounds shrink as they dry), so don't worry if the hole isn't filled perfectly the first time. Let each coat of compound dry (read the directions; some can dry in just two hours).

Don't believe spackling labels that say you don't have to sand. You will need to. You'll have to sand between coats if there's any excess compound. After the final coat, use fine-grit paper.

5 CUT AROUND GLUE SPOTS

Mirrors and paneling are sometimes installed with an adhesive backing to help hold them in place. But when you take them down, the glue sticks to the drywall. Don't try to pull it off—you'll tear the drywall face, making rips across the wall. Instead, cut around the glue with a utility knife, cutting through the drywall face.

Scrape off the glue with a putty knife. You'll still tear the paper, but the tears will be confined to the outline you cut into the drywall. Use sandpaper on small areas of glue that won't scrape off. Fill gouges that you made in the wall with joint compound (see "Seal Torn Paper," p. 169).

CUT OUT WALL CRACKS

When homes settle, drywall cracks sometimes shoot out above or below windows and above doors. You can't just cover or fill the cracks with joint compound—they'll come back. Instead, fix the cracks with joint compound and mesh tape. Mesh tape gives you less buildup than paper tape and is plenty strong. Protect the window or door trim with masking tape before starting the fix.

To fill the crack, use a utility knife to cut a V-shaped groove along its entire length **(Photo 1)**. Fill the groove with joint compound, let it dry, then sand it flush with the wall. Place mesh tape on the crack **(Photo 2)**. Apply joint compound over your tape and feather it out 2 to 4 in. on each side of the tape. Let the compound dry, then apply a second and third coat, feathering it out 8 to 10 in. from the tape with a 10-in. taping blade.

1. Cut a V-shaped groove in the crack, removing everything that's loose, even if it means cutting all the way through to the back of the drywall.
2. Fill the groove with joint compound, then cover it with mesh tape, then cover it with another layer of compound.

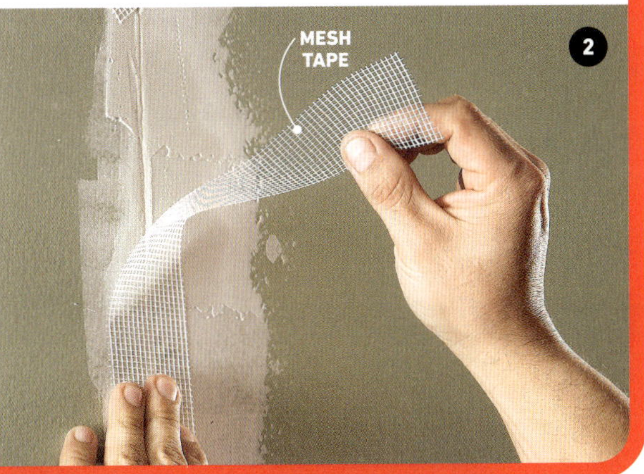

6 FIX HOLES FAST WITH AN ALUMINUM PATCH

The old method of repairing large holes was to cut out a square in the drywall, attach wood backing and then screw on a new patch of drywall. Aluminum patches are a faster, easier solution. Cut the patch so it covers the hole by at least 1 in. on each side, then place it over the hole. One side is sticky to adhere to the wall. Cover the patch with joint compound. Let it dry overnight, then recoat.

7 BLOCK STAINS WITH SPECIAL PRIMER

Don't expect regular primer or paint to cover marker or crayon marks; they'll bleed through even several coats of paint. The same goes for water stains. First try to wash off the marker or crayon with a Mr. Clean Magic Eraser dipped in warm water. If that doesn't work, cover the marks with stain-blocking primer. Apply the primer with a roller so the texture will match the rest of the wall. Buy a cheap disposable roller and then throw it away when you're done.

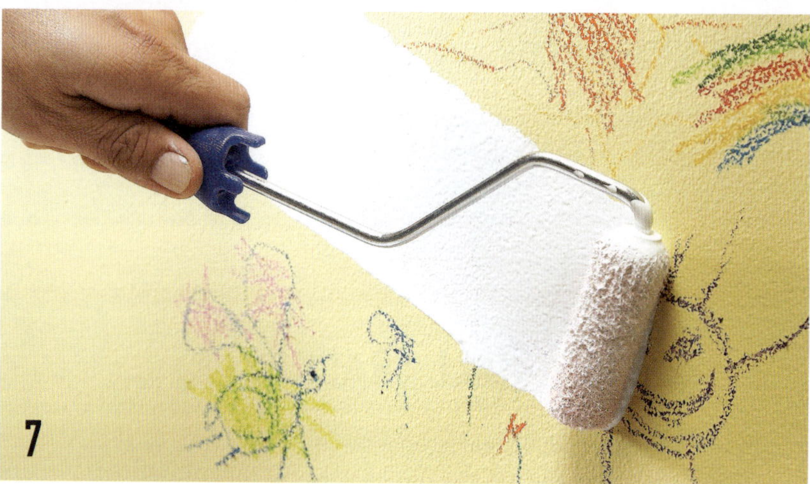

REPLACE LIFTING TAPE

Tape will lift off the wall if there isn't enough joint compound underneath to adhere it to the drywall. You'll have to cut away the loose tape and replace it. Start by cutting through the paint and joint compound to remove every piece of loose tape. Go beyond the cracked area. Peel away the tape until you see the underlying drywall **(Photo 1)**. Then fill the hole with joint compound and wait for it to harden. Embed mesh or paper tape in joint compound over the hole **(Photo 2)**. Extend the tape a few inches past the hole on each side. Once it's dry, apply a second coat and feather it to blend the patch with the wall.

1. Cut away loose tape with a utility knife. Be aggressive and cut past where the tape has lifted away from the wall.
2. Place a strip of tape in joint compound a few inches past and directly over the patch. Apply joint compound over the top of the tape.

Make Exterior Paint Last

Painting the exterior of a house takes a lot of time—you won't want to do it again soon! The key to a long-lasting paint job is solid prep work, and here are 17 tips that get the job done.

By Brad Holden

1

1 CLEAN SIDING AND TRIM

Dirty surfaces won't hold paint. Remove dirt, mildew, cobwebs and anything else that isn't meant to be there. Do the cleaning in stages. Start by applying a solution of bleach, water and a cleaner such as JOMAX (a bleach activator), using a garden sprayer. Next, remove weathered paint and dirt using a pressure washer. Be careful, as you can damage siding and trim with a pressure washer. If you don't feel confident, a siding cleaner and scrub brush will do the job. Thoroughly rinse to remove any cleaner residue and let the surfaces dry.

2 SCRAPE

After the surfaces have dried completely, scrape off any remaining loose or flaking paint. Applying new paint over flaking paint will cause it to peel far sooner than it should. Before scraping, pound in any nail heads that could nick your scraper blade. You can buy a hardened steel scraper or, for about twice the price, you can buy a carbide scraper. Carbide holds an edge far longer than hardened steel. With either option, buy a couple replacement blades so you don't have to sharpen as often. You can sharpen a carbide blade using a diamond stone.

3 REMOVE OLD CAULK

While you're scraping, check the caulking around windows, doors and trim. If the caulk is in good shape and still adhering, leave it in place. If not, dig it out with a 5-in-1 tool (shown), utility knife or putty knife.

4 SAND OFF RIDGES

After scraping, sand any sharp paint edges, blending them with the surrounding surface. If you don't blend them in, the sharp edges will create thin, weak areas in the new paint. Brush away any dust created by sanding, and then rinse the siding and trim thoroughly.

5 REPAIR DAMAGED SURFACES

Don't paint over rotten or insect-damaged wood. Even

if it covers, the paint won't last. Replace or repair any damaged wood. Fill nail holes and other small imperfections with exterior wood putty. Sand off excess putty after it's dry.

6 CREATE A GAP BETWEEN TRIM AND CONCRETE

Boards that come in contact with concrete won't hold paint for long. Water on the concrete wicks up into the wood, loosening the bond between the wood and your paint. To remedy this, trim any wood so that it's about ¼ in. above concrete.

7 KEEP SPACE BETWEEN TRIM AND SHINGLES

If trim or siding contacts the shingles, water will wick into the wood and the paint won't last. Lay a ¾-in.-thick spacer on the shingles and cut any trim or siding to create a gap between the wood and the shingles.

8 SPOT-PRIME

Prime nail heads, putty and knots before priming the whole surface. These areas are more difficult to cover, so they need a little extra attention.

9 PRIME ALL BARE WOOD

You can get good results with oil or latex primer. For bare woods with a high tannin (a dark, natural pigment) content, such as cedar and redwood, use a stain-blocking exterior primer. Stain-blocking primers prevent "bleed-through" of tannin as well as stains from old, rusty nails.

10 CAULK ALL CRACKS AND GAPS

Caulk around windows, doors, trim and anywhere else water could get behind a painted surface. Use interior/exterior paintable latex caulk. Be sure to prime first; primer adheres to bare or slightly dirty surfaces much better than caulk.

11 DON'T FORGET THE THRESHOLD

The bottom of a wood doorjamb will rot prematurely if you don't caulk the line where the threshold meets the jamb.

8

9

10

11

12 SEAL END GRAIN

When you install or expose new wood, seal any end grain with a paintable water repellent, such as Woodlife Classic clear wood preservative. Allow the repellent to dry according to the directions, then prime and paint.

13 KEEP VEGETATION TRIMMED

Plants that come into contact with your exterior walls hold moisture against the paint, which can lead to compromised paint and rotting wood. That means more repair work, more money and more frequent painting.

14 WAIT FOR GOOD PAINTING WEATHER

Avoid painting on hot days, in direct sun and in windy weather. Ideal temperatures for painting are between 50 and 90 degrees. Temperatures below 50 degrees can prevent the paint from adhering to the surface properly. Hot weather, wind and direct sun all cause paint to dry too quickly, preventing adequate penetration of the primer and/or paint. It can also cause oil paint to blister. When possible, work in the shade, following the path of the sun throughout the day. Never paint when rain is imminent or right after it rains. Painting a damp surface can cause paint to bubble.

15 KEEP AN EYE ON YOUR PAINT JOB

Whenever you're out doing yard work, check in on your paint. Look closely for areas of cracked or peeling paint, or wood that might be rotting. With a little spot maintenance, you can extend the life of your paint job by a few years.

16 EASE SHARP EDGES

Sharp edges won't hold paint; there just isn't enough surface area. If you install any new wood, be sure to give any sharp edges a slight round-over. It doesn't take much; a single pass with a sanding block is usually sufficient.

17 DON'T STALL ON PAINTING

Primer loses its bonding properties with prolonged exposure to UV light. After priming, you have a window of time to apply paint. Check the label on your can, as the amount of time can vary among manufacturers. We checked with two major companies. One said that paint must be applied within one week; the other said anywhere from four to six weeks.

6 Tips for Painting Interior Woodwork

Brushing on a silky smooth finish takes patience and attention to detail. Here's how.

By Carl Hines

Having trouble getting your paint to look smooth? Welcome to the club. Painting woodwork so it has a flawless, glossy sheen is challenging. In this article, we'll show you some techniques and tricks that'll produce top-notch results.

For great painted woodwork, surface preparation and good brushing technique are essential. We'll show you how to accomplish both, plus what to add to the paint to help it lie smoother.

Many pros still rely solely on oil-based paints because they dry slowly and allow brush marks to flatten out. But you can achieve similar results with high-quality latex paint. Today's formulations cover and brush out well. You won't have the strong odor of oil that'll drive you out of the house for days. And latex also offers the advantage of fast drying and easy soap and water cleanup.

PRO TIP Stiff putty knives work better for scraping; flexible putty knives work better for filling.

Latex paint is available in a range of sheens from flat to high gloss. Because you want your wood trim to wear well, we usually recommend eggshell or semigloss. The downside to these shiny finishes is that every bump and scratch shows through. Good prep is critical.

PREPARATION, PREPARATION

A coat of paint won't fill or hide cracks, chips and other surface defects, and it won't smooth an existing rough surface. You have to fill and smooth the woodwork before you paint.

Wash the woodwork with a trisodium phosphate (TSP) solution or substitute to remove grease and grime. Mix according to the directions on the package and scrub with a sponge or rag. Be sure to rinse well with clear water to remove residues.

Next, examine the surface for loose and cracked paint that will need scraping. Many scraper types are available, but a 2-in. stiff putty knife works well for small areas **(Photo 1)**. When you're done scraping, you'll be left with a rougher surface and a few more scratches and gouges than when you started. Don't worry—you'll fix these areas next.

For dents and chips deeper than about ⅛ in., we like to use a two-part polyester resin. One example is Minwax wood filler. It sticks well, doesn't shrink and sands easily. It's also the best material for rebuilding chipped corners. Auto body fillers also work well.

Scoop out an amount the size of a golf ball onto a scrap piece of wood or cardboard. Add the correct amount of hardener (follow the directions) and mix thoroughly but quickly **(Photo 2)**.

1 GET RID OF OLD PAINT

Remove all loose or cracked paint with a stiff putty knife. Work in various directions to get underneath the loose paint.

Caution: Paint dust and chips from lead paint are hazardous. If your home was built before 1977, the year lead paint was banned, call your local public health department and ask about paint testing details and safe scraping, sanding and cleaning techniques.

2 MIX FILLER

Fill nicks and gouges with a two-part wood filler. Mix it thoroughly (following label directions) with a 2- or 3-in. flexible metal or plastic putty knife.

3 FILL BLEMISHES

Pick up a dab of putty with the knife and apply it to the gouges. Hold the knife at an angle and press the filler in the scraped area. Leave the filler slightly higher than the surrounding surface.

4 SAND FLUSH

Sand the filler flush to the painted surface with a medium sanding sponge or 100- or 120-grit sandpaper. Make sure to get rid of all ridges. Then finish-sand with 180-grit sandpaper or a fine sanding sponge. Spot-prime the filler and any bare wood.

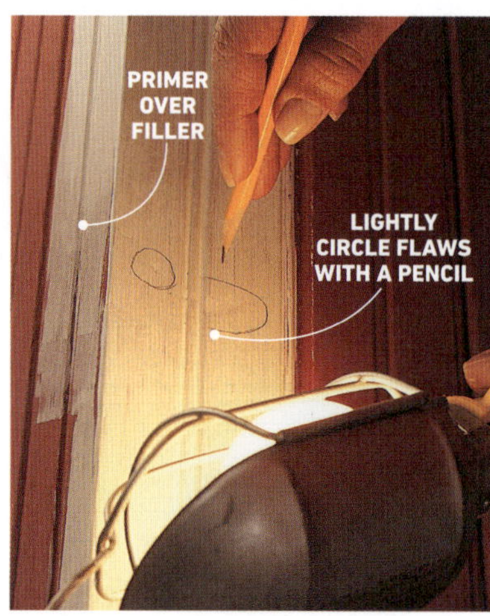

5 CHECK FOR IMPERFECTIONS

Hold a utility light close to the surface, and circle any imperfections with a pencil. Fill, sand and spot-prime these areas. Finally, lightly sand the entire surface with the 180-grit paper to ensure that the new paint will stick.

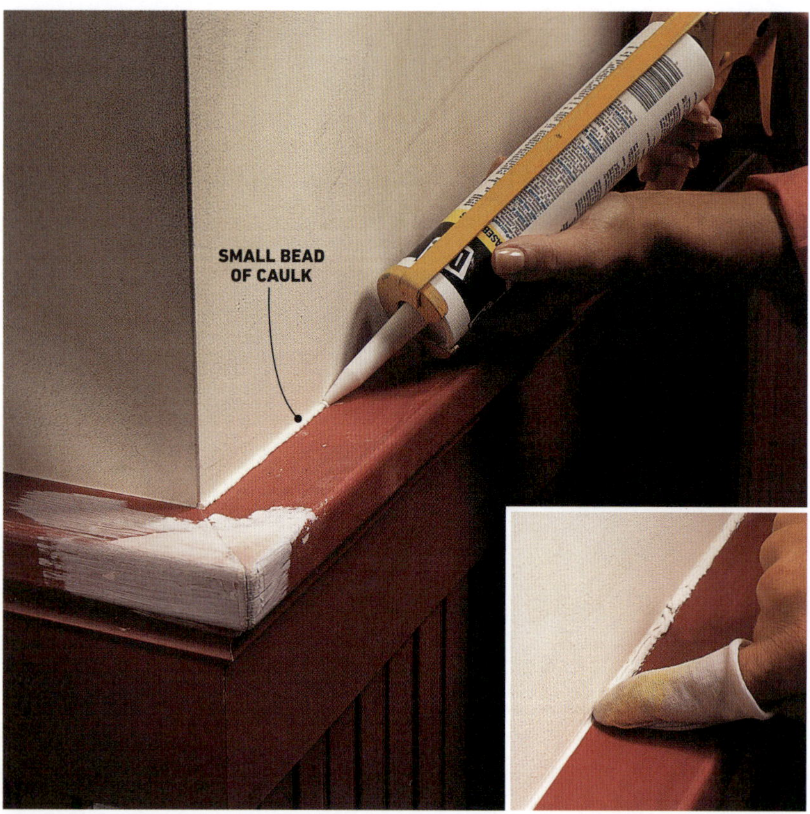

6 CAULK THE GAPS

Apply a small bead of paintable caulk to the crack between the wood and the wall. Smooth the caulk with a damp rag wrapped around your finger. Wipe the edges to remove any ridges of caulk.

PRO TIP Brush marks in the old paint are particularly annoying and have to be sanded out, not filled.

Most of the resins only have a 5-to-10-minute working time.

For finer scratches and chips, use spackling compound. (Ready Patch by Zinsser is one brand used by many pros.) Don't use a lightweight compound; it doesn't stick to painted wood as well.

"Spot-prime" the filler and any bare wood with a latex primer. This step is worth the effort because it helps you see any imperfections. Check your work by holding a bright light (trouble light or flashlight) close to the woodwork **(Photo 5)**. Every small bump and scratch will jump out. Circle the defects with a pencil, then go back to the filler and sanding steps. Spot-prime and finish-sand these reworked areas.

Prep work requires patience, especially when you have to go back to an earlier step. What you decide is acceptable here is what you'll get in the finish coat. But keep in mind that the most critical eye will probably be yours.

Finish up the prep work by lightly sanding all areas that haven't been scraped or primed. Use 180-grit paper or the fine sanding sponge. This will smooth out previous brush marks and scuff the surface to help the new coat of paint stick. Then wipe down the entire surface with a damp cloth to remove all the dust.

CAULK

Now that the filling, sanding and priming are done, caulk any long cracks and gaps **(Photo 6)**. Use an acrylic latex caulk; it adheres well, remains flexible and cleans up with water. Cut the caulk tube at the very tip to leave a very small hole. You'll have better control of the caulk. Apply a bead of caulk that protrudes slightly, then wipe it with a damp cloth wrapped around your finger. Wipe excess caulk off the cloth so you don't smear it on either side of the joint. You may have to wipe several times to produce a smooth, clean caulk line.

THE PAINT AND THE BRUSH

Don't undermine all the time and effort you've put into the prep work by using cheap brushes and paint. Buy the best. With proper cleaning, a quality brush will last for years. In most cases, you'll find the highest quality paint and tools (and good advice) at specialty paint stores.

While we recommend latex, it does have one weakness: It dries quickly. The longer the paint remains wet, the better it flows and flattens, leaving a smooth surface. We recommend that you use an additive that slows down the drying process and helps the paint lie smooth. (Floetrol is one common choice.) Always read the directions for the amount to add.

For best results from brushing, don't dip directly from the can. Pour a quart of the paint into a 4- or 5-qt. pail. This is your working paint that will move around with you. Add the measured amount of additive and mix well **(Photo 7)**. From this pail you can dip and tap your brush without splattering. Good-quality paints are ready to use out of the can and don't need thinning with water. Be sure to have the paint store shake the can so it's well mixed, then stir the paint occasionally as you use it.

BRUSHING TECHNIQUE

The sequence in brushing is to quickly coat an area with several brush loads of paint, and then blend and smooth it out by lightly running the unloaded brush tip over it (called tipping). See **Photos 9-11**. Try to coat a whole board or section, but do not let the paint sit more than a minute before tipping.

CHOOSING A BRUSH

As with paint, buy quality when you shop for brushes. You'll spend about $10 to $15 per brush. Some of our favorites for trim are a 2½ in. straight brush and, for detail work and cutting in, a 1½ in. angle brush. Which brush to use is an individual choice. For latex, buy a synthetic bristle brush with "exploded" tips.

A good brush draws a decent "load" of paint into the bristles and applies it smoothly.

7 USE ADDITIVES
Pour a quart of paint into the pail and add a latex additive for smoother results. Follow the label's instructions for the correct amount. Mix thoroughly.

8 APPLY PAINT TO THE BRUSH
Dip the brush bristles 1 to 2 in. into the paint to load the brush. Lightly tap the tip of the brush against the sides of the pail to shake off excess paint.

9 BRUSH FROM THE TOP Start at the top of the board with the loaded brush and stroke down toward the middle. When the brush begins to drag, stop and reload.

10 EVEN IT OUT Lightly set the tip of the brush against the paint and lightly stroke down the whole length of the board. Hold the brush almost perpendicular to the surface.

11 LET IT SIT The fine brush strokes left after tipping will flow together until the paint begins to skin over.

The more paint the brush carries, the faster you'll coat the woodwork. But you want to avoid dripping. So after dipping, tap the tip of the brush against the pail, like the clapper of a bell **(Photo 8)**. For a drier brush, try dragging one side over the edge of the pail.

Hold the brush at about a 45-degree angle, set the tip down where you want to start and pull it gently over the surface with a little downward pressure **(Photo 9)**. Here's where the good brush pays off. The paint will flow smoothly onto the surface with little effort on your part.

A common mistake is to force paint out of the brush after it becomes too dry. The goal is a uniform thickness but not so thick as to run or sag. With practice, you'll quickly find the ideal thickness. If the new color doesn't hide the old, it's better to apply a second coat than to apply the paint too thick. Continue the next brush load from where your last stroke left off, or work backward, say from an inside corner back into the wet paint.

When "tipping," avoid dabbing small areas as this leaves marks in the paint. Make long strokes. The brush will leave a slight

PRO TIP Always use painter's masking tape. It's less likely to damage the surface when removed. Don't leave it on for more than a couple of days or it'll harden and be tougher to remove, and might rip the paint.

track of parallel ridges, but they'll lie down before the paint begins to skin over **(Photo 11)**.

MASKING OFF AND CUTTING IN

Often the boards you're painting butt against a different paint color or a wall. There are a couple of ways to leave a sharp, crisp line.

Masking off with tape is one method. Lay painter's tape tight to the line where your new coat of paint will end **(Photo 12)**. Push the tape tight against the surface with a stiff putty knife to prevent the wet paint from bleeding (running) underneath the tape. Brush the woodwork, letting the paint go partially onto the tape, then tip. Remove the tape when the paint is dry.

The pros can usually skip the masking tape and just cut in with a brush; it's faster. With some practice and a steady hand, even an amateur can get very sharp lines. Learn with a smaller brush (1½ in.) and use a wider brush as you gain control. Dip the brush and scrape one side on the pail. Hold the dry side of the brush toward the line and slowly draw the brush along **(Photo 13)**. Support your arm to steady it, and keep the stroke moving. Use gentle downward pressure; you want the bristles to splay out slightly as you stroke. You'll find you can control the paint line by varying the pressure you apply to the brush.

When the brush is dry, reload and start where the previous stroke ended. Sometimes you'll have to go back over a section where the paint is shy of the line. Complete cutting in and then coat the rest of the piece.

12 PROTECT ALREADY PAINTED AREAS Apply painter's masking tape to protect finished surfaces before brushing on the second color. Carefully position the tape and push it tight against the surface with a stiff putty knife. Be sure the paint underneath has thoroughly dried.

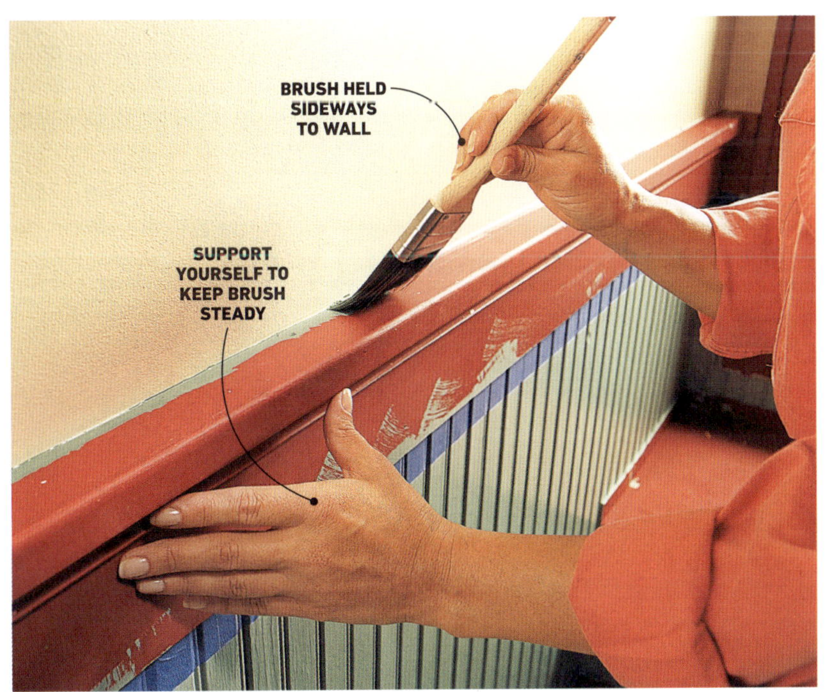

13 CUTTING-IN Load the 1½ in. brush with paint and drag one side over the edge of the pail. Holding the dry side of the brush toward the wall, carefully set the tip of the brush close to the wall. Apply a little pressure and pull your brush along the line. Guide the paint up to the line by manipulating the pressure and position of the brush's tip as you pull it along.

Remove Paint from Trim

Paint drips on your natural woodwork are a pain, but don't despair. Here's how to get rid of the drips without damaging the wood.

By Ryan Van Bibber

SUNDAEMORNING/GETTY IMAGES

1 USE A PAINT SCRAPER

A few dried paint drips on natural trim can make a whole room look shabby. But you don't need to strip the woodwork to get rid of them. You can remove paint drips—and the streaks of old paint that make edges of trim so hard to repaint—just by scraping, even if the paint has been dry for years.

First, scrape the paint with a metal putty or utility knife. Paint doesn't stick well to varnish, and often the paint drips will just pop right off. Use a razor knife for corners. Finally, clean up any residue by rubbing the wood with denatured alcohol. You can use matching stain or a stain marker to touch up any light spots.

Scraping removes the big blotches but sometime leaves paint in the wood grain. For that, you may need to use a little paint remover. Start by taping off the wall and removing the largest blotches. Next, scrub off the remaining paint.

2 AVOID DRIPS NEXT TIME

Masking tape does a good job of protecting woodwork—if it's applied well.

Clean off all the dirt and grime along the edge of the trim with a damp rag. Hold the tape tight against the wall and roll it out so the tape covers the edge. Press the tape against the wood with a putty knife along the entire length. Use painter's tape that's at least twice as wide as the trim and leave it flared out to protect the face of the trim from drips.

When you're done, either remove the tape immediately while the paint is still wet or wait until the next day when it is totally dry. If you pull it free when the paint is partially dry, you may peel off bits of fresh paint along with the tape.

SKILLS IN PRACTICE

How to Paint a Ceiling

It's one of the toughest painting jobs in a house, but experts are on-hand with their best tips

By Jeff Gorton

Ceilings present unique painting challenges. For starters, they're usually much larger than any single room wall and are often illuminated with raking light that accentuates even the smallest flaw in your paint. Add to that the challenge of working overhead and things can get messy in a hurry. That's why we called in Bill Nunn, a painting consultant who has been painting for 35 years, to help you out with his best ceiling painting tips.

1 USE A STAIN-BLOCKING PRIMER TO COVER FLAWS

Roof leaks, overflowing sinks, tobacco smoke and big spills can all leave ugly ceiling stains or dinginess that is impossible to conceal with plain old paint. But cover the stain with a coat of stain-blocking primer and your troubles are over.

Bill's all-time favorite is white pigmented shellac. You can buy spray cans of pigmented shellac, but Bill prefers brushing it on. Just don't forget to pick up some ammonia or denatured alcohol to clean your brush. If you're painting over a ceiling that's yellow from smoke, roll a coat of shellac over the entire ceiling before painting with latex.

2 SAND BEFORE YOU PAINT

Over time, and as the layers of paint build up, bumps and crud can get stuck to the ceiling. On untextured ceilings, Bill starts with a quick once-over sand with 100-grit drywall sanding paper. This helps ensure a perfectly smooth paint job and increases paint bonding. The easiest way to do this is with a sanding pole. When you're done sanding, wipe the ceiling with a damp sponge to remove the dust.

3 CUT IN BEFORE YOU ROLL

Cutting in before you roll allows you to cover most of the brush marks with the roller. Bill likes to carefully brush paint along the edge of the ceiling a section at a time. He'll cut in about 10 linear ft. and then roll that section. This method has a couple of advantages over cutting in the entire room at once. First, the cut-in section will remain wet until you roll, so it blends in better. Bill says it's also simply less boring to alternate between cutting in and rolling.

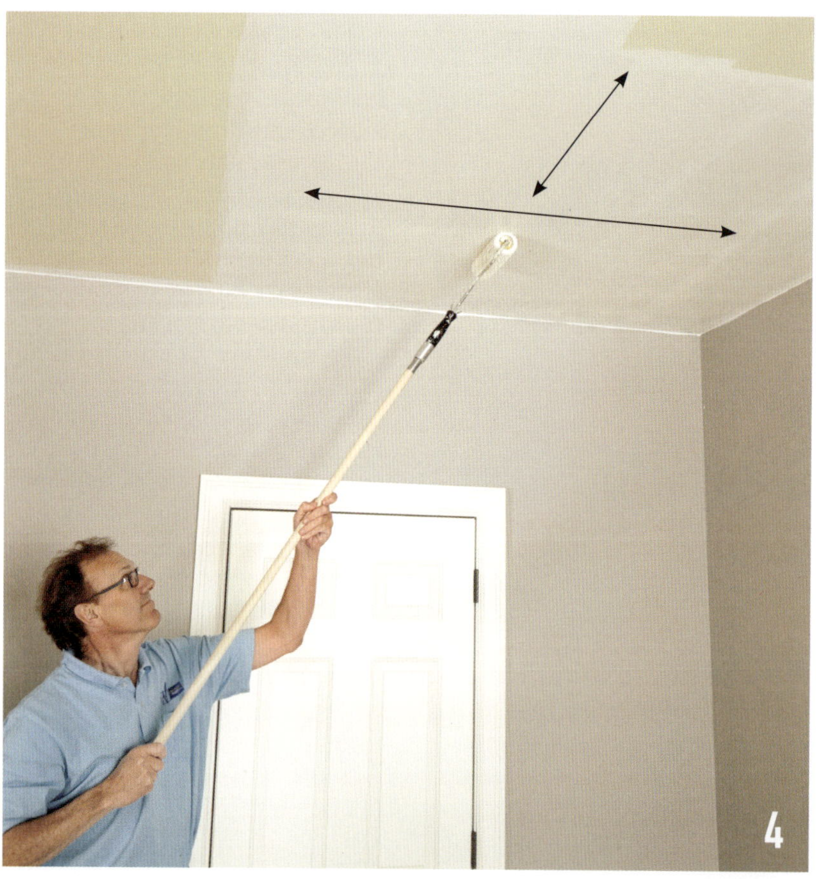

PRO TIP Bill prefers to move everything out of the room and cover the floors with drop cloths before painting a ceiling. But if this isn't possible, he groups furniture in the center and covers it with painter's plastic. Sometimes it may be necessary to make two or more small groups so that you can reach over them with the roller.

4 ROLL BOTH DIRECTIONS

There are a few tricks to getting a smooth, consistent coat of paint on the ceiling. First, work in sections about 5 or 6 ft. square. Move quickly from one section to the next to make sure the paint along the edge doesn't dry before you roll the adjoining section. This is called keeping a wet edge, and is the key to avoiding lap marks. Bill says you'll get the best coverage by immediately rerolling each section at a right angle to your first roller direction as you go.

5 BUY SPECIAL CEILING PAINT

While there are exceptions, in general you'll get the best results with paint that's formulated for a ceiling application. For a ceiling, you want paint that doesn't spatter, has a long open time (dries slowly), and is flat instead of glossy. Most ceiling paints are formulated with these qualities. And of course you can have ceiling paint tinted if you want a color other than "ceiling white."

6 LAP YOUR CUT-IN ONTO THE WALLS

If you're painting your walls anyway, lap the paint onto the walls a little bit. Then when you paint the walls, you can err on the side of leaving a little ceiling color showing when you cut in and it won't be noticeable. Some painters like to skip this cutting-in step and save time by mashing the roller into the corner instead. Bill objects to this method because it's sloppy, builds up excess paint in the corner and can leave runs or a thick paint line on the wall.

7 DON'T BE AFRAID OF COLOR

You may not want to paint your ceiling yellow, but don't be afraid to deviate from plain old white. Bill says painting the ceiling a color can make a small room seem bigger, or a room with a high ceiling seem more intimate. Plus, it's just much more interesting. Ask at any full-service paint store for help in choosing complementary wall and ceiling colors, or search online for examples of rooms you like.

7

8

8 YOU DON'T NEED AN EXPENSIVE POLE

Bill is sort of old-school when it comes to equipment and actually prefers low-tech solutions. You can buy all kinds of fancy extendable paint poles, but Bill prefers a simple wooden broom handle. And his reasons are simple. They're cheap and light and do the job.

9

9 ROLL GENTLY ON TEXTURED CEILINGS

Painting textured ceilings is a bit of a crapshoot. If the texture has been painted over already, it's probably safe to paint again. If the texture has never been painted, there's a risk the water in the paint could loosen the texture, causing it to fall off in sheets. A lot depends on the quality of the texturing job. If you have a closet or other inconspicuous area, do a test by rolling on some paint to see what happens. If the texture loosens, painting over the larger ceiling is risky.

Bill has a few tips for painting over texture. If possible, spray on the paint—it's less likely to loosen the texture than rolling. But spraying in an occupied house is usually impractical. Bill says the best tip for rolling on paint is to avoid overworking the paint. Just roll the paint on and leave it. Don't go back and forth with the roller, as this is likely to pull the texture from the ceiling. If the ceiling needs another coat of paint, wait for the first coat to dry completely. Then roll another coat perpendicular to the first one using the same careful technique.

10 USE A THICK, PREMIUM ROLLER COVER

Here's a tip that applies to most paint jobs but is even more important for ceilings. You want to get as much paint on the ceiling as you can in the shortest amount of time possible while minimizing spatters. To do this, you need the best roller cover you can buy. Bill's favorite is a ½-in.-nap lambswool cover. If you've never tried a lambswool roller cover, give it a chance and experience the difference. If you're worried about the cost, keep in mind that lambswool covers are easy to clean and can last a long time if you take good care of them.

CHAPTER 6

Woodworking

TOOL SPOTLIGHT

WOODWORKER'S FINISHING KIT

Technique is important for achieving consistent results, but quality tools and materials are equally important. Woodworker Jay Cork shares his go-to's.

MAGNIFYING GLASS/LIGHT
A magnifying glass with a light helps me spot blemishes.

TACK CLOTH
Tack cloths are meant to clean the surface between coats. I've never liked the store-bought ones, but a microfiber cloth dampened with solvent has never failed me.

SANDING BLOCKS
I love this sanding block from *woodcraft.com*. The block uses the same 5-in. discs as my sander, and it's form-fit for my hand.

SPATULA KNIVES
With some types of grain, the color difference requires two or more tones of filler. I use small art knives to achieve that detail.

RUBBER SQUEEGEE
For larger areas, a rubber squeegee will help spread the filler into the grain. This grout tool that I found at a hardware store does the same job.

COLORED PENCILS/MARKERS
Use colored pencils or markers to create grain lines on a repair.

VERSATILE WOOD DYE
TransTint wood dye is soluble in both alcohol and water. I use it to tint shellac or a water-based finish. Go easy—a little goes a long way!

STEEL WOOL
When used between coats, Briwax "0000" oil-free steel wool won't contaminate the finish. I never use steel wool on bare wood; the iron can cause little black stains that will never come out.

FESTOOL SANDPAPER
Festool "Granat" is hands-down the best sandpaper I've ever used. It's more expensive, but you'll save money using it.

EPOXY PUTTY
Epoxy putty is a great choice for repairing damaged furniture, but beware—it doesn't take stain exactly like wood.

BRUSHES
I find that a verystiff, natural-bristle brush gives me greater control for brushing polyurethane.

PAINTING PYRAMIDS
Painting pyramids keep your project elevated and stable—but be careful. I once sanded a piece while it was still on the pyramids and the points dug in on the back side.

NITRILE GLOVES
In the past I've used blue latex gloves. But I discovered these ultra-durable Venom Steel nitrile gloves. I'll be using these from now on.

BLOXYGEN
Bloxygen displaces oxygen with an inert gas. Spraying it into a can of finish as you put the lid back on keeps the finish from going bad.

TWEEZERS
Dust, hair, brush bristles and even insects can all ruin your finish. If you catch the culprit quickly with a pair of tweezers, the finish should level back out.

CHISEL
A sharp chisel is for more than just wood. I use one to shave off drips and runs after the finish has dried.

TIMBERMATE WOOD FILLER
Timbermate is a water-based wood filler made from wood flour. It can be thinned out with water for use as a grain filler, and it shrinks less than any other filler I've used.

PREVAL SPRAYER
When topcoating with epoxy, I like to have a Preval sprayer filled with denatured alcohol. A little spritz will help settle bubbles and other surface blemishes.

MINERAL SPIRITS AND DENATURED ALCOHOL
Certain finishes require specific solvents. I use denatured alcohol for thinning shellac and epoxy. Mineral spirits can be used for thinning oil-based finishes and for cleaning.

7 Shop Class Lessons You Should Master

Nail the basics to become a better woodworker

By Ethan O'Donnell

1

1 ACCOUNT FOR WOOD MOVEMENT

Sure, wood's a pretty tough material all around, but it's still highly susceptible to temperature and moisture fluctuations from the surrounding environment. This phenomenon, known as wood movement, can result in contraction and expansion across the grain. When the humidity is high, wood absorbs moisture and swells. When humidity drops, wood shrinks.

The movement is gradual, but it can cause big problems in your woodworking projects, so you have to account for it in your woodworking projects. There are several ways to do that, some of them depending on the type of project and where it will sit once finished. The most important tactic for dealing with wood movement is to let it sit and acclimate in your shop. The time can vary depending on the size and thickness of the lumber and whether or not its kiln dried.

2

2 HOW TO USE A HAND PLANE

A hand plane is a great tool for woodworking projects, large and small, and it's definitely a skill you should have learned how to handle in shop class.

Here's a quick refresher: Hold the plane at a slight angle to the wood and then plane along the same direction as the wood grain whenever it's possible. Planing against the grain will cause the blade to catch and tear or splinter the wood.

3

3 UNDERSTAND NOMINAL DIMENSIONS

For many of us, the moment we learned that a 2×4 board is actually 1½ x 3½ in. was simply mind-blowing. The reason for the contradicting measurements is that the board has been planed down to eliminate irregularities. At one point, many years ago, 2×4s actually were 2 x 4 in., but their rough surfaces made them very difficult to stock and handle. The old terms, such as 2×4 or 4×4, are still commonly used today, and are known as the nominal size of the board. Nominal sizes are still used simply because they're easier to say and they stick to tradition. Now, most big box stores will list the nominal size, as well as the actual sizes of lumber to cut down on confusion.

4

5

TOOLS: UNCLEPODGER/GETTY IMAGES

4 FIX MITER JOINTS

In shop class, many learn the satisfying skill of cutting a miter joint that closes up perfectly and maintains a true 90-degree angle. If your miter skills are rusty, here's a quick fix for a slightly open miter joint: Rub the shank of your screwdriver along the miter at a steep angle, from both sides of the joint. Chances are, you'll be the only one that knows it wasn't perfect to begin with.

5 EASY NAIL PILOT HOLES

Often when you are nailing small finishing nails into moldings or other projects, the nail will split the wood unless you drill a pilot hole first. However, tiny drill bits have a habit of breaking after just a couple of uses.

So rather than using a drill bit, drill the perfect-sized pilot hole using the nail itself. Simply clip the head of the nail off with lineman's pliers for thicker nails or use wire cutters for thinner ones; then place the headless nail into the drill. Drill the hole with this nail pilot hole hack, and then drive in a nail.

6 MAKE TABLE SAW-QUALITY RIPS WITH A CIRCULAR SAW

Even if you have your own table saw, sometimes it's easier to rip large sheets of plywood with a circular saw. The trick to a perfectly straight cut is to clamp a straightedge to the plywood and use it as a guide for your saw. On most circular saws, the distance between the edge of your saw's base and the blade is 1½ in., so you can simply position the straightedge 1½ in. from your cutting line. But measure this distance on your saw to be sure.

You can buy a straightedge or use the factory edge of a plywood sheet. If your straightedge only has one straight edge, be sure to mark it to avoid using the wrong or crooked side.

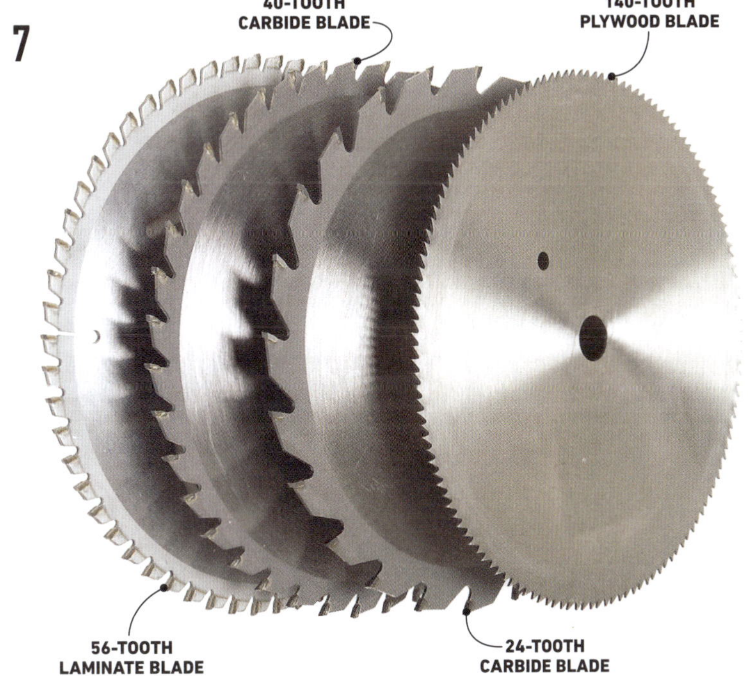

7 CHOOSE THE RIGHT CIRCULAR SAW BLADE

As long as they're sharp, any of these four 7¼ in. circular saw blades will make smooth rip cuts in plywood and reasonably good crosscuts. In general, the more the teeth, the smoother the cut. The disadvantage of the 140-tooth plywood blade is that the teeth will dull much faster than the teeth on the three carbide blades. This is especially true if you cut particleboard. The 40-tooth carbide blade is a good all-around blade. However, if you have a project that calls for a lot of fine cuts in expensive plywood, don't hesitate to buy the special 56-tooth laminate-cutting blade.

Get the Most from Your Drill Press

Thirteen hacks to do more with this workshop staple

By Brad Holden

A drill press is a simple, one-job tool, right? Some might even call it "boring." But as is often the case with tools, many tinkering minds have come up with clever ways to use this humble shop staple. Here's how to use your drill press to its full potential.

1 SET THE TABLE FOR PERFECT "PERPENDICULARITY"

A drill press can only drill perfectly straight holes if the table is perfectly perpendicular to the spindle. Here's an old machinist's trick to make your table spot-on. Make about a 30-degree bend in a ¼-in. steel rod about 2 in. from the end. Cut it to a length that will reach the outer edges of your table when the short end is in the chuck. Chuck in the rod and then turn the chuck so that the rod's end is oriented toward either edge of the table. Raise the table until the rod just touches the surface and then lock the table. Turn the chuck to position the rod on the opposite edge of the table. Adjust the tilt of the table until the rod touches both edges equally. Lock the tilt adjustment nut and never adjust it again. (Find out how to drill angled holes on p. 202.)

2 ADJUST BELT TENSION TO LIMIT VIBRATION

After you've changed speeds, or if your drill press has excessive vibration, check the belt tension. You should be able to deflect the belt with your finger no more than ½ in. midway between pulleys. To adjust the tension, loosen the motor lock, move the motor forward or backward and then tighten the lock again. Some drill presses have a tension adjuster lever to move the motor.

3 CHECK YOUR SPEED FOR EFFECTIVE DRILLING

Detailed charts are available online with information about speed, bit types, diameters and materials being drilled. But here are two general rules: Decrease the speed as the bit diameter increases, and slow way down for steel. Some high-end drill presses have a variable-speed dial on the front. Otherwise, you'll change speeds by changing

the belt position on the pulleys located under the top cover. On most drill presses, a graphic under the lid shows the speeds associated with different belt positions. To change the belt positions, first release the motor lock to take the tension.

4 NO-FUSS DEPTH SETTING

Mark the desired depth on the edge of your workpiece. Lower your spindle until the bit reaches the mark, then set the depth stop.

5 MAKE A CLAMP BAR FOR SMALL PARTS

To safely drill small parts, you need a way to hold them. A clamp bar is a fast solution. Predrill a screw hole in the end of a 1×2, and screw it to the table where needed. This pivoting bar lets you squeeze the workpiece against the fence while keeping your hands out of the way. For dowels, cut a V-notch in the bar to keep them from sliding. A hand screw clamp also works well for small parts, again with a V-notch for dowels.

PLUNGE AND RELEASE TO CLEAR THE FLUTES

Don't bore a hole in a single plunge. The bit's flutes will fill up with sawdust, create heat, slow down drilling and dull the bit prematurely. Instead, drill in small increments, raising the bit often to release the sawdust. If the sawdust doesn't come out on its own, blow it out.

6 ADD A BIGGER TABLE FOR BETTER SUPPORT

Most drill press tables are small and not ideal for woodworking, so try adding a larger table. Two thicknesses of MDF will suffice. On the table shown, the top layer of MDF is assembled as a frame. This allows for a replaceable sacrificial insert where all the drilling happens. The insert is offset so that only one quadrant is centered under the chuck. This lets you use all four quadrants of the insert before you need to replace it.

7 SECURE WORKPIECES WITH TOGGLE CLAMPS

Sometimes—such as when you're drilling steel—you need to firmly clamp your workpiece to the table. I use a pair of toggle clamps (about $6 each at Harbor Freight). I just screw them directly to the table where needed.

8 CLEAR DEBRIS QUICKLY WITH AN AIR NOZZLE

I've tried shop vacuums and dust collection setups on my drill press, but they're not very effective. I've found the best thing for clearing dust off the table and out of the bit's flutes is compressed air. I hang an air nozzle from an eye screw on the underside of the table.

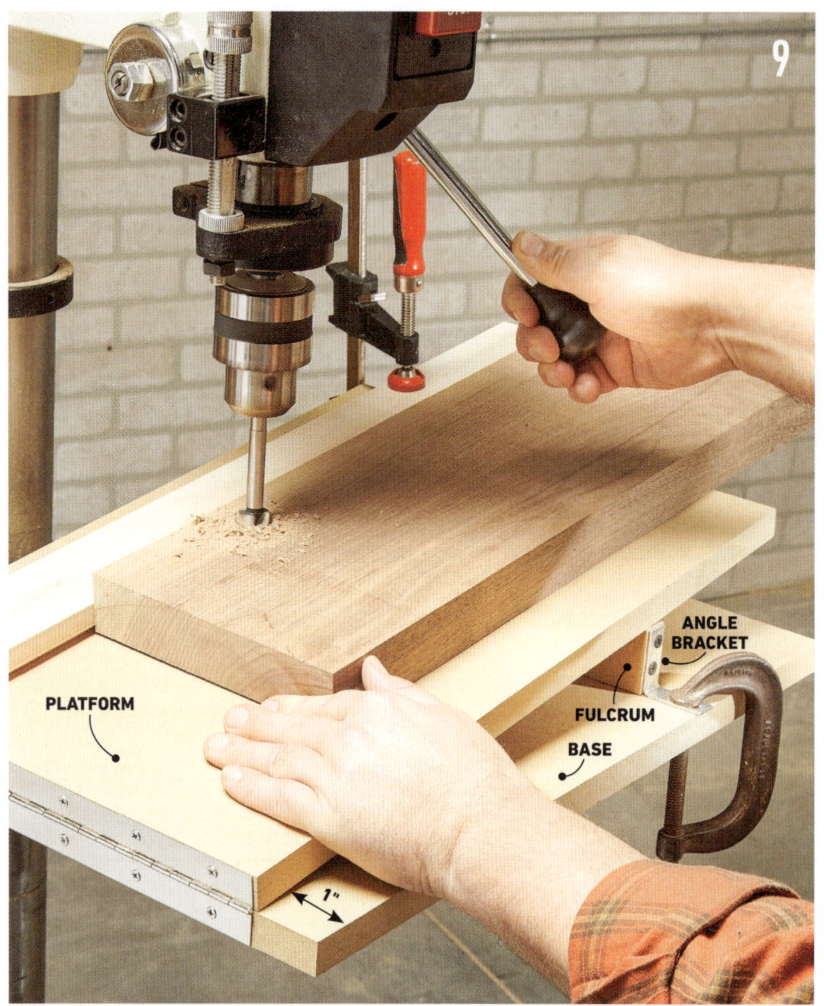

9 DRILL ANGLED HOLES WITH A HINGED TABLE

To drill shallow angles, don't tilt the table. Instead, make a hinged platform. Join two pieces of MDF together at one end with a piano hinge. The platform is 3 in. narrower, centered on the base. The fulcrum is 1½ in. tall, and its length is the same as the platform's width. Fasten a 1½-in. angle bracket to each end of the fulcrum. To use, slide the fulcrum to create the desired angle, and then clamp or screw the angle brackets to the base.

10 MAKE A DUST CHANNEL FOR ACCURATE DRILLING

When you're drilling, sawdust collects between the fence and the workpiece, preventing your workpiece from registering against the fence for subsequent holes. Make a ¼ x ¼-in. rabbet on the fence's bottom edge so the dust has a place to go and won't interfere with drilling accuracy. Likewise, when you're clamping stops to the fence, leave them ¼ in. above the table's surface.

11 STABILIZE ROUND STOCK WITH A V-BLOCK

To drill a hole or a straight line of holes in a cylindrical object, use a shop-made V-block. To make one, set your table saw or circular saw blade to 45 degrees, and then make two passes to create the "V." Leave a little extra length on the dowel, screw the end of the dowel to the V-block and cut that end off later when you're finished.

12 BUILD A SANDING TABLE IN 5 MINUTES

A set of sanding drums is a handy addition to your drill press. One advantage this setup has over a spindle sander is that you can set the height of the drum to utilize the entire sanding surface. All you need is a piece of plywood with a cutout sized for the sanding drum you're using. Swing the table off to one side and clamp the sanding platform into place.

13 DRILL EVENLY SPACED HOLES

One of many ways to drill evenly spaced holes is to use a shelf standard attached to a fence. Tap a finish nail into the edge of your workpiece and clip off the head so that no more than ⅛ in. is left protruding. Mark the starting hole on the workpiece and drill it with the nail engaged in the shelf standard. Move the workpiece however many spaces are needed on the shelf standard for each consecutive hole.

Sharpen Tools

Five tricks to get razor-sharp chisels, bits and more

By Jeff Gorton

If sharpening your blunt chisels sounds like drudgery, we can help. We'll show you some cool sharpening tips and tools that will motivate you to tune up the edges on all the dull tools in your shop.

We don't have space here to teach every sharpening step, but we've collected tips to help you get started on the most common sharpening tasks. For more info, go to *familyhandyman.com* and search for the topic you're interested in.

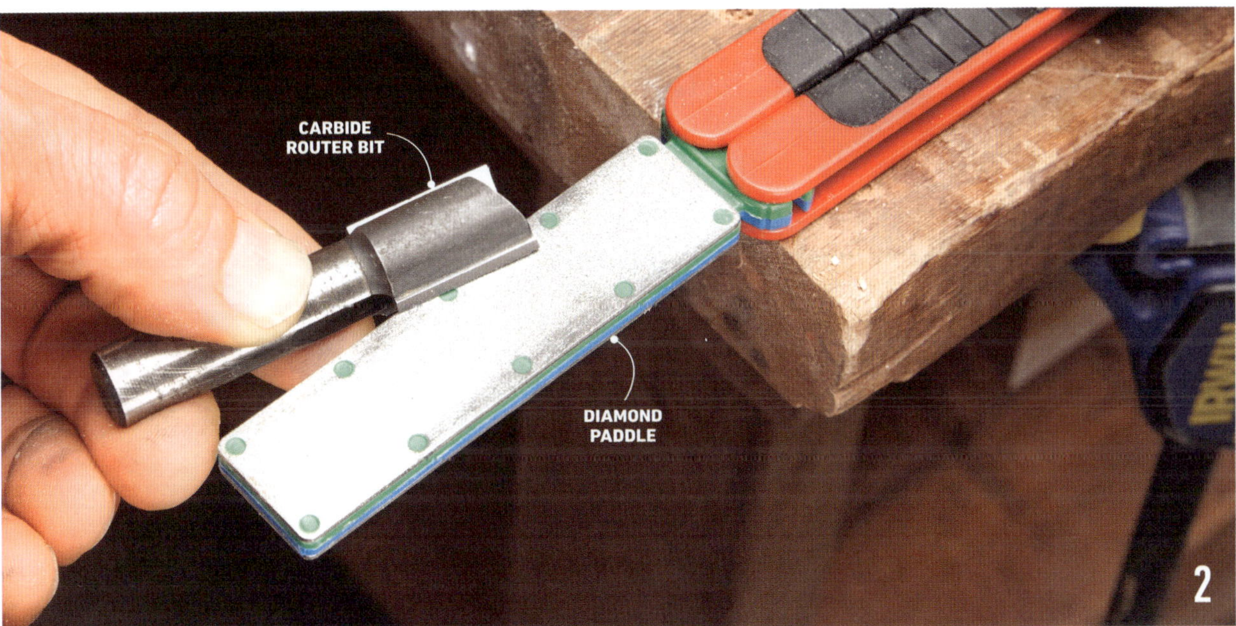

1 FLATTEN THE BACK OF CHISELS AND PLANE BLADES

It's impossible to get a sharp edge on a chisel or a plane if the back of the blade isn't flat. If you're using the glass and sandpaper method of sharpening **(Tip 5)**, press the back side of the blade against the sandpaper and move the blade back and forth, being careful to hold it perfectly flat. Sand the back of each blade until it's uniformly shiny along the cutting edge. Do this with each grit as you move through the progression from coarse to fine. You can use the same technique with any natural or diamond sharpening stone.

2 TUNE UP CARBIDE ROUTER BITS WITH A DIAMOND PADDLE

Chipped or severely dulled carbide router bits require professional sharpening, but you can restore a slightly dulled edge with a diamond paddle. The one we're using is available online and at sporting goods and woodworking stores for about $20.

To avoid changing the cutting profile of the bit, sharpen the back of the cutters only. A handy method is to clamp the diamond paddle to your workbench and move the bit back and forth over the diamond-impregnated surface. Start with the coarser-grit side of the paddle. Then switch to the fine side. The sharpened carbide should have a consistent shiny band along the cutting edge.

TRIANGULAR
BASTARD-
CUT FILE
SPADE
BIT
3

Drill
Doctor
350X
4

3 IT'S EASY TO KEEP YOUR SPADE BITS SHARP

Most of us reach for a spade bit instead of our expensive Forstner bits when it's rough material that needs drilling. But this abuse takes a toll. Luckily, a spade bit doesn't have to be sharpened with precision to work better. A few strokes along the bottom with a file and you're back in business.

Clamp the bit in a vise and file the cutting edges, making sure to maintain the existing angle. A tapered triangular file works well for many sizes of spade bit.

4 DON'T THROW AWAY THOSE OLD DRILL BITS

If you've ever tried to sharpen a drill bit on a grinder, you know what a hit-and-miss proposition it is. It's hard to maintain the correct angle, keep the chisel point centered and avoid burning the bit.

Drill Doctor offers several versions of a special tool that makes drill-bit sharpening almost foolproof. The least expensive tool (about $60) is perfect for the home shop. You simply follow the instructions for chucking the drill bit into the tool and rotate it on the grinding wheel to sharpen. Go to their website to compare features of the different models and to get tons of great information on sharpening drill bits.

5 FOOLPROOF CHISEL AND PLANE SHARPENING

There's nothing quite like working with a razor-sharp plane or chisel, and also nothing more frustrating than trying to use dull ones. Arkansas or Japanese stones are the traditional tool, but they're expensive to buy and take practice and skill to use. But there's an easy and inexpensive way to get great results without stones or much practice. The key to success is the honing guide, which ensures a consistent bevel. The guide we're using (about $15 at woodworking stores) works for both chisel and plane blades. You'll also need a 12-in. square of ¼-in. plate glass to provide a perfectly flat honing surface. You can order one at almost any hardware store, but be sure to have the sharp edges sanded smooth. You'll glue sandpaper to the glass and use it like a sharpening stone.

Use spray adhesive to attach half sheets of silicone carbide sandpaper to the glass. Cover one side with 220- and 320-grit paper and the other with 400- and 600-grit. The sharpening angle is determined by how far you extend the blade before clamping it to the guide. Dimensions on the side of the guide show where to set chisels and planes to maintain 25- and 30-degree angles.

Clamp the blade in the guide and roll it back and forth on the coarsest paper until the edge is uniformly shiny. It should take only 15 or 20 seconds. Repeat this process for each progressively finer grit.

Clamping Tips

Successfully secure your project, no matter the size or shape

1 CLEVER SOLUTIONS, BETTER RESULTS

First things first. Here are three basic types of clamps that belong in any workshop:

Pipe clamps are the everyday high-pressure workhorses of woodworking. They cost about $15 per set, plus a few bucks more for pipes. Because you can quickly screw the clamps onto different lengths of pipe, one set of pipe clamps does the same work as several lengths of bar clamps. Buy pipes in 2-, 3- and 4-ft. lengths and you'll be ready for most situations.

Bar clamps are quicker and easier to use than pipe clamps. Light-duty bar clamps are perfect when you need a long reach and moderate pressure. They cost $10 and up.

Spring clamps are the fastest helpers for holding your work in place or doing light-pressure clamping. They're usually the cheapest option too.

2 PREVENT CLAMP STAINS WITH WAX PAPER

The moisture in glue triggers a reaction between iron and chemicals in wood (called tannins). The result is black stains on the wood, especially with tannin-rich woods such as oak or walnut. A strip of wax paper creates a barrier between the clamp and the wood. I also use wax paper to keep glue off my cauls.

3 LONG-JAW HAND SCREW

Extend the reach of your hand screw clamps with a couple of lengths of scrap wood. Screw the jaw extensions to the side of your hand screw clamp and away you go. Works great and couldn't be easier.

Rockwell
Model 15 Drill Press
HAND SCREW
CLAMP
EXTENSION
3

4 NO-CLAMP VENEER TRICK

Gluing down veneer is tough. You have to apply even pressure over every square inch. There are fancy tools for this, but for small veneer jobs, try this trick: Apply a thin coat of wood glue to both the substrate and the back of your veneer. Let the glue dry. Then position the veneer and use a hot iron (no steam) to reactivate the glue. Then press the veneer into place. The bond is almost instant and very strong.

5 ONE CAUL REPLACES MANY CLAMPS

Thin, flexible parts require lots of clamps to achieve a consistently tight fit. Or you can use a caul. Something like this solid-wood edging on plywood would have needed a clamp every few inches. But with a stiff caul to spread the clamping force, you can use fewer clamps, spaced far apart.

4

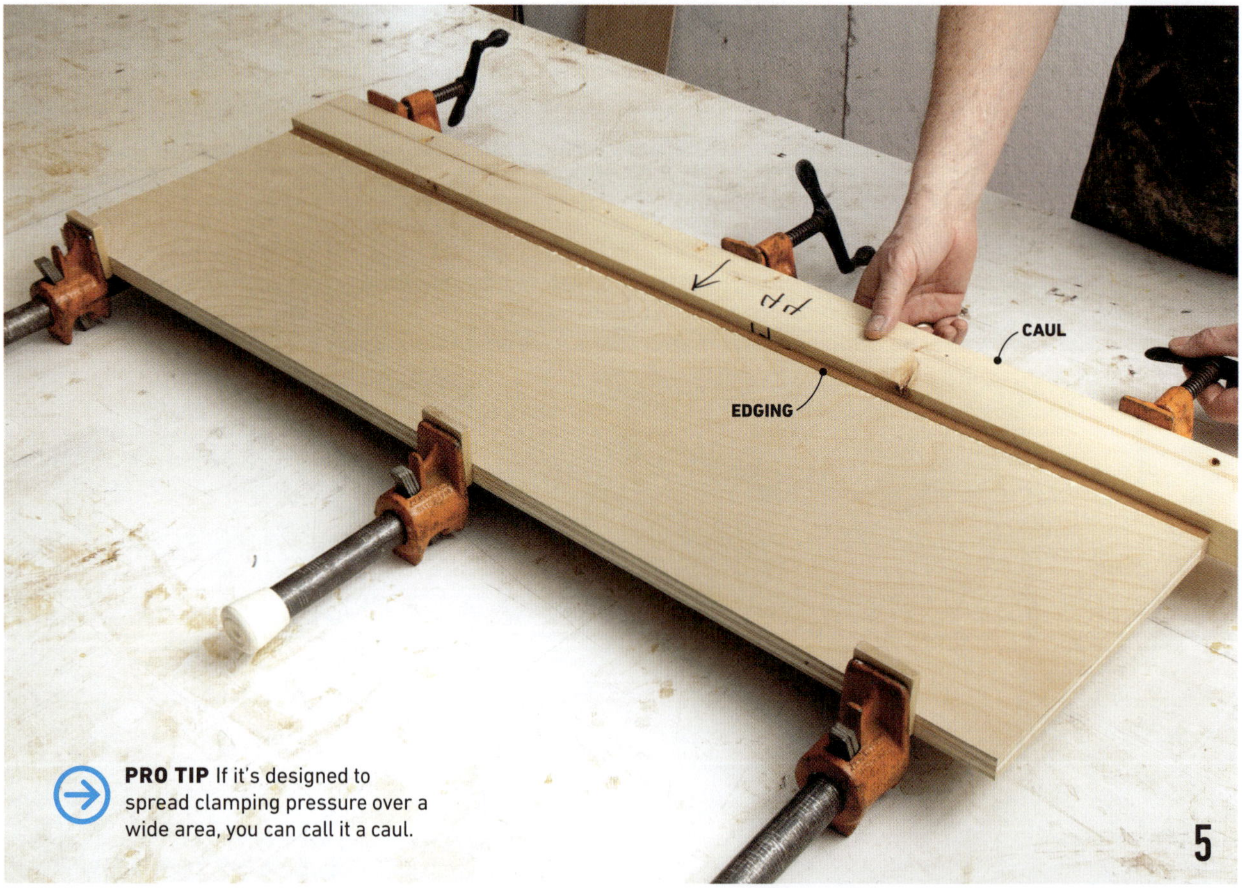

CAUL

EDGING

PRO TIP If it's designed to spread clamping pressure over a wide area, you can call it a caul.

5

6 CAULS KEEP GLUE-UPS FLAT AND FLUSH

As you squeeze boards together with pipe clamps, they sometimes arch or slip out of alignment. Pairs of upper and lower cauls are the solution. Lightly squeeze the cauls with bar clamps, then you can tighten the pipe clamps, then tighten the cauls a little bit more. Repeat these adjustments until the boards are joined flush and flat.

Two-by-fours make great cauls. Carefully select ones that have a slight bend, or "crown," along the narrow 1½-in. edge—but no twist or warp. A crown is an advantage because it creates extra pressure in the middle of the caul. Be sure to label all your cauls with an arrow marking the direction of the crown and the caul's length.

7 SHIFT CLAMPS TO SQUARE

To check the squareness of a cabinet frame or box, try taking diagonal measurements. If the measurements aren't equal, shift the position of the clamps. In this photo, the shift is exaggerated for clarity. In most cases, a slight shift will do the trick. Sometimes, shifting just one clamp will pull the assembly into square.

8 WATER PRESSURE

Some woodworkers keep a stack of bricks in the shop for those times when weight is better than clamps. But plastic buckets make even better weights. Filled with water, they provide a lot of weight. When empty, they're light, easy to store and handy for other jobs.

Edge-Gluing Boards

Here's how to get great results with minimum hassle

Gluing boards together to make wider panels is a handy woodworking skill that's easy to learn. Woodworkers with well-equipped shops often buy rough lumber and then rip, plane and joint the lumber to get straight edges for tight-fitting joints. But you can get the same results by carefully choosing boards from a home center or lumberyard. Look for boards with similar color and grain patterns. Then sight down the edge of each board to be sure it's straight. Finally, make sure the boards are flat and not twisted.

1 ARRANGE BOARDS FOR THE BEST APPEARANCE

For projects like tabletops where one side of the glued-up boards will be more visible, choose the best-looking side of each board to face up. If the boards vary in shade, arrange them so differences blend as well as possible. For example, don't put a dark board between two light ones. Finally, flip the boards end for end and shuffle them until their grain patterns look natural and pleasing. When you're happy with the results, draw a "V" across the boards with chalk or pencil. If you're assembling several panels, also number them. When it's time to glue the boards together, simply align your marks to make sure the boards are properly arranged.

2 APPLY AN EVEN BEAD OF GLUE

You can use white or yellow woodworking glue for interior projects. For projects exposed to moisture, always use a glue that's resistant to water. Spread a ⅛-to-3⁄16-in.-dia. bead of glue along the edge of one board. For an even bead that's perfectly centered on the edge, hold the glue bottle with one hand and, with your other hand, grab the spout. Move the glue bottle along the board quickly, letting your index finger ride along the board as a gauge to keep the bead of glue centered. Use a spring clamp to hold the board upright while you apply the glue. You only need to apply glue to one of the two boards being joined.

USE JUST ENOUGH GLUE

Using too much glue won't adversely affect the strength of the joint, but it will make a mess that will require extra time to clean up. The goal is to apply just enough glue so that when the boards are clamped there will be an even, 1⁄16-in.-wide bead of squeezed-out glue along the length of the joint. Avoid getting glue on the board faces to make it easier to finish too.

PRO TIP Cover the top of the clamps with masking tape to avoid staining the boards and to make cleanup easier.

3 SLIDE GLUED EDGES TOGETHER

Press the two boards together and slide them back and forth against each other. This is the best way to spread the glue evenly on the edges of both boards.

4 INSPECT THE GLUE JOINT BEFORE CLAMPING

Separate the boards and inspect the edges. The goal is to have a thin, even layer of glue on each edge. If there are areas where the glue is thin or missing, apply a little more glue before clamping the boards together.

5 DON'T SKIMP ON CLAMPS

A good glue joint should have an even bead of glue squeezed-out along its entire length. Add clamps to areas where there is no excess glue.

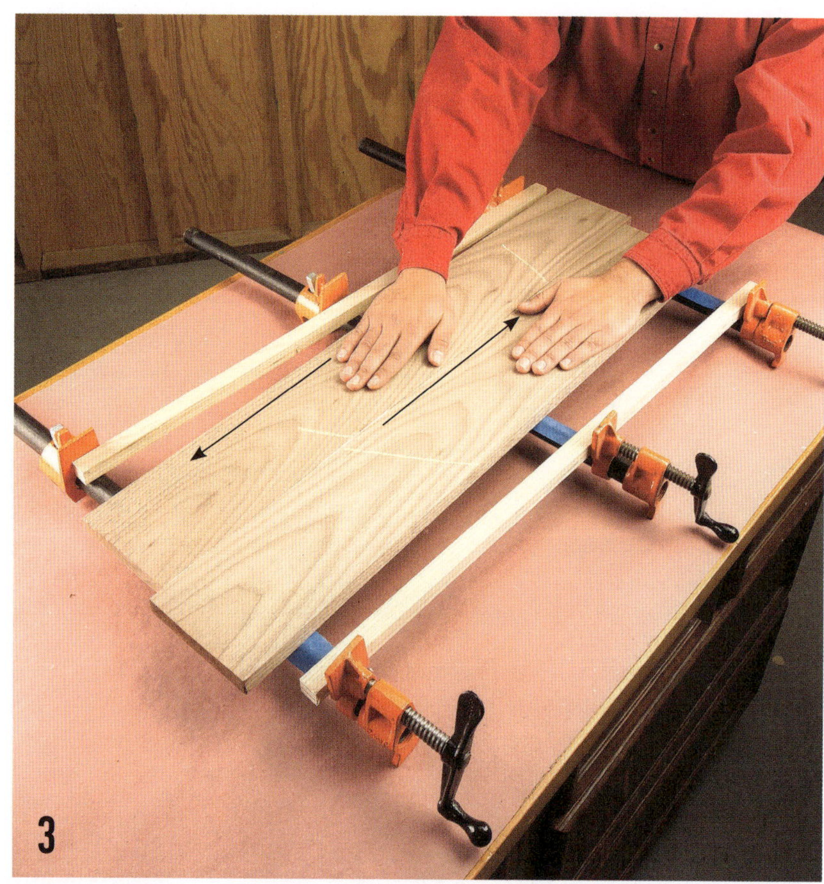
3

4

5

6 ALIGN THE TOP SURFACES CAREFULLY

You'll save yourself tons of sanding by making sure the top surfaces are as close to perfectly flush as you can get them. There are a couple of tricks to make this easier. First, glue and clamp only one joint at a time. It takes a little longer because you will have to wait for the glue to set up before removing the clamps and adding the next board. But it's much easier to get good results if you focus on one joint at a time. Second, start clamping at one end and work your way along the boards, making sure the top surfaces are flush as you tighten the clamps. Feel the surface with your finger and adjust the boards up or down until the tops are flush with each other. Then apply enough clamping pressure to close any gaps and squeeze out about a 1/16-to-1/8-in. glue bead.

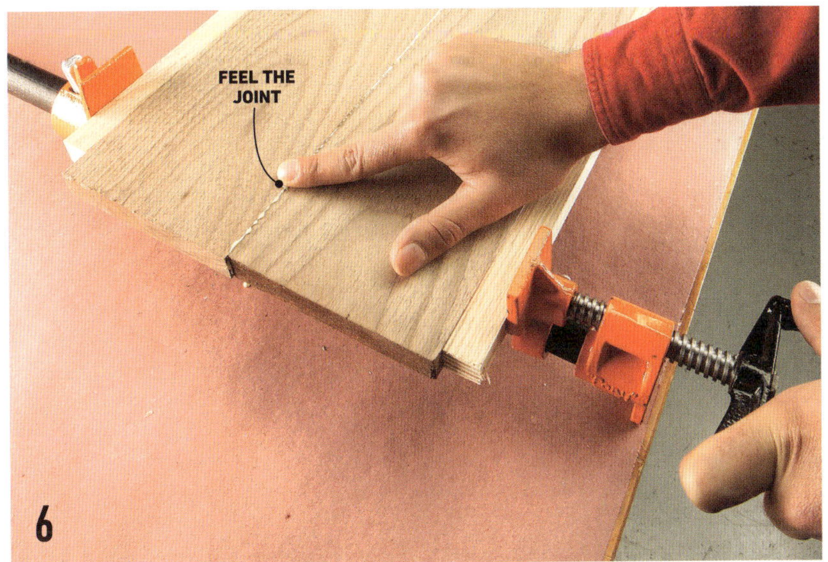

7 SCRAPE GLUE WHILE IT'S SOFT

At room temperature and average humidity, the glue that was squeezed-out will be ready to scrape in about 20 minutes. Wait until the glue changes from liquid to a jellylike consistency. Then scrape it off with a chisel or putty knife. If the clamps are in the way, you can safely remove them after about 20 minutes in normal conditions. Handle the glued-up panels carefully, though, since the glue won't reach maximum strength for several more hours.

8 DON'T WALK AWAY FROM BOWED GLUE-UPS

Glue-ups that turn out bowed are impossible to flatten after the glue completely sets. Hold a straightedge across the glued-up boards to make sure they're flat. Try flattening them by driving shims between the boards and the clamps. If the assembly is bowed up, add another clamp on top of the boards.

PRO TIP Place strips of wood between the clamps and the boards to protect the edges of the boards.

Easier Hand-Sanding

Special tools and high-quality sandpaper produce great results with less effort

By Jeff Gorton

I know, you're probably thinking, "Yuck, I hate sanding." But the truth is that with top-quality sandpaper and a few special tools, sanding by hand can be made a lot more pleasant. Sure, sanding by hand is a little slower than power sanding. But it's quieter and doesn't spew dust all over the place. And besides, there are some places that you can't reach with power sanders. In this article, we will tell you how to choose the best type of sandpaper for the job and show you some of our favorite hand-sanding tools.

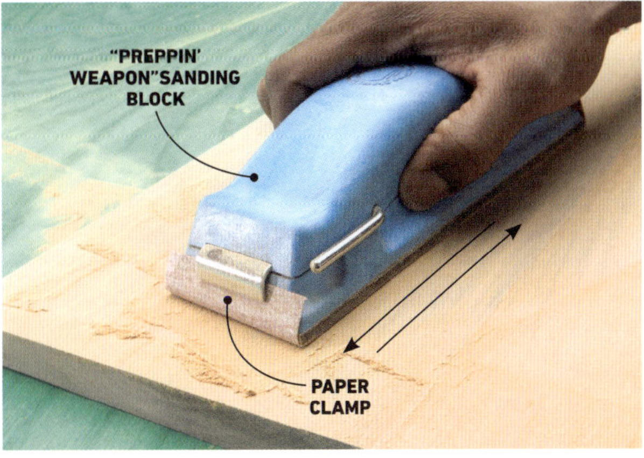

CHOOSE THREE GRITS

When you sand, you're scraping away material from the surface to remove imperfections or to shape and contour edges. The goal is to start with the sandpaper that's just coarse enough to remove the worst defects easily. Starting with sandpaper that's too coarse will mean extra sanding later with finer-grit papers to remove the deep scratches left by the coarse grit. On the other hand, if you start with sandpaper that's too fine, it'll take forever to sand out defects. In most cases, 80 grit paper is a good starting point for sanding planed or shaped wood. Start with 100-grit if the wood is already smooth with no deep scratches, planer marks or other surface defects.

Both 80- and 100-grit leave a network of fine scratches behind, so the next step is to sand with a little finer grit. This replaces the scratches with smaller, less visible ones. If you started with 80-grit paper, skip to 120-grit paper, or if 100 then to 150. Finally, sand with 220-grit sandpaper. For most types of wood, this is the finest grit you will need. Wood with very dense grain, such as ebony, may require one additional sanding step with 320- or 400-grit paper to eliminate visible scratches. Here are the two grit progressions we usually recommend: 80/120/220 and 100/150/220.

USE A SANDING BLOCK FOR FLAT SURFACES

It's tempting to just fold a piece of sandpaper and go to work. But you'll get better results with far less effort if you use a sanding block. The block distributes sanding pressure more evenly and maintains a flatter surface. A block also lets you bear down harder. You can make a sanding block by cutting a small square of rigid foam or gluing a thin layer of cork to a wood block. Or you can buy a simple rubber sanding block at almost any hardware store, paint store or home center. But for the ultimate in hand-sanding convenience and efficiency, consider ordering a sanding block like the one we show above. Its shape conforms comfortably to your hand, and the well-designed clamps make it easy to install quarter sheets of sandpaper.

The biggest mistake I see people make when they use a sanding block is failing to change paper often enough. To encourage more frequent paper changing, use a straightedge and utility knife to cut to size a bunch of paper sheets in each of the grits you'll be using. With exact-size sheets on hand, it'll be easy to change the paper often—as soon as you notice it isn't cutting efficiently.

In general, it's best to sand with the wood's grain, especially for the final grits. But to remove deep scratches and stains, it's OK to angle across the grain, up to about 45 degrees for the initial sanding. This goes contrary to popular opinion, but it's a good method to remove material quickly. But before switching to the next finer grit, sand with the grain to remove all cross-grain scratches from your project.

FOAM PIPE INSULATION AND SWIMMING NOODLES MAKE GREAT SANDING PADS

Soft, flexible foam makes a great base for sandpaper because you can easily squeeze or compress it to fit a variety of shapes. Wrap sandpaper around scraps of foam pipe insulation to sand medium-size coves. For large concave surfaces, use scraps of foam swimming noodles. These are easy to cut with a bread knife. You can even stick paper to the inside surface of pipe insulation to make a sanding pad for dowels and other cylindrical shapes.

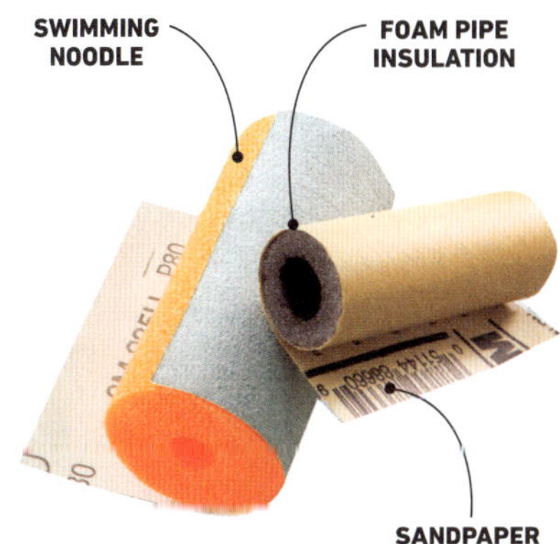

SAVE YOUR FINGERS; TRY CONTOUR SANDING GRIPS

Contour sanding grips make it easier to sand molding profiles because you can get a good grip and the shape stays consistent as you sand. We're sanding a coved edge created with a router. You can buy a set of these shaped rubber sanding pads for about $6. Simply choose the one that fits the profile you're sanding and wrap sandpaper around it. I like to use sandpaper with pressure-sensitive adhesive on the back and stick it right to the pad.

STICK SANDPAPER TO A PUTTY KNIFE TO REACH INTO TIGHT CORNERS

It's difficult to sand "with the grain" into tight corners without scratching the adjacent wood. For these hard-to-reach areas, wrap an adhesive-backed sanding disc over the edge of a flexible putty knife. Trim the sandpaper flush to the edge of the putty knife. Otherwise you can use spray adhesive to mount regular sandpaper or buy a sandpaper roll with adhesive backing.

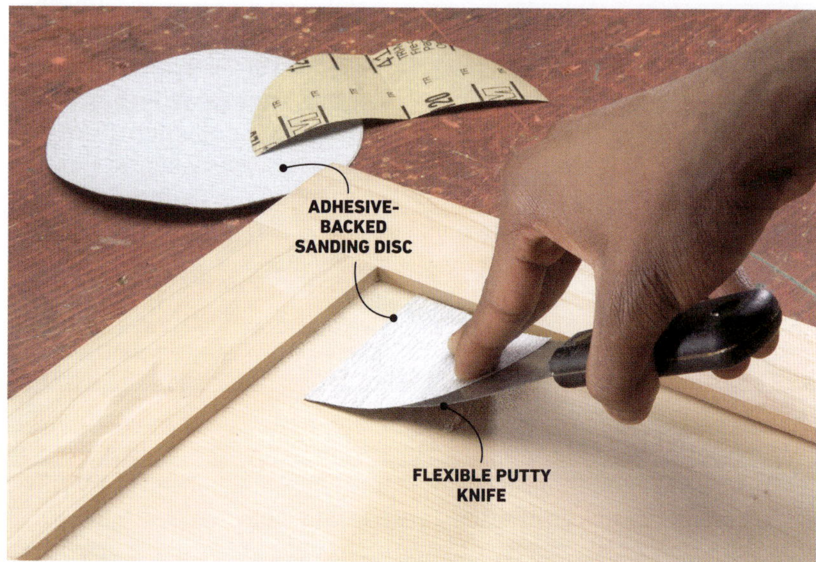

BUY "CLOG-RESISTANT" SANDPAPER FOR SANDING PAINTED SURFACES

Paint and resinous wood such as pine will clog most types of sandpaper quickly. To avoid using reams of sandpaper, look for sandpaper labeled as "clog-resistant" or "no-clog." It's coated with a soapy film, called stearate, that sheds as you sand, taking the paint or resin with it and leaving the grit exposed for more efficient sanding. This "no-load" paper is easy to recognize. Look for a mottled gray or colored surface. Brown aluminum oxide and yellow garnet sandpaper are not coated and will clog easily. Clog-resistant sandpaper costs a little more, but it's worth it because it lasts three or four times longer and saves you sanding time.

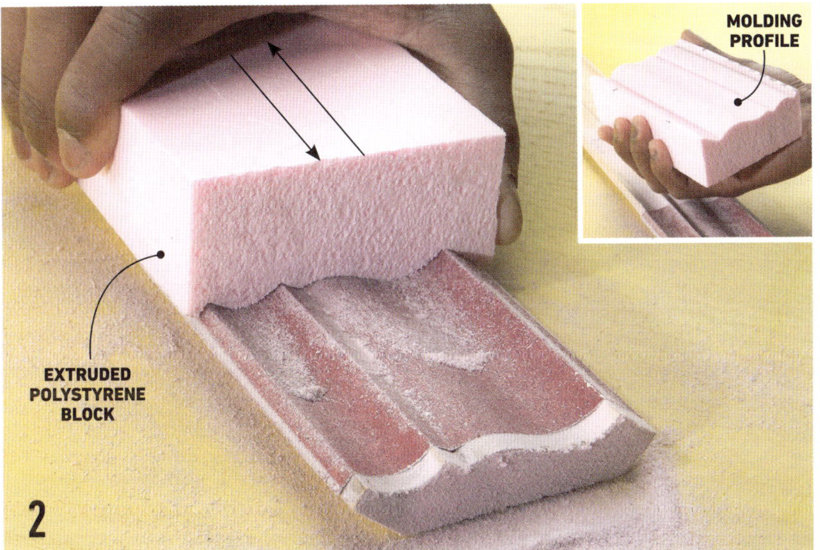

MAKE A CUSTOM SANDING BLOCK TO SPEED UP SANDING OF COMPLEX SHAPES

Scraps of rigid foam insulation (extruded polystyrene) make great sanding blocks and have the advantage of being easy to shape. The photos show how to make a sanding block that conforms to your molding profile. Make three blocks while you're at it. Then glue three progressively finer grit papers to the blocks to complete your sanding sequence. If you don't have any extruded polystyrene, ask for scraps at a local building site or look for a damaged sheet at a home center or lumberyard.

This profile sander has one drawback. It's difficult to fit the sandpaper tightly into the sharp corners of the custom-shaped block. It can round-over the edges on some molding profiles. Prevent this by slicing through the sandpaper with a utility knife in the "creases" and pressing it tight to the block with a putty knife. The other solution is to cut the custom-shaped block into sections to eliminate the parts that could round over a sharp profile. Sand these areas separately with a square sanding block or a small piece of folded paper.

1 MAKE A MOLD

Spray the molding and the back side of a 120-grit sandpaper with spray adhesive. Stick it to the molding. Press it into recesses with the blade of a putty knife.

2 SHAPE THE BLOCK

Rub the rigid foam insulation over the sandpaper until it begins to conform to the molding.

3 ATTACH SANDPAPER

Coat the foam block and the back of the sandpaper with spray adhesive. Then carefully stick the sandpaper to the block and sand the molding.

4 Simple Joinery Options

Make strong, long-lasting joints without years of practice or a big budget

By Brad Holden

Traditional hand-cut joinery requires skill and a great deal of practice to master. But are those fancy joints necessary? Nah. I still use mortise-and-tenons or dovetails when a project calls for it. But for most projects, I just need joinery that's strong and simple.

My go-to methods include four different techniques: dowels, pocket screws, biscuits and the Beadlock system. But there's no reason to have all of them in your arsenal. Most serious woodworkers choose one or two, become proficient and use them for nearly all their joinery. These four methods are strong enough for most typical joinery, and they're all very affordable.

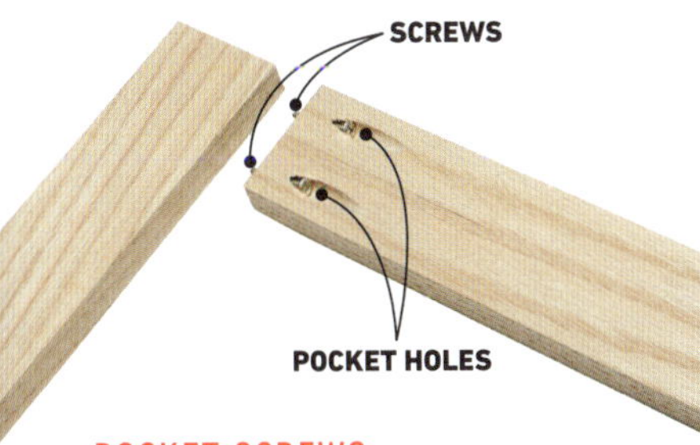

POCKET SCREWS

You can get a basic pocket hole kit for about $30. You'll need a supply of different lengths of special self-drilling washer-head screws (coarse threads for softwoods, fine threads for hardwoods).

You may have a drill/driver already, which is the only tool that's necessary. That's a big plus. It saves you money as well as space in your shop. Once you've become a convert, you can pick up more clamps, accessories and jigs to really step up your production. The only downside to pocket screws is that without special clamps, they don't automatically align parts during assembly.

Pros
- Fast
- No large clamps required
- Benchtop or portable

Cons
- Visible holes
- Parts alignment not automatic

1 DRILL THE HOLES

Clamp the workpiece in the jig and drill the steeply angled holes. This unusual jig has two pairs of holes: one for thinner stock and one for thicker. The included drill bit bores a flat-bottom hole with a short pilot hole at the center to guide the screw. A stop collar regulates the hole depth.

2 DRIVE THE SCREWS

Apply glue, clamp the parts into alignment and drive the screws. Some pocket hole jigs are portable. You can clamp them to a workpiece that's too large to put on your workbench.

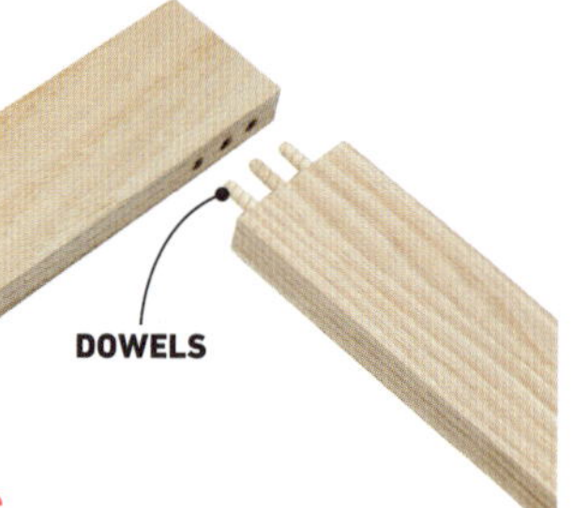

DOWELS

A solid, easy-to-use doweling jig will set you back about $70. As with the pocket hole method, the only tool you'll need is a drill. Then you'll also need a supply of dowels. The dowels for joinery are different from the standard dowel rods you can find at a hardware store. Joinery dowels are grooved to keep glue from getting trapped in the bottom of the hole and preventing the parts from pulling together.

Unlike pocket screws, dowels align the parts and make both sides of the joint look the same (that is, no exposed screws). That's good when both sides will be visible.

Pros

- Automatic alignment in both directions
- Mating dowel holes can be positioned anywhere using dowel centers

Cons

- Clamping required and slow

1 DRILL THE HOLES

I use the Dowl-It jig which is self-centering, with an integrated clamping mechanism. Mark the hole locations on both parts, clamp the jig and drill the hole.

2 INSERT THE DOWELS

Apply glue to the dowels and mating parts. Press the joint together and clamp. You can use shims with this jig to drill holes for offset parts. When necessary, use dowel centers to mark the starting points for drilling into the adjoining part.

1

2

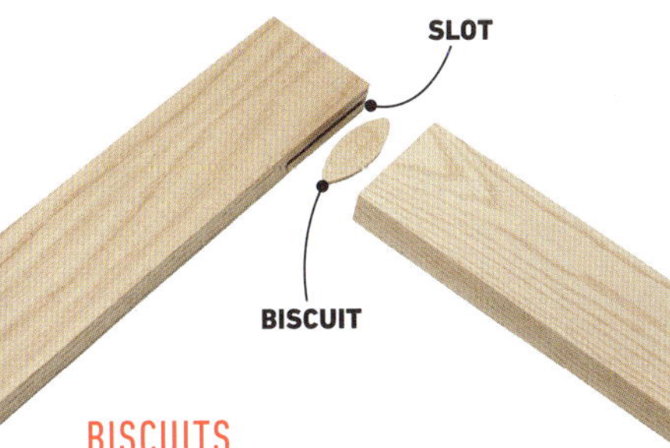

BISCUITS

A plate (aka biscuit) joiner runs anywhere from $70 to $700. The $700 variety is really nice, but it's not necessary for an amateur woodworker. A modestly priced model works just fine. A plate joiner cuts a semicircular slot in adjoining parts so they can accept a plate/biscuit, which is then glued into place. Biscuits come in different sizes to accommodate various part dimensions.

Pros

- Fast
- Easy to use
- Easy to offset parts
- Effective dust collection
- Automatic alignment in one direction

Cons

- Clamping required
- Parts can slide during clamping

1

1 CUT THE SLOTS

Mark joint centerlines on adjoining parts. Set the plate joiner to the desired cutting height, and set the cutting depth to match the biscuit size you're using. Line up the guide mark on the joiner's fence with your mark and plunge the cut. The latest version of this Ryobi plate joiner costs around $100 on Home Depot's website.

2

2 INSERT THE BISCUITS

Apply glue to the mating surfaces and in the slots. Insert the biscuit, press the joint together and clamp.

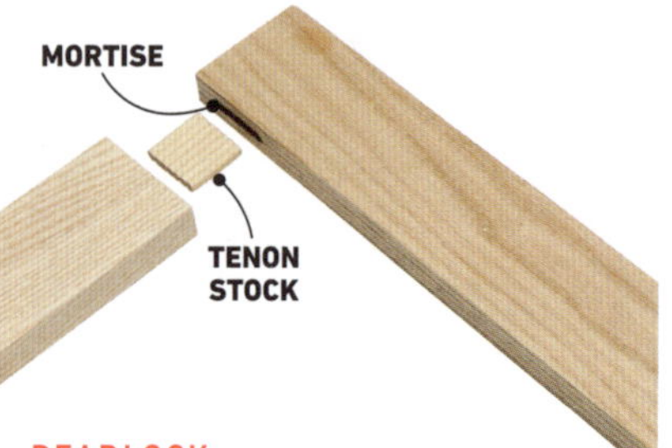

BEADLOCK

A Beadlock jig facilitates drilling mortises in adjoining parts—again, using only a drill. This is one of many "loose tenon" systems. Instead of the tenon's being cut from one of the adjoining parts, precut tenon stock is glued into a mortise in both parts.

Beadlock mortises are just a series of overlapping holes, and the tenon stock looks like a stack of dowels. You can buy tenon stock, or you can buy router bits to make your own tenon stock. But you will need a router table for that, and it's a bit fussy.

Pros

- Easy to use
- Automatic alignment in both directions
- Extremely strong

Cons

- Slow
- Clamping required

1 DRILL THE MORTISES

Mark the joint centerline on both parts, position the jig using its alignment guide and then clamp the jig into place. Drill the first set of holes, slide the drilling block to its second position and drill the second set of holes. Repeat the process on the mating part.

2 INSERT THE TENONS

Apply glue to the mating parts and the Beadlock tenon. Press the joint together and clamp.

JOINT STRENGTH TEST

We made 24 x 24-in. L-joints from red oak for all four of these joinery methods. Then we applied increasing tension with a turnbuckle and measured the failure point with a scale.

While admittedly not very scientific, the results were very surprising. And it's always fun to break things!

Breaking Point

Our joints failed at the following stress levels:

ITEM	LBS.
Pocket screws	85
Dowel joint	83
Biscuit joint	61
Beadlock joint	121

POCKET SCREWS
The pocket screw joint is the only one that didn't break at the glue joint. The wood broke instead!

DOWELS, BISCUITS AND BEADLOCK
While the Beadlock joint was the strongest, these three joints eventually failed the same way: The glue joint broke and the wood pulled free of its reinforcement.

BOTTOM LINE

Strength should not be your main consideration. All of these methods are plenty strong for typical woodworking uses.

Unless the joint has to be especially strong, choose your method on the basis of speed or convenience rather than on strength.

Get a Glass-Smooth Finish

Follow these tips for a professional result every time

By Jay Cork

My early projects with finishing furniture and instruments weren't pretty—I ruined some valuable furniture. I've learned a lot since then, working with some of this country's top experts in wood finishing. Now I'd like to share some of that knowledge with you.

If there's one thing I've learned while practicing wood finishing, it's that your patience is always rewarded; there are few shortcuts to achieving great results. But that's not a bad thing. In fact, I find that I really enjoy slowing down and pacing myself. When I get in a hurry and cut corners, I always regret it. Here are the steps that I never skip when completing a woodworking project.

1

2

1 DE-WHISKER BEFORE WATER-BASED STAIN

Any water-based stains and finishes can cause the grain to rise like whiskers. To avoid this, "de-whisker" the wood before staining. Mist it with water, but avoid oversaturation; just spray and wipe with a towel. After the wood dries completely, sand with 220 grit and it will be prepped and ready to finish.

2 SHAVE AWAY RUNS

When you see a run, your first instinct may be to grab a piece of sandpaper. Don't! Sandpaper can damage the area around a run and make things worse. I prefer using a very sharp chisel to remove drips or runs in finish. If you spot a run as your project is drying, wait! Let the finish dry first before you fix it.

JAY'S TIPS FOR A FANTASTIC FINISH

- **Start with gloss:** A satin finish is simply a gloss with tiny particles in it. Those "flatteners" make the finish less shiny. But too many layers of satin can obscure the grain, causing the finish to appear dull. To avoid this, I start with at least two coats of gloss then apply one last coat using satin. That gives me good depth and luster in a finish.
- **Sand between coats:** Modern polyurethanes don't require sanding between coats for adhesion, but I still recommend it. Remove the dust before the next coat. It's tempting to use an orbital sander. Don't! Sanding by hand with 320 grit is the way to go.
- **Never use compressed air to remove dust:** Compressed air is very good at blasting away dust after sanding, but it's a really bad idea. Here's why: Compressors often contain moisture, oil and small particles of rust. All it takes is a microscopic drop of oil to produce "fish eye" in a finish. Use a lint-free rag with mineral spirits instead.

3 HIDE A REPAIR WITH FAKE GRAIN

Sometimes repairs don't blend in because the grain lines have been interrupted. I use colored pencils and markers to make fake grain to disguise the repair. This skill takes time to master, so my advice is to practice! It's a really fun challenge. Buy many brown shades, not just a couple, and don't forget red and yellow. Start with lighter colors. You can always go darker!

4 SET UP LOW-ANGLE LIGHT

Proper lighting for finishing is hard things to get right. It might be perfect from one perspective but useless from another. I've used floor lamps or utility lights as a source of reflected light, but the reflection was too small. Then I had a better idea—I attached a 4-ft. LED light fixture vertically to a stand. It stands opposite me as I work, always giving me a long line of reflected light in the finish.

3

4

6

7

5

5 MY FAVORITE FINISHES

When finishing a tabletop, oil-based polyurethane is what I prefer. I love the classic amber hue that oil provides. Another advantage: Oil-based finishes can be thinned much more than water-based poly. I find thinning the final coat fifty-fifty really helps level it out. For highly figured wood, rubbing in a few coats of boiled linseed oil (and letting it dry completely) before the polyurethane topcoat can give the figure even more depth.

I use shellac on virtually every finishing project. Zinsser SealCoat is a wax-free clear shellac that works very well as a sanding sealer or prestain conditioner. I also love General Finishes Arm-R-Seal because I can apply it with a brush, wipe it on or even spray it. General Finishes Gel Topcoat in satin gives a very attractive, hand-rubbed sheen.

6 RUB OUT WITH STEEL WOOL

Gently rubbing out the final coat of satin finish with "0000" steel wool and a little soapy water will produce the silkiest, smoothest finish you've ever felt.

7 SEE WITH YOUR FINGERS

The most important lesson I learned when cutting my teeth refinishing cars, furniture and musical instruments was to not trust my eyes. Our fingers are far more capable of sensing minute details. Even before the finishing process begins, my fingers will tell me very quickly if my joints are all glued evenly or if there are any rough spots that need to be addressed.

GRAIN FILLING: WHAT, WHY AND HOW?

Red oak, hickory and ash are the most common species with "open grain." While beautiful, they don't take a finish evenly. No matter how much you sand, they'll still have a bumpy texture. If you want a perfectly smooth finish, you'll have to fill the grain.

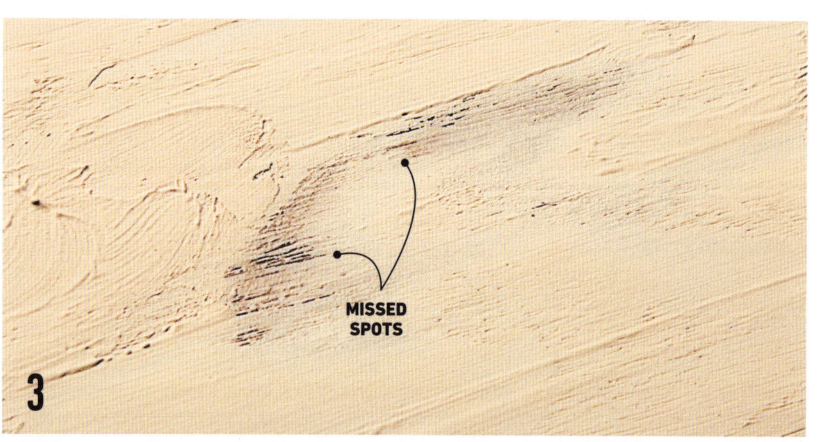

MY FAVORITE FILLER

I've tried many grain filler products, but the only product I use now isn't even a grain filler; it's marketed as a water-based wood putty. Timbermate is made from wood flour and available in many species. It will accept stains, dyes and finishes just like the wood around it. It ages the same as wood, which makes me confident that my project will look good the day I complete it, as well as years down the line.

1 MIX IT BY HAND

I start with two big scoops of Timbermate wood putty in a plastic food container. Wearing nitrile gloves, I slowly add water and mix it with my fingers. This takes time; mix until those last little clumps are dissolved.

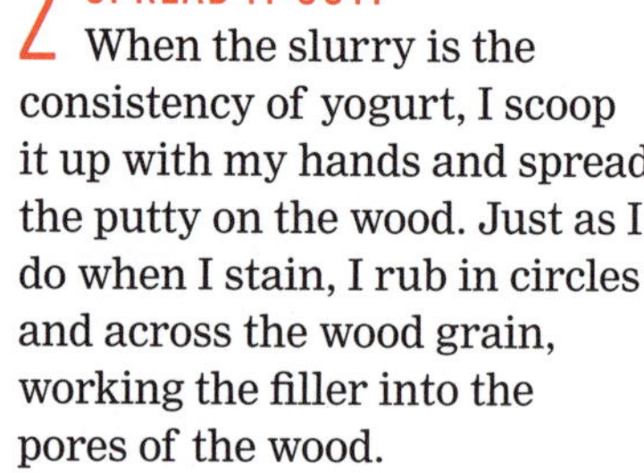

2 SPREAD IT OUT!

When the slurry is the consistency of yogurt, I scoop it up with my hands and spread the putty on the wood. Just as I do when I stain, I rub in circles and across the wood grain, working the filler into the pores of the wood.

3 GET THE SPOTS YOU MISSED WITH A SECOND COAT

Applying a second coat produces the best results; it covers little spots that were missed. I'll even start the second coat of putty before the first one is completely dry so the slurry remaining in my container doesn't dry out.

4 SAND LIGHTLY!

I like to wait a day before sanding so the moisture has a chance to evaporate. I've achieved the best results using a random orbital sander that has effective dust collection, and variable speed so I can slow it down. I start with 80-grit paper and stop at 220.

5 SEAL WITH SHELLAC

Shellac is very versatile! Because it's compatible with all finishes, it's used as a barrier between water- and oil-based stains and topcoats. I use thinned shellac as a prestain conditioner. I'll also use it after grain filling to even out the absorption rate of the filler and wood, so the stain or topcoat lies down evenly. In addition, shellac can be used alone as a stunning topcoat, but that's for another article.

5

SKILLS IN PRACTICE

Build a Table Saw Sled for Crosscuts

This gadget makes even wide crosscuts safe and simple

By Travis Larson

CAUTION You must remove your blade guard when using this sled. Keep your hands well away from the blade.

Figure A
Plans for a table saw sled

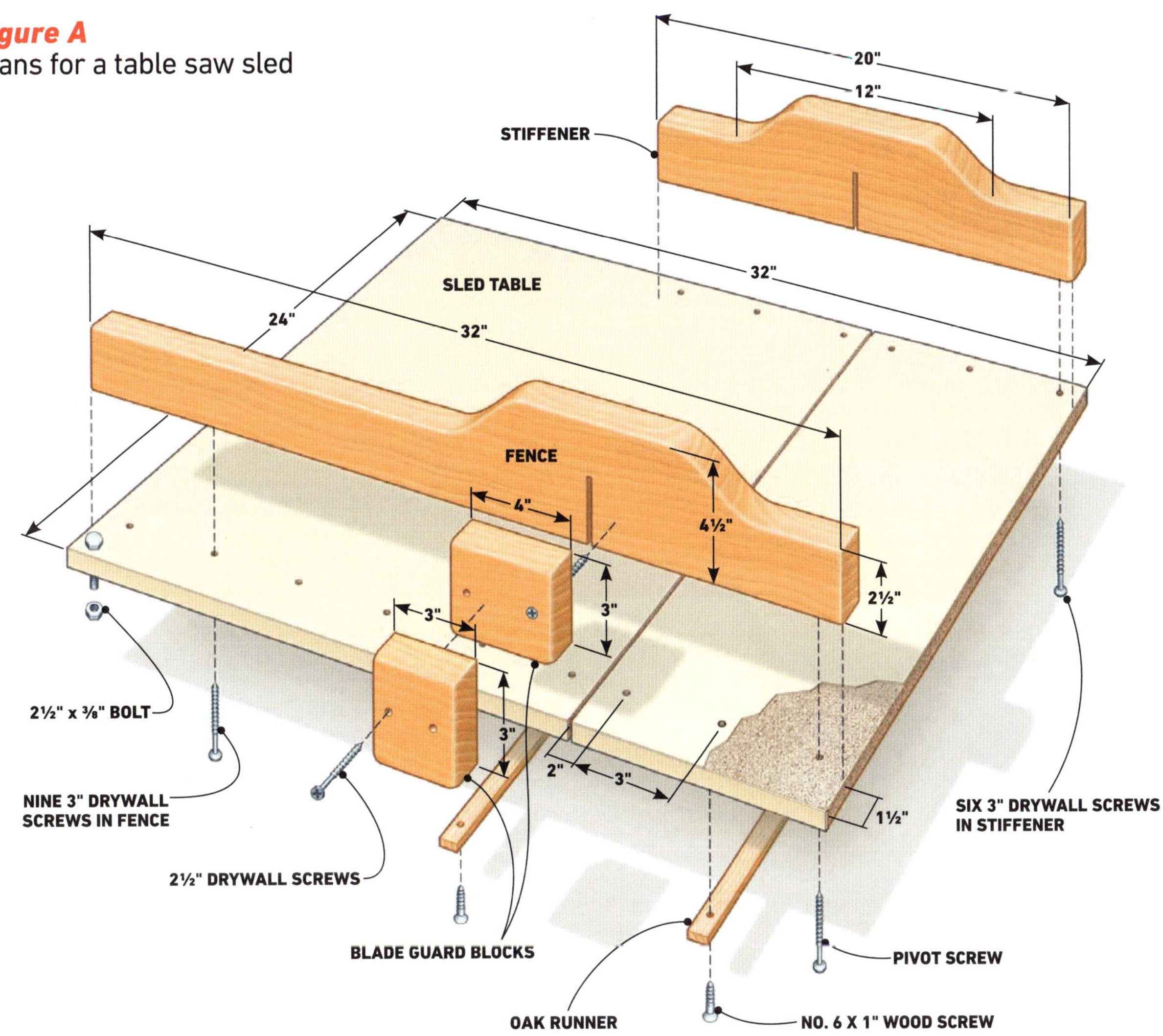

Many custom cabinetmakers and furniture makers use only a well-tuned table saw for all their precision cuts. Their secret for making perfect crosscuts and miter (angle) cuts is to use a table saw sled even on wide boards.

A sled is a movable contraption that slides in the table saw's factory-machined miter gauge slots. The workpiece then rests against a wooden fence at the front of the sled, a setup that keeps the work from slipping and ensures a clean, perfectly square cut every time. Read on and you'll see how to use it for specialty cuts too.

Although the miter gauge that comes with your saw can be used for crosscutting, it's less safe and accurate than a well-made sled. You can buy a factory-built sled too, but only if you're willing to cough up $200 to $350. And it won't perform any better than a $20 homemade unit.

cont. on p. 237

Materials

- One 4-ft. length of 24-in. wide closet shelving
- 6 ft. of clear 2x6
- 4 ft. of 1⅛ x ¼-in. oak lattice
- Double-faced tape
- A handful of 2½ in. and 3-in. drywall screws
- Fifteen 1-in. No. 6 wood screws
- Two 2½ in. x ⅜-in. bolts
- Three ⅜-in. nuts, four ⅜-in. washers, one ⅜-in. lock washer
- Varnish

Tools

- Circular saw
- Screw gun with No. 2 Phillips drive bit
- Jigsaw
- ¹⁄₁₆-in. drill bit
- ⅛-in. drill bit
- ⅜-in. drill bit
- Countersink bit
- Carpenter's square
- Four clamps

1 MARK THE SAW SLOT

Cut a 32-in. length of 24-in. wide shelving using a carpenter's square and circular saw (or your table saw if you have an extended fence). Place the cut shelving on the saw with the edge hanging 2 in. over the left side of the saw table, and draw a left runner guideline even with the edge of the miter gauge slot. Also draw a line to mark the blade path.

2 MAKE THE RUNNERS

Rip the oak lattice to the same width as the miter gauge slots. Hand-sand or plane the runners so they'll slide easily in the slots without binding. Cut them all to the same length as the depth of your sled.

3 ATTACH THE FIRST RUNNER

Clamp the left runner even with the line and clamp a straightedge tight against the runner to keep it straight while you mount it. Drill 1/16-in. pilot holes and then you can countersink holes and fasten the runner with five 1-in. No. 6 evenly spaced wood screws.

PRO TIP Attach a "flag" of tape ¾ in. from the end of the drill bit to prevent you from drilling through the sled table.

4 SCREW ON THE SECOND RUNNER

Sprinkle sawdust in the right slot, press double-faced tape onto the second runner and lay it tape side up into the slot (the sawdust shims the runner above the table surface so the tape will stick to the sled bottom). The strip should be flush with the infeed edge of the saw table. Align the sled table with the infeed edge of the saw table, then lower the fixed left runner into the slot and lower the right side of the sled onto the taped runner. Carefully lift the sled off the saw, then screw on the second runner.

5 CREATE FENCE AND STIFFENER

Using a jigsaw, cut a 20-in. long 2×6 for the stiffener and a 32-in. long 2×6 for the fence to the dimensions shown in **Figure A**. We used a coffee cup to mark the layout curves. Sand the parts, round over the edges with a router and seal them with varnish.

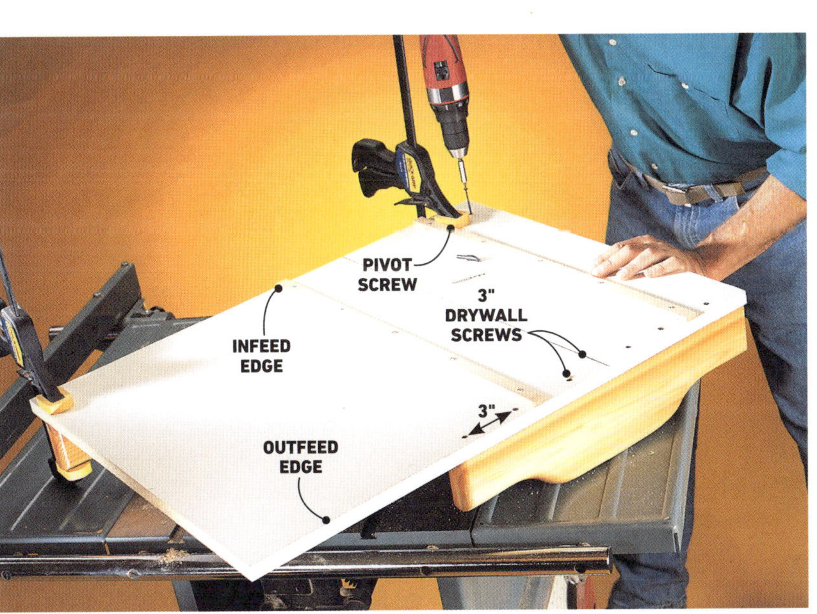

6 CONNECT THE STIFFENER

Clamp the stiffener flush with the outfeed edge, keeping the right end of the stiffener even with the right end of the sled table. Drill pilot holes (⅛ in.) and countersink holes and screw the stiffener through the sled bottom with 3-in. drywall screws spaced every 3 in. Keep the screws 2 in. away from the blade path. Clamp the fence 1½ in. back from the infeed edge (see photos) of the sled table. Install only one pivot screw at the right end of the fence and leave the clamp on the left side.

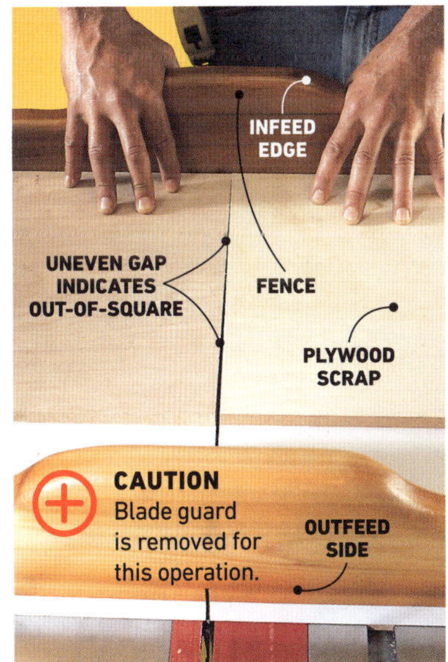

7 CHECK THE FENCE

Square the fence with a straight-edged piece of plywood. Raise the blade and cut through a piece of scrap plywood, stopping the cut at the fence. Check for square by flipping over half the plywood and look for a gap.

8 ADJUST THE FENCE
Gently tap the fence to adjust it and make another test cut in a new scrap. Repeat this step until the two halves meet perfectly. Then flip over the sled and fasten the fence as you did the stiffener.

USING YOUR SLED SAFELY

Using a sled is a bit more dangerous than operating a table saw conventionally because the factory-made blade guard must be removed, exposing the spinning blade. To make the sled safer and keep you digitally intact, we built in a couple of safety features. The first is a set of blade guard blocks **(Photo 10)** attached behind the fence. These keep the blade from getting at your hands after it passes through the cut. The second is a stop bolt **(Photo 9)** in the front, left corner of the sled table. Another stop bolt is anchored in the saw table itself. The sled automatically stops when the bolts meet after you complete a cut and before the blade penetrates the guard box. Working together, they shield the blade to protect your hands.

But remember, no system is fail-safe. You need to avoid dangerous practices such as:

- Crosscutting long boards that are hard to support.
- Cutting angles freehand when the back of the board isn't firmly against the fence or an anchored jig **(Photo 15)**.
- Clamping the board so that your hands are less than 4 in. from the saw blade.
- Attempting to cut severely warped or curved wood that won't rest directly on the sled table.
- Raising the blade higher than ⅛ in. above the wood to make a cut.
- Pulling the sled backward out of the workpiece before letting the blade come to a complete stop. After you complete a cut, always shut off the saw before you remove the workpiece.

cont. from p. 234

You can build this sled in just over a couple of hours. You'll need 3 ft. of Melamine (which is plastic-coated particleboard) closet shelving material, 5 ft. of straight 2×6 lumber, hardware and 4 ft. of oak lattice.

SIZE THE SLED TO FIT YOUR NEEDS

This sled is designed for either a 10-in. cabinet saw or a contractor's saw (not the portable benchtop saws). These saws feature larger tables, which can handle a sled this size. This sled will handle everything from the most delicate cuts to stock up to 19 in. If you own a benchtop model, consider building a smaller sled that will work for small projects such as picture frames or shadow boxes.

MELAMINE CLOSET SHELVING MAKES A CHEAP AND STABLE BASE

Melamine is a great material to use for your sled base. Choose a 24 in. width for a full-size sled like ours, or 12 in. if you're going to make a mini sled. Melamine is cheap, easy to find at home centers and doesn't warp with variations in humidity the way plywood sometimes does. The only drawback is that you must keep it dry or the edges will swell up like a pro wrestler on steroids. As a precaution against moisture, seal the edges with varnish.

For the fence and stiffener, select any piece of 2×6 wood that is straight-grained (the grain runs in parallel lines) and clear (knot free); see **Photo 8**. I sorted

9 BOLT ON SAW TABLE STOP

Drill a ⅜-in. hole in the left corner (see **Figure A** for location) and install a 2½-in. long, ⅜-in. dia. bolt positioned as shown in **Figure A**. Raise the blade to full height and cut through the sled table and fence, shutting off the motor when the blade exits the table. (Keep your hands well away from the path of the blade while you're making this dangerous cut.) Drill a ⅜-in. hole through the lip of the saw table and anchor a 2½-in. long, ⅜-in. bolt with two nuts, washers and a lock washer. Adjust the bolt until the head is centered on the sled table stop bolt.

PRO TIP When drilling metal, first use a center punch to make a divot to keep your drill bit from wandering. Then, to avoid overheating and dulling larger drill bits, work your way up to the ⅜-in. hole by starting with a ⅛-in. bit, then using a ¼-in. bit, then a ⅜-in. bit.

10 INSTALL BLADE GUARD BLOCKS

Precut and finish the two blade guard blocks (see **Figure A** for dimensions). Center the first block on the saw path and screw it to the fence with two 2½-in. drywall screws. Center and screw the second block to the first block, offsetting those screws from the first guard block screws.

11 MAKE A CUT

Standard, 90-degree crosscuts are the bread-and-butter cuts this sled is designed to make. With the saw off, set the blade height to cut no higher than ⅛ in. above the wood. Pull the sled back, lay your workpiece against the fence and line up the blade with your cutting mark. Turn the saw on, hold the wood against the fence and slowly push the workpiece through the saw. After the cut is completed, slightly separate the two halves from the blade and shut off the saw. Let the blade coast to a complete stop before you remove the wood.

12 MAKE IDENTICAL CUTS

Screw a stop block to a 1×4 and screw or clamp the 1×4 to the fence for repetitive, identical cuts that exceed the table saw fence rip capacity.

PRO TIP Keep the stop blocks ⅛ in. above the sled table so sawdust won't pile up against the block and make your length cuts inaccurate.

through cedar at the lumberyard until I found two pieces of wood that had 36-in. long clear sections. Sealing these before assembly will also prevent warping caused by humidity and keep them free of grime. The last nonhardware ingredient is a 1⅛-in. wide, ¼-in. thick oak lattice, to be used for the runners that fit in the miter gauge slots on the saw table.

REPETITIVE CUTS

Woodworking projects frequently require a zillion identical-length boards. Measuring each one is time-consuming and inaccurate. The solution is your new sled, fitted with stop blocks. Push each board against the block, make a pass through the wood, then set it aside and grab the next piece of stock. Little cuts shorter than the sled fence are easy. Just clamp a stop block directly to the sled fence **(Photo 13)**. For longer lengths, you need to extend the fence with a 1x4 and stop block, or clamp a block to the table saw fence **(Photo 12)**.

BE EXACT WHEN MACHINING THE RUNNERS AND PLACING THE FENCE

While you can be a little sloppy on most of this project, you have to be very careful with two procedures:

1. The runners must be precisely sized and positioned. Take your time and mill the runners **(Photos 2-4, p. 234-235)** so they easily slide in the miter gauge slots without any binding or slop. Sneak up on the runner widths by ripping off small amounts of wood until you get the perfect fit. Ripping thin, narrow boards is dangerous, so be sure to use push sticks (not your fingers) when sawing. Most slots are about ⅜ in. deep, so the ¼-in. thick runners glide just above the bottom of the slot.
2. The fence has to be absolutely square to the saw's blade path.

13 SAW PAST THE SLED FENCE

Clamp a stop block to the table saw fence for repetitive cuts that are longer than the sled fence but shorter than the maximum table saw fence width.

Caution: Position the stop block so the wood you are cutting leaves the block before it meets the blade.

Warning: Don't ever use the table saw fence without a stop block for length cuts. It's a dangerous kickback hazard!

14 SLICE AT A 45-DEGREE ANGLE

Use a 45-degree architectural square to cut a perfect 45-degree, 12-in. long jig from a piece of scrap plywood. Screw the jig stock to a separate piece of plywood held tight against the fence to hold it in place for safe cutting. Screw a 1×2 flush with the back edge of the jig with 1⅝ in. drywall screws **(Photo 15)**. Hold the right-end screw 3 in. away from the tip of the triangle.

Use a straight-edged scrap piece of plywood against the fence to square the sled **(Photos 7 and 8, p. 235-236)**. When you flip over half of the plywood and push the two cut edges together, any gap will be double the size of a regular out-of-square error.

GET THE MOST FROM YOUR SLED

A sled can go beyond square crosscuts to take on specialty cuts too. With a couple of cutting jigs (attachments), you can make multiple identical cuts. Perfect miter cuts of any angle are easy and fast, as are dadoes (you can use a dado blade to cut grooves, too) and rabbets (open-ended grooves on board edges). Clamp or screw stops and jigs right to the fence or to the sled table itself to make your table saw a multitask tool.

15 USE A MITER JIG

Clamp the miter jig to the sled fence with 2 in. of the jig tip projecting past the right side of the saw path, then cut off the tip. This gives you room to move wood back and forth to fine-tune lengths. Grip cutting stock firmly against the jig and use it as a guide for cutting 45-degree angles.

CHAPTER 7

Plumbing

TOOL SPOTLIGHT

Plumber's Toolbox

A longtime plumbing professional shares a look inside her toolbox

By Harrison Kral

Judaline Cassidy is a New York City-based plumber who has been working in the trades for more than 25 years. Over the course of her career, Judaline has become an advocate for women in the trades and gained valuable insight into what it takes to be a plumber. We spoke with her to get a better idea of her daily life on the job, and asked her to give us a look at the most indispensable tools she keeps in her toolbox. Here are some of the most essential tools Judaline brings with her every day on the jobsite:

CHANNELLOCK PLIERS

Judaline's go-to pair of pliers is a set of little Channellocks. The compact pair of pliers is a versatile tool Judaline can use for a variety of tasks, while also small enough that she can easily carry it around in her pocket.

BANDANNA/BEANIE

When she's on the jobsite, Judaline wears either a bandanna or a beanie, depending on the weather. Her favorites are a beanie from Carhartt and a bandanna from Tools and Tiaras, which Judaline founded. The organization is dedicated to giving a helping hand to young girls and women who want to pursue a nontraditional trade.

PIPE WRENCH

No plumber's toolbox is complete without a quality pipe-wrench. Judaline carries around one of Ridgid's Heavy-Duty Straight Pipe Wrenches. They have an adjustable hook jaw that fits a wide range of pipe diameters.

FOUR-WAY SCREWDRIVER

If you're only going to carry a few tools with you, make one of them a multitool. Judaline always has a four-way screwdriver from Milwaukee on hand while she's working. It's a versatile tool that comes with eight bits and three nut drivers.

TAPE MEASURE

Trying to work with a low-quality, banged-up tape measure can really slow down a project. That's why Judaline always has this trusty, Milwaukee 25-ft. Stud Tape Measure. The blade features an anti-tear coating and its reinforced frame can withstand a drop from up to 80 ft. in the air.

PIPE WRENCH: RIDGID TOOLS;

Clearing Out Stubborn Drain Clogs

How to investigate and fix a blocked drainage pipe without making a call to a professional

By Jeff Gorton

Clogged drains are always a hassle, but some, like a plugged P-trap under the sink or a stopped-up toilet, may only require a wrench, a plunger and a little elbow grease to unclog. But sometimes the clog is deep in the drainpipe and requires more work and powerful tools to root it out. We'll show you how to find and clear out these clogs, which are often hidden in the drain system under your floor.

The job of clearing clogs in the larger drain lines found under the floor isn't for everyone. In the first place, you'll spend money to rent the large drain-cleaning auger required, and you have to be strong enough to heft the machine and to wrench loose those old, corroded cleanout plugs. Then there's the mess, and the half-day you'll spend running for rental equipment and various plumbing parts.

So why would anyone in their right mind attempt to clear out under-floor drains? Well, some of us thrive on challenge and love the satisfaction of solving a problem. If this isn't motivation enough, consider that pro drain cleaners will charge considerably more than your equipment rental fees, depending on the problem, and you may have to miss work. However, some clogs require the services of a pro, and it's worth the unexpected day off. Call your plumber if you suspect the main drain to the street is clogged by tree roots or caved-in pipes.

Figure A
Under floor drain system

CAUTION
Don't use a small, hand-operated drain snake to clean large drains. It's not up to the task, and may even cause a larger problem by getting tangled or breaking off in the drain.
MAIN STACK
KITCHEN DRAIN LINE
UPSTAIRS BATH DRAIN LINE
DRAIN-CLEANING MACHINE
CLEANOUT OPENING
MAIN STACK CLEANOUT FITTING
FOOT-OPERATED SWITCH
GFCI
CLEANOUT PLUG
LAUNDRY DRAIN LINE
½" CABLE
CLOG
MAIN DRAIN TO STREET
FLOOR DRAIN LINE
PRO TIP We show a house with a full basement, but the information applies to houses built on slabs and over crawl spaces as well.

1 TAKE OUT THE BACKFLOW DEVICE
Remove the backflow preventer to gain access to the floor drain trap for cleaning. Drive a chisel against one of the notches in the retaining ring, turning it counterclockwise to unscrew it.

2 VACUUM THE TRAP
Suck out sand and dirt with a wet/dry vacuum. Loosen stubborn dirt or retrieve other yucky stuff with a coat hanger or small hand-powered drain snake.

3 CLEAR THE PLUG
Unscrew the cleanout plug in the side of the floor drain with a pipe wrench, slip-joint pliers, or as a last resort, by chiseling it out with a cold chisel.

To remove drain cleanout plugs, you'll need a large slip-joint pliers or pipe wrench, and if they're especially stubborn, a hammer and cold chisel. You'll have to rent a drain-cleaning machine to clear drain lines. You'll also need heavy leather (not cloth) gloves, safety glasses, a shop vacuum, a bucket and rags, hand cleaner and Teflon plumbing tape. You may need a heavy-duty grounded extension cord to reach an outlet.

FINDING THE CLOG

The first step in clearing a clog is locating it. This often takes trial and error, but use these pointers to get you started. If only one fixture is clogged, the problem is either in the trap or drain line leading from that fixture. If a group of fixtures is affected, look for the clog in a location downstream from where their drains join. **Figure A** (previous page) shows the drain system under the floor of a typical house. Notice that a clog in the location shown would affect the kitchen and laundry drains, but not the upstairs bath that drains into the main stack. A clog in the larger main drain would cause all the drains to stop working.

As many of us have discovered the hard way, a clog in the drain system under the floor often results in wastewater backing up onto the floor through the floor drain. To prevent this backup, many floor drains are fitted with an insertable backflow preventer that allows water down but not up. **Photo 1** shows one method of removing the ball-type backflow preventer to gain access to the floor drain trap for cleaning.

If cleaning the fixture trap doesn't solve the problem, and you've determined that the clog is in one of your under-floor drains, then you'll have to rent a drain-cleaning machine. With it, you can punch through the clog,

4 RUN THE CABLE

Unplug the drainpipe leading from the floor drain by using a ½-in. cable inserted through the cleanout opening. Start the process with a general-purpose drilling or retrieving tool attached to the cable, and complete the job with a finishing tool.

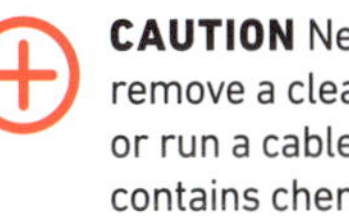

CAUTION Never attempt to remove a clean-out plug from, or run a cable into, a drain that contains chemical drain cleaner. Call a pro instead.

5 OPEN THE CLEANOUT PLUG

Drive corroded cleanout plugs counterclockwise using a cold chisel and heavy hammer. If this doesn't work, break out the plug with the hammer and chisel, being careful not to let any pieces fall into the drain. Wear gloves and safety glasses, and be prepared for a possible flood of wastewater (yikes!).

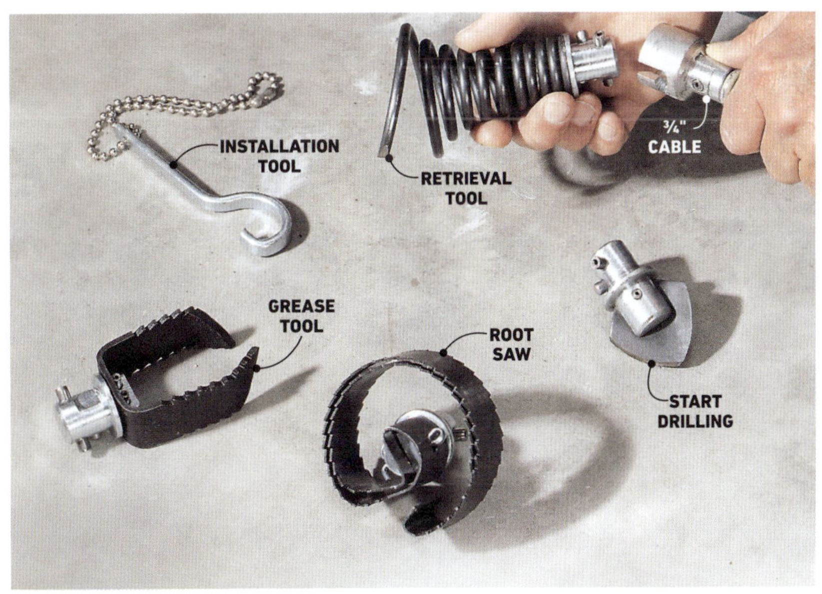

6 ATTACH THE RIGHT TOOL

Connect a cleaning tool to the cable. Use the starting drill to bore through a clog, the retriever to snag rags or other items, the grease tool to cut through grease and soap and clean up the sides of the pipe, and the root saw to cut through roots.

snag and retrieve an obstruction, or cut through solid roots or very stubborn clogs.

REMOVING CLEANOUT PLUGS

The first thing you have to do to work on an under-floor drain is remove the cleanout plug. Removing a plug from a corroded steel or cast iron fitting is a real chore. Try using a pipe wrench with a steel pipe slipped over the handle to increase leverage. If this doesn't work, you'll have to resort to chiseling **(Photo 5)**.

Note: Removing the cleanout may release a flood of backed-up wastewater, so be prepared with buckets and rags, and stay clear.

After you've conquered the clog and it's time to replace the old cleanout plug, use a new plastic rather than metal plug, and don't forget to use Teflon plumbing tape to seal the threads. If the cleanout fitting is too damaged or corroded to use a threaded plug, install a Real-Tite or other PVC plug instead **(Photo 10)**. These plugs meet code.

7 FIND THE CLOG
Feed the cable into the drain with the motor off until you can't push it any farther. Then start and stop the motor with the foot switch as you slowly feed cable into the drain. Let up on the foot switch immediately if the cable stops turning or you think you've reached the clog.

RENTING A DRAIN-CLEANING MACHINE

Before you head to the rental store, attempt to determine the location of the clog, or be able to describe the symptoms.

For smaller drain lines, from 1½ in. to 3 in. in diameter, use a ½-in. cable. Larger main drains require a ¾-in. cable. Ask your rental agent to recommend the correct machine and show you exactly how to use it. Also ask for safety instructions. Inspect the machine to make sure the motor and pulley are covered with a guard. Ask the rental agent to test the built-in ground fault circuit interrupter (GFCI), check the cord for fraying or wear, and make sure the cable is not bent, kinked or tangled. Ask for an assortment of cleaning tools **(Photo 6)** and a description of their use. These machines are very heavy; a large machine with 100 ft. of ¾-in. cable can weigh 215 lbs. You'll need help getting it in and out of your car and house.

Some rental machines use a cable that's dual-wound and has a self-feeding feature. Since we aren't demonstrating the use of this particular machine, ask your rental dealer for safety and operating instructions.

OPERATING A DRAIN-CLEANING MACHINE

These machines are incredibly powerful, and dangerous if safety precautions aren't followed. Read and follow the instructions provided with the equipment.

Position the machine 2 to 3 ft. from the cleanout opening, plug it into a grounded outlet or 12- or 14-gauge grounded extension cord, and make sure the switch on the motor is in the "Forward"

8 ADJUST THE CABLE

Flip the switch on the motor to "Reverse." Then use the foot switch to run the motor in reverse for a few revolutions of the cable cage. This will relieve tension that may have built up in the cable when it hit the clog. Switch the motor back to "Forward."

Note: The only other time you should reverse the motor is when the cable gets stuck and will not turn in the forward position.

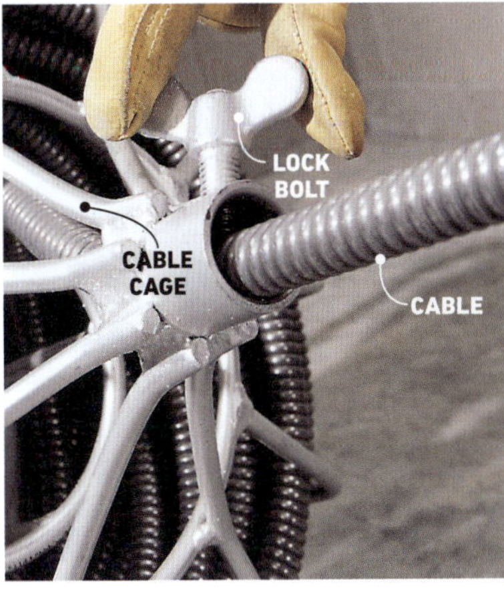

9 BREAK THE CLOG

Chew slowly through a clog by following these steps:

1. Tighten the lock bolt that secures the cable.
2. Depress the foot switch, running the machine in "Forward" while you hold the cable.
3. Loosen the lock bolt, feed a little more cable into the drain and retighten the bolt.
4. Repeat this process until you cut through the clog.

position. Put on heavy leather gloves and safety glasses and make sure you aren't wearing any loose clothes, belts, jewelry or anything that could become entangled in the cable.

Position the foot-operated switch where you can step on it while you're feeding cable into the drain. Practice starting and stopping the machine with the foot switch to get the hang of it.

Keep both hands firmly on the tool's cable and slowly feed it into the pipe as you stop and start the motor with the foot switch **(Photo 7)**. Feel for an increase in cable tension and listen for the motor to slow or the built-in safety clutch to slip. All of these signs indicate you've reached a clog. Stop immediately when you sense a change. **Photos 7-9** show you how to operate the machine in a safe fashion.

Caution: Do not allow tension to build up in the cable. This will happen if the cutting head hits a snag and stops turning, but the motor and its cage continue to rotate. Torque builds until the cable suddenly twists, potentially wrapping around your hand or arm like a steel boa constrictor. This can happen quickly and without warning, so proceed slowly and carefully as you feed the cable into the drain.

If you have the time after boring through the clog, clean the sides of the pipe by attaching a finishing tool to the cable and running the full length of the cable down the drain. Then use a hose to run water down the drain as you retrieve the cable. The hose and water will flush any leftover debris down the drain and rinse gunk off the cable as you reel it in.

10 CLOSE THE CLEANOUT PLUG

Replace the cleanout plug. Use a RealTite plug as shown, or similar product, if the fitting threads are damaged or for easier access in the future. Push the new plug into the cleanout fitting, and tighten the thumbscrew or Allen bolt in the middle of the cover to complete the seal.

Tips for an Easy Faucet Install

14 ways to make upgrading your fixtures easier

By Bill Bergmann

The instructions in the box with a new faucet tell you everything you need to know for a normal installation. Trouble is, there's no such thing as a normal installation. Every job has its own complications.

To get solutions to some of the most common problems, I sat down with Joe Barnes, a second-generation master plumber who faces these kinds of faucet situations every day. Use these expert tips to make faucet replacement an easy half-day job instead of an all-day ordeal.

1

2

1 LOW-FLOW PROBLEMS?

If your faucet has weak pressure or flow, a new faucet probably isn't the solution. Here's how Joe tracks down the source of the trouble:

- If both the hot and the cold are weak, the aerator is probably clogged. Simply remove it and clean it to solve the problem.
- If either the hot or the cold (but not both) is weak, then faulty supply lines, shutoffs or supply pipes are the problem. Supply hoses or shutoff valves are easy enough to replace. Fixing faulty or antiquated plumbing is a larger job, but it can benefit other fixtures in the home that have low water pressure issues.

2 MEASURE BEFORE YOU SHOP

Before you choose a new faucet, check the configuration and spacing on your sink. If you have a three-hole configuration, measure from the center of each handle to determine your spacing. Standard spacing is typically 4 or 8 in. If you want a single-hole faucet but your sink includes three holes, no problem. Many faucets include a cover plate to conceal the other two holes.

3

3 GET A BASIN WRENCH

A basin wrench gets at all the impossible-to-reach nuts below the faucet. Joe uses a basic version of this tool, but many plumbers like Ridgid's EZ Change Faucet Tool. It will reach those difficult nuts and handle just about any other fitting you might encounter during a faucet install.

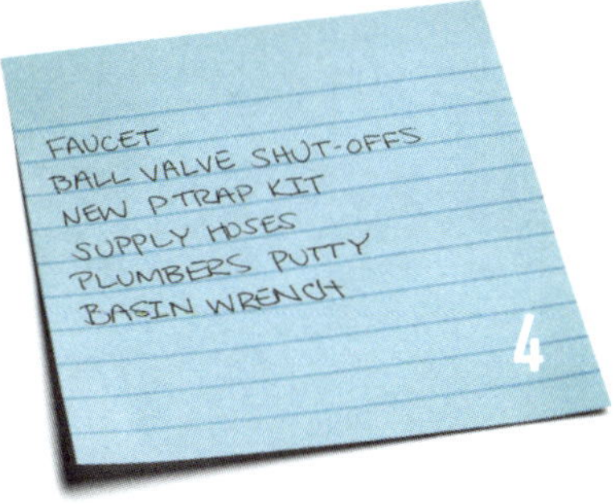

4

4 GET EVERYTHING YOU NEED

When you pick up a new faucet, bring a list of every possible install item you could need. Joe says if he's headed to a job he hasn't seen, he'll be sure to have every potential part along. One trip to return a few things is far easier than multiple runs for the stuff you don't have.

LOOK FOR EASY-INSTALL FEATURES

Many manufacturers have easy-install faucets; it's worthwhile finding one. Joe likes Delta's EZ Anchor mounting system because you don't need to reach under the sink for mounting. American Standard faucets with the Speed Connect feature are also easy to install. Its drain stop mechanism has only four parts, instead of up to 14 for a standard assembly. These and other new faucet designs make for a quicker and stress-free install process.

5 REPLACE YOUR SUPPLY LINES

Never reuse old supply lines. The last thing you want is water damage from an old failed supply line. Even if the hoses are newer looking, Joe will replace them because the rubber washers can fail over time. Quality supply lines with a braided stainless steel casing may cost a bit more, but they're well worth it in the long run.

6 CUT STUBBORN CONNECTIONS

If you find rusted mounting nuts or other encrusted, petrified connections that won't budge, go ahead and cut them. An oscillating tool or rotary tool with a metal-cutting blade works well for this.

7 REPLACE YOUR P-TRAP

Make space under the sink by taking out the P-trap. Reusing an old P-trap can be a messy ordeal, so Joe usually includes a new trap assembly on his installs. The cost of a plastic P-trap kit is minimal, and you'll get peace of mind knowing all the fittings are new and clean. Keep in mind that some bath sink drains are 1¼ in., and kitchen sink drains 1½ in. Be sure to get the right size. Joe sees a new P-trap as cheap insurance against a series of callbacks.

8 INSTALL THE FAUCET FIRST

If you're installing a brand new sink, mount the faucet to the sink before dropping the sink into place. Having everything in plain view always makes for better connections, and you'll spend less time you spend on your back.

9 USE PLUMBER'S PUTTY

Some manufacturers suggest using silicone caulk to seal a faucet or drain, but it can be difficult to apply and can stain natural stone. Joe prefers plumber's putty. It's easier to work with, and the non-staining variety won't leave blemishes. Roll and knead the putty before you use it so it compresses more easily. He says it's far easier to repair a faucet assembly that was installed with putty. Silicone is as much an adhesive as it is a sealant, and can make pulling things apart a pain.

10 CLEAN OFF YOUR SINK DECK

To ensure a good seal between the sink and the new faucet, be sure to clean up the footprint of the old faucet. Scouring powder works well for soap scum and other tricky crud. For tougher lime or rust deposits, a rough pumice stone is usually the best remedy.

11

AERATOR

12

11 GET LEAKPROOF CONNECTIONS

Each connection requires a different amount of torque to tighten. Over-tightening the slip nuts on a plastic waste line can strip the threads and make for a leaky connection. Always hand-tighten these connections. For flexible supply lines, the standard recommendation is to get them finger tight, then give them a quarter turn with a wrench. But Joe usually gives them a half turn and has never had an issue.

12 REMOVE THE AERATOR AND FLUSH OUT SEDIMENT

Plumbing work knocks sediment loose inside pipes. Be sure that sediment doesn't clog your aerator or valves. Joe always removes the aerator and then lets both the hot and the cold run for a minute to flush the lines before reinstalling the aerator.

13 DON'T SKIMP ON THE TEFLON TAPE

A 40-ft. roll of Teflon tape is cheap, so don't be stingy with it. Make sure you wrap all threaded connections clockwise several times. When you thread on that nut, it should feel tight, and the clockwise wrap will keep the tape from unraveling as you tighten the connection. Putting plumber's grease on male thread connections on the faucet and supply lines will aid in installation and make them easier to remove.

14 CHECK FOR LEAKS

Once everything is connected and the water is back on, do a leak check. Wipe it all down with a dry rag, and then blot the connections with toilet paper to see if there is any evidence of a slow leak. Close the drain and fill the sink up to the overflow several times and drain to ensure there are no leaks.

TEST THE SHUTOFFS

Almost every faucet is connected to shutoff valves beneath the sink. But those old valves often don't work, and it's best to know that before you begin. If your shutoffs don't stop the water flow, you can repair them or replace them. Or you could turn off the water to the whole house at the main shutoff valve while you replace the faucet. For help with those jobs, find more information at *familyhandyman.com*.

Ultimate Guide to Pipe Fittings

If you're doing a plumbing installation or repair, you'll need to buy pipe and pipe fittings. Here's some help figuring out which fittings you need.

By Chris Deziel

I doubt there's a DIY plumber out there who has not experienced the frustration making multiple trips to the hardware store to complete a repair. I certainly know that I have.

Putting together a network of pipes of different diameters and materials can be like assembling a puzzle. Sometimes you don't know exactly which fitting to buy until you reach the part of the puzzle where you need it.

Plumbing fittings vary by size, purpose and material. You often must tie together pipes of different materials with transition fittings. Materials in common use today include copper, PVC and CPVC, PEX, ABS, galvanized steel and cast iron, and they can mostly all be connected to each other with appropriate fittings.

With all the different pipe sizes and materials out there, things can get confusing. Fittings for water lines are different than those for drain and waste lines. It's no wonder professional plumbers don't go anywhere without a truck full of fittings. It's their magic cupboard, letting them complete installations and repairs much more efficiently than amateurs like me.

WATER LINE FITTINGS

PEX is quickly becoming the material of choice for most water lines. But PVC, CPVC and copper are still in common use, as is galvanized steel outdoors.

The three reasons for PEX's popularity are its flexibility (it can bend around corners), durability and ease of assembly. You simply push your PEX pipes and fittings together rather than gluing (PVC and CPVC), soldering (copper) or screwing them (galvanized steel).

Here are the fittings you're most likely to need when assembling or repairing water lines:

- **Coupler:** Joins two lengths of pipe in a straight line. Whenever you cut a pipe during a repair, you'll need a coupler to put it completely back together.
- **Bend:** For changing pipe direction. Common bend angles are 90 degrees, (aka elbows) or 45 degrees. Bends are typically made of the same material as the pipe except for PEX bends, which are made from brass or hard plastic materials.
- **Tee:** Shaped like the letter "T" with two parallel ports and a perpendicular one. It's used for adding a branch line. When the branch line is a different size than the main one, you can easily make the connection with a reducing tee fitting.
- **Reducing adapter:** Another way to join pipes of different diameters. It may be shaped like a bell (that's common for copper and galvanized pipes) or fit inside the larger pipe (more common for plastic). The first type is called a bell adapter, and the second a reducing bushing.
- **Union:** A type of coupler you can take apart. Its large threaded nut holds together the two halves of the pipe its connecting. You can use one in place of a coupler in any situation where you want to temporarily disassemble the pipes.

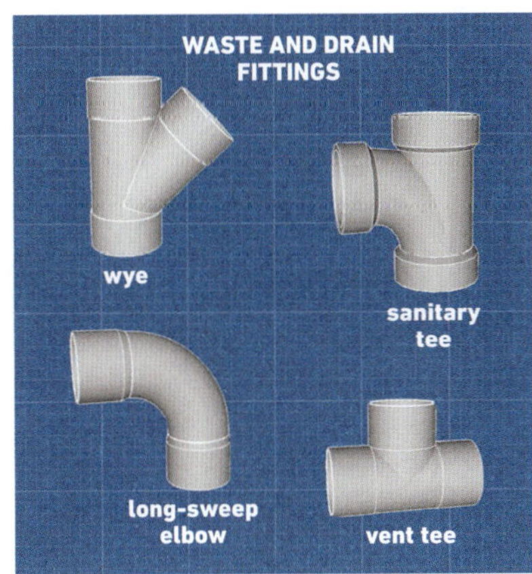

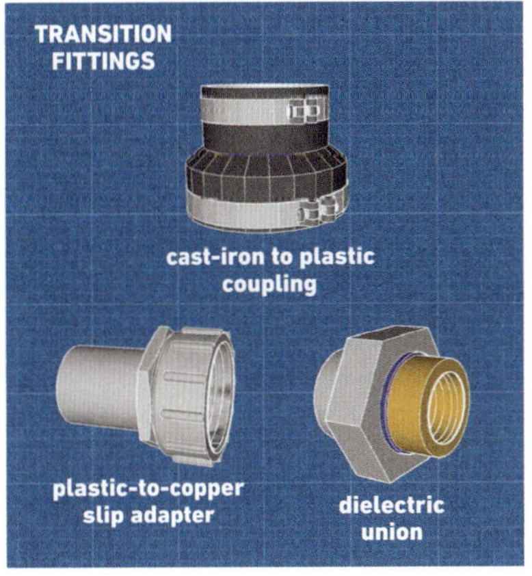

- **Threaded adapter:** To join a pipe with a glue or solder slip joint to one with threads, you'll need a threaded adapter. It can have male or female threads. Threaded adapters join plastic pipes to each other, or copper to itself or to brass.
- **Compression fitting:** This lets you join plastic or copper pipes without glue or solder. Most feature a ring that fits around the pipe and a nut that tightens onto the fitting, wedging the ring into the gap between the pipe and fitting. Compression fittings allow for easy pipe repair. Most modern faucet and toilet shutoff valves have compression fittings.

WASTE AND DRAIN FITTINGS

Cast iron was a common material for drain pipes in the first part of the 20th century. They are usually connected with couplers that feature rubber gaskets that are surrounded by a stainless steel sheathing.

These days, most drains are made with PVC or ABS plastic. Plastic drain fittings are usually glued, but the ones you might need to remove temporarily, like cleanout plugs, are threaded.

Here are the most common drain fittings. The list doesn't include couplers and ordinary bends, because they're similar to the ones used for water pipes and serve the same purposes.

- **Long-sweep elbow:** Makes a 90-degree bend in a longer arc than an ordinary elbow to allow water to flow more smoothly. It's used for connecting vertical drain lines to horizontal ones and horizontal lines to horizontal ones.
- **Straight tee:** Performs the same function as tees for water lines, but are seldom used for drain lines. They're mostly for vents when you need to tie horizontal pipes to vertical stacks.
- **Sanitary tee:** Also called a santee, this has a sweep on its perpendicular port to promote water flow in the direction of the sweep. Use it to connect a horizontal waste line to a vertical one, but not a vertical one to a horizontal one. That's the job of a wye.
- **Wye:** Shaped like the letter "Y," a wye does the same job as a sanitary tee, but with less chance of backflow. This is the fitting you need to connect the vertical drain from your sink or toilet to the sewer. You can also use it to connect a horizontal waste pipe to a vertical one.

TRANSITION FITTINGS

Whether you're connecting PVC or CPVC pipes to copper, cast-iron pipes to ABS or galvanized pipes to copper, you'll need a transition fitting. In some cases, you can do it by taking two threaded adapters of different materials and screwing them together. But it's often easier to use an adapter specifically made to couple them, assuming you can find one.

- **Plastic-to-copper slip adapter:** It has male copper threads on one end and a PVC or CPVC slip joint on the other. After soldering a female thread adapter to the copper pipe, you screw in the adapter and glue the plastic pipe to the slip joint.
- **Dielectric union:** Used for mating copper or brass to galvanized steel, it has an insulating washer that keeps the pipes separated electrostatically to prevent more corrosion. Dielectric unions are most commonly used when installing a new water heater.
- **Cast-iron to plastic coupling:** These are also widely known as Fernco couplings after the company that makes most of them. They consist of a rubber cylinder that is surrounded by a stainless steel sheath and two or more threaded pipe clamps that can be tightened simply with a screwdriver.

Do's & Don'ts of Soldering Copper

Tricks to complete your job in less time—and with fewer leaks

By Jeff Gorton

DO Keep nearby soldered joints from melting by wrapping a wet rag around them. Wet and wring out a 2-in.-wide strip of cloth and wrap it around the fitting you want to protect. The wet rag will absorb most of the heat and prevent the solder in the existing joint from melting.

DO Use MAPP gas to speed up the job. Lead-free solder melts at a higher temperature than the now-banned lead-based solder. MAPP gas torches burn hotter than propane, making them a better choice for modern solder. Five to 10 seconds of heating with a MAPP gas torch is all that's required before you can feed solder into most ½-to-¾-in. pipes and fittings. Be careful, though. It's easier to overheat a joint with MAPP gas. If the flux turns black and the solder won't flow into the fitting, the joint is overheated.

MAPP GAS TORCH

DON'T Solder too close to wood or other flammable material without protecting it from the flame.

DO Use a flame protector. These small flame-retardant blankets are available at hardware stores and home centers. You hang one behind the joint you're working on to insulate the flammable material and help prevent fires. In a pinch you could use a piece of sheet metal instead. Wetting the area around the soldering job with a spray bottle of water also helps prevent fires. Always keep a fire extinguisher nearby and ready as a safety precaution.

DON'T Reuse old fittings. Recycle them instead. It's time consuming and difficult to take apart and clean old fittings. And there's a good chance they'll leak.

DO Buy new fittings instead. You'll get better results in less time.

DO Use tinning flux. It works just like standard flux but contains a bit of silver solder powder that melts under heat. The resulting thin layer of solder helps ensure a leak-proof joint. Tinning flux is available at most hardware stores and only costs a little more than standard flux.

DON'T Feed too much solder into the joint. It's tempting to melt a few inches of solder into a joint as extra insurance. But excess solder can puddle inside pipes, restricting water flow, and can form small balls that break loose and damage faucet valves.

DO Use about ½ in. of solder for ½-in. pipe and ¾ in. for ¾-in. pipe. Here's a tip. Bend the end of the solder at a right angle, leaving a few inches below the bend. The bend makes it easier to gauge how much solder you've used.

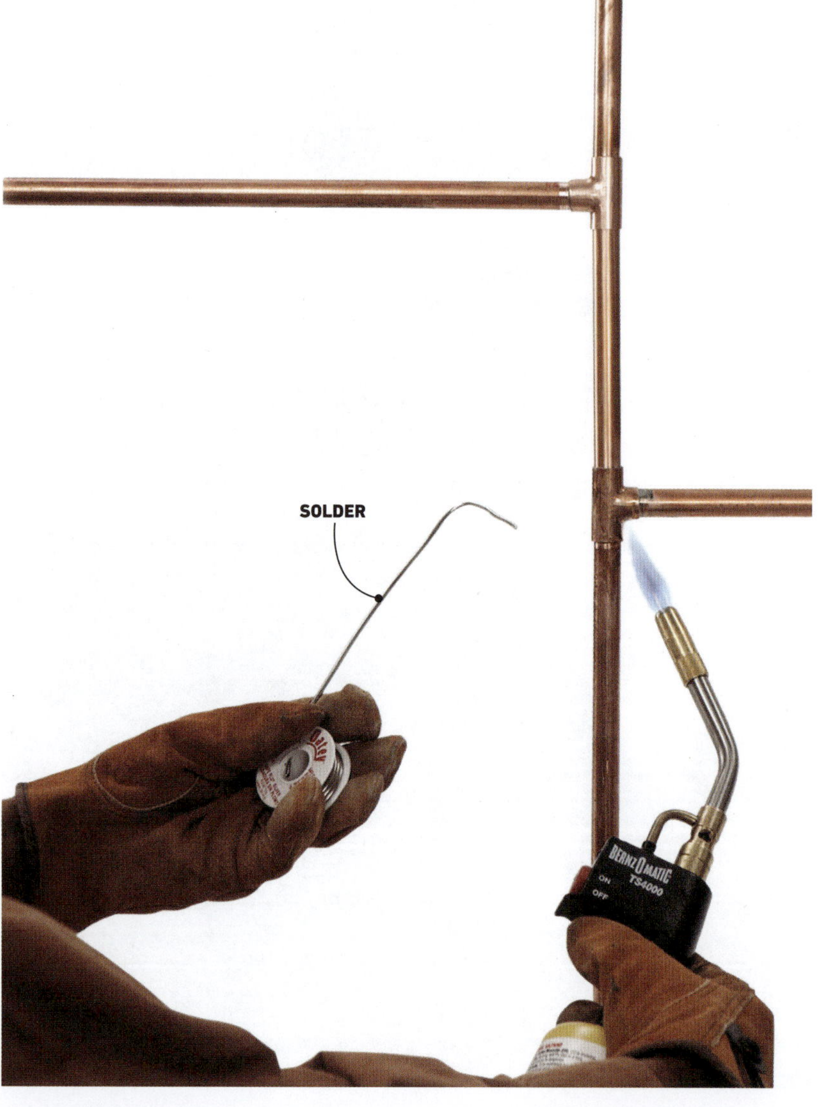

DO Cut, flux and assemble a section of pipes and solder them all at once. Use pipe straps to support the pipes if necessary. Be careful to clean and flux the end of every pipe and the inside of the fittings before assembling. Then before you start soldering, press the pipes firmly into the fittings to make sure they're fully seated. Start soldering at one end of the assembly and move methodically from one joint to the next.

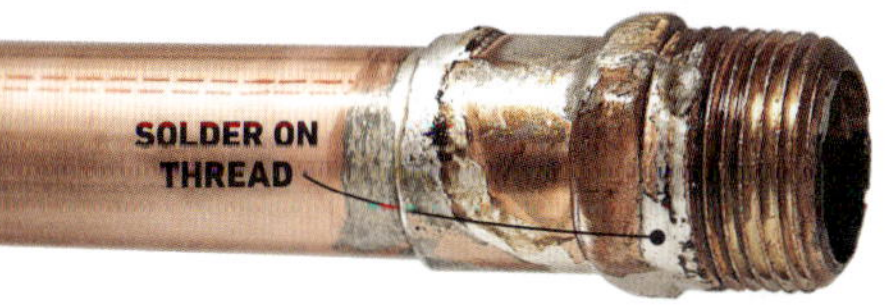

DON'T Get solder on threaded fittings. It can clog the threads, preventing a good seal with the matching part.

DO Follow these steps to avoid the problem. If the threaded fitting is positioned so that solder will run down onto the threads, solder the pipe and fitting at a workbench instead so you can keep the fitting pointed up. If you have to solder a threaded fitting where the solder will flow onto the threads, wipe excess flux from around the joint after you assemble. Extra flux can run down onto the threads, causing the solder to follow it.

DON'T Try to solder pipes with water in them. When you're repairing or tying in to existing copper pipes, it's common to find a small amount of water in them even after you close the valve and drain the pipes. Soldering a joint in pipes that contain even tiny amounts of water is nearly impossible. Most of the heat goes into turning the water to steam, so the copper won't get hot enough to melt the solder.

DO Stop the trickle of water with a pipe plug. Push the plug into the pipe with the applicator tube provided. When you're done soldering, dissolve the plug by holding the torch under the spot where the plug is. You'll find inexpensive plugs at home centers and hardware stores.

An old trick was to stuff a wad of soft white bread into the pipe to temporarily stop the trickle of water. This works, but you run the risk of clogging aerators and valves with the partially dissolved bread.

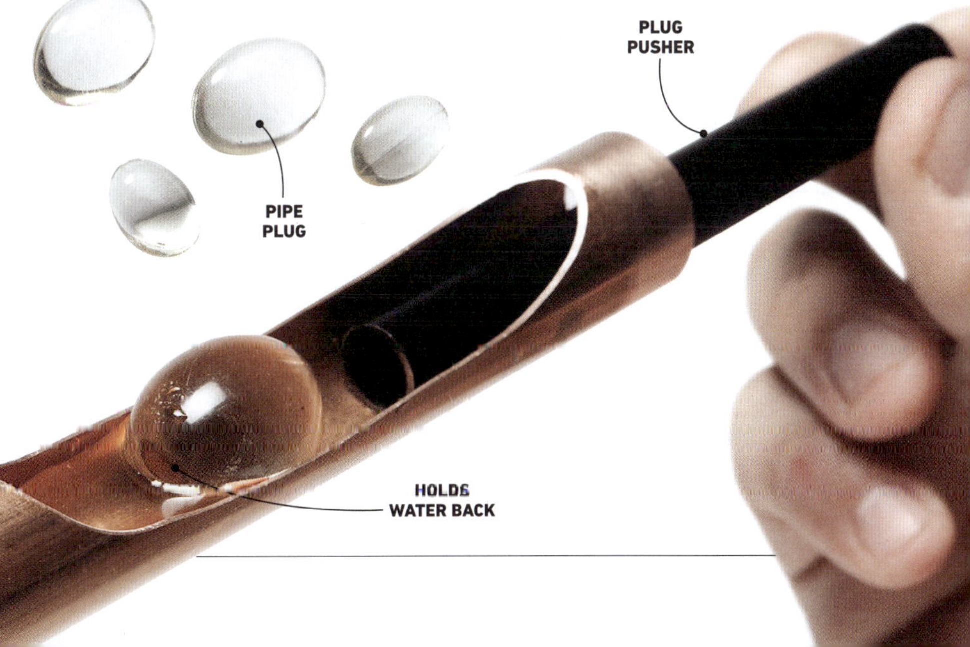

Finish Up a Plumbing Job

Take these steps to wrap up any project with confidence

By Gary Wentz

When the job is done and you're ready to pack up your tools, take the time to do a final check for tiny leaks and sediment lingering in the lines. There's no 100% prevention for either problem, but if you take a few precautions, you can reach 99% certainty. And that's about as good as life gets.

1 FLUSH BEFORE YOU CAULK

A small leak at the toilet flange leads to a puddle. But if that puddle is dammed up by caulk around the toilet base, it may not show up for months. So before you caulk, flush a couple times and probe for leaks with a strip of paper.

2 DETECT DRIPS WITH PAPER

Paper towels or newspaper are great leak locators. You'll immediately see or even hear leaks as soon as a drip of water hits the paper.

3 STRESS-TEST DRAIN LINES

To test drain lines under a sink, don't just turn on the faucet. Instead, completely fill the sink. (Fill both bowls on a double sink.) Then open the drain to release a gush of water. In humid conditions, fill the sink with lukewarm to hot water. The hotter the water, the less dense it is, so it will show leaks faster.

4 DON'T GET FOOLED BY CONDENSATION

In high humidity, a cold water line will sweat, making it almost impossible to detect tiny leaks. Here's how to work around that: Run the water just enough to fill the line. Then take a coffee break while the water in the pipe warms to room temperature. When it's warm enough, wipe the pipe dry and look for leaks. Condensation may also be caused by cold water in drain lines.

5 LOCATE LEAKS WITH TISSUE

A wet spot on a tissue is a lot easier to see than a small droplet on a pipe. So wipe with a tissue and look at it after each swipe.

6 CHECK SINK RIMS

Dribble water around a sink rim to check the seal. Rim leaks rarely show up right away, so wait a few minutes before inspecting from below.

7 FLUSH BEFORE YOU CONNECT

Sediment trapped in a fill valve can make a toilet fill slowly or run constantly. To flush out this sediment, run water into a bucket before you connect the toilet to the supply line.

WHAT YOU DO DEPENDS ON THE PIPES

There's no need to flush every step on every job. It depends on the age and type of plumbing. In a newer home with PEX plumbing, for example, you might only have to remove the aerators before flushing.

Old galvanized steel pipes, on the other hand, usually contain a lot of debris and call for just about every trick in the book.

5

6

7

8 LET IT RUN

When flushing lines, you'll be tempted to shut off the water after 10 seconds. That's not long enough. One minute is the minimum. In a large house with long runs of supply pipe, let it flow for several minutes. Better to waste some water than to repair plugged faucets.

9 START AT A HIGH-VOLUME, LOW-RISK VALVE

To flush out debris, you need a high-volume flow of water. That makes outdoor hose bibs and washing machine supply lines great for this purpose. These faucets have another advantage too: Unlike kitchen or bath fixtures, they have big, simple ports that are less likely to get plugged or damaged by sediment. Just keep in mind that any faucet you choose for flushing should be downstream from the work area. And watch out! Washing machine hoses often have screens that can become plugged. Luckily, they're easy to remove and clean.

10 PROTECT THE SHOWERHEAD

Low-flow showerheads have tiny openings that can be plugged by a single particle. So run the tub faucet before the shower. In a dedicated shower (no tub spout), remove the showerhead and flush the line.

11 FLUSH HOT AND COLD SEPARATELY

To get maximum flow through a single-handle kitchen or bath faucet, swing the handle to one side and run the water full blast. Then switch to the other side and do the same.

12 FLUSH OUT SEDIMENT

Water supply pipes contain sediment: corrosion, mineral deposits, pipe dope or solder. Plumbing work shakes that stuff loose. Water flow will carry that loose grit to fixtures—and possibly plug them. To prevent that, run water through the lines to flush out the sediment.

13 REMOVE AERATORS

Small particles that flow through a faucet often get caught in the aerator. So always unscrew the aerator and run the water after a plumbing job.

SKILLS IN PRACTICE

Wood-Fired Hot Tub

A soothing soak in your own backyard

By Joe Cruz

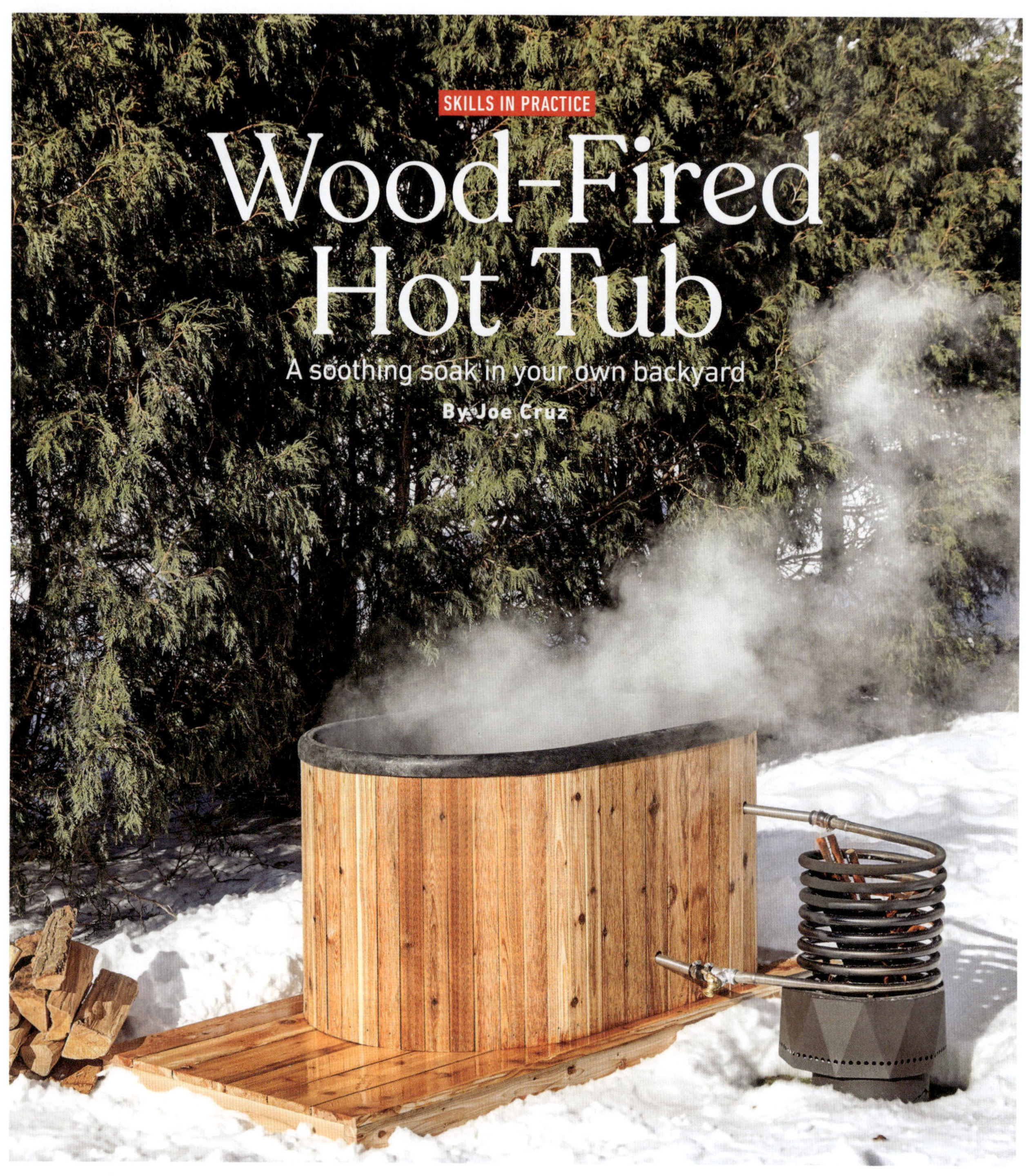

Whether it's summer or winter, you don't need to go to a resort to enjoy a relaxing soak in an outdoor hot tub. For a relatively small price, you can build this hot tub in your own backyard and take a dip whenever the mood strikes. Fill the tub with a garden hose, light a fire to heat the water, hop in and relax!

1

2

THE TUB

I chose this Rubbermaid stock tank for a few reasons. First, it's deeper than the metal tanks that I saw. Second, the plastic itself is a more comfortable temperature in hot or cold weather than metal. Third, its rounded top edges have a larger radius than the edges of metal tanks, so they're more comfortable to rest your arms on.

Lastly, you'll find it much more comfortable to lean back against the angled ends of the stock tank than the straight sides of a metal tank. This tank had molded-in brackets for supporting it on a wood frame. I didn't like the look, and they would've made it harder to clad the tank, so I cut them off with a multi-tool.

1 CUT THE PLATFORM

Set the stock tank upside-down diagonally on one end of a 4 x 8-ft. sheet of plywood. This lets you get the platform and a tub cover from one 4 x 8-ft. sheet. With your pencil at a slight angle as shown, trace around the perimeter of the stock tank. Cut out the platform with a jigsaw. Cut the cover the same size.

2 BUILD UP THE BASE

Cut treated 2x4s to form an elongated octagon. Secure the all the 2x4s to the platform with water-resistant wood glue and exterior screws.

What It Takes

TIME	COST	SKILL LEVEL
2 days	$500+	Intermediate

TOOLS

Jigsaw, miter saw, table saw, router with flush-trim bit, router table, bead and cove router bit set, carpenter's square, caulking gun, hot glue gun, drill, 1¼" hole saw, ¼" spade bit, rubber mallet, screwdriver, garden hose

THE WATER HEATER

To heat the water, we used a wood-fired thermosyphon heat exchanger. This ¾-in. stainless steel coil circulates the water in the tub without the need for a pump. It's based on natural convection, called thermal siphoning. Cold water enters at the bottom of the heater and expands. Convection moves the heated water upward, pushing it through the coil and out into the tub; at the same time the heated water is replaced by cooler water below. So no need for power—just dry wood.

You can purchase a 60-ft. roll of ¾-in. copper tube and bend a heating coil yourself. But it would cost about the same as the coil I found online and had delivered.

Materials

ITEM	QTY.
4' x 8' x ¾" plywood	1
1½" x 3½" x 8' green treated (2x4)	2
¾" x 3½" x 8' cedar (1x4)	3
¾" x 2½" x 8' cedar (1x3)	12
100-gal. poly oval stock tank	1
Stainless steel coil heat exchanger	1
Stock tank drain plug	1
Smokeless fire pit	1
4' x 8' x 1" pink foam insulation	1
Tube of construction adhesive	1
Exterior wood glue	1
1¼" construction screws	1 box
1½" finishing screws	1 box
Plumber's tape	1 roll
Drain valve	1
¾" galvanized tee	1
¾" rubber couplers	2

3 TRIM THE BASE

Trim the 2x4 base so that it's flush to the edge of the platform. Use a jigsaw or a router with a flush-trim bit.

4 ADD MOUNTING BLOCKS

Cut plywood squares to fill the areas between the reinforcement ribs on the bottom of the stock tank. Secure the plywood using construction adhesive and a few self-tapping screws through the ribs into the plywood edges.

5 ATTACH THE BASE

Apply construction adhesive to the plywood squares. Set the assembled base on the upturned stock tank and center it. Secure the base with 1¼-in. screws through the platform into the plywood squares you installed in the previous step.

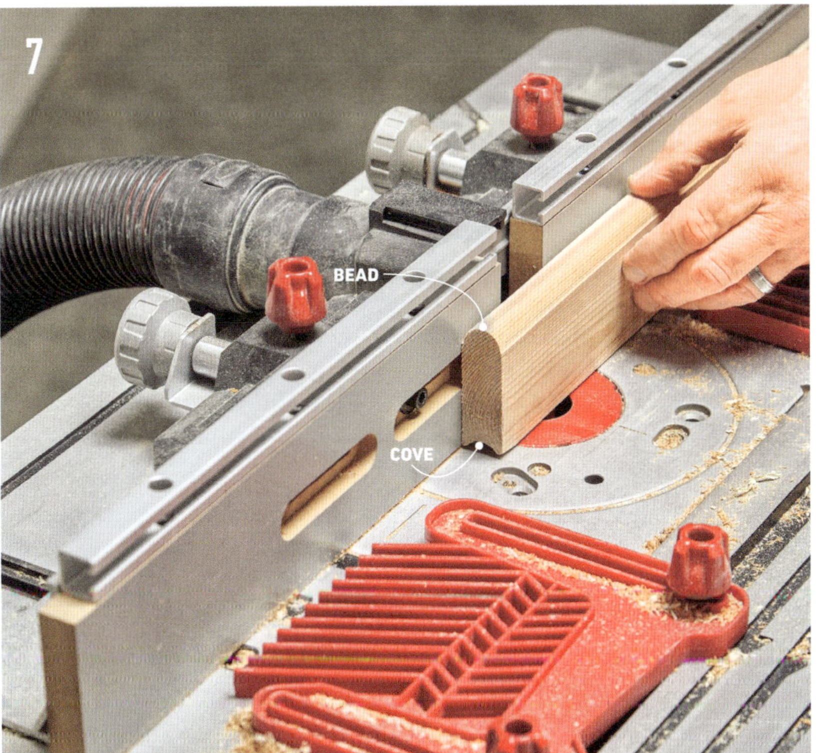

6 INSULATE THE TUB

Cut 1-in.-thick insulation to size using a table saw or utility knife. Make kerf cuts in the insulation on the pieces that curve around ends of the tank to allow the insulation to bend without breaking. Attach the foam insulation to the stock tank with a combination of hot glue and construction adhesive.

7 MAKE THE CLADDING

Using a router table, rout a bead on one edge of all the cladding boards and then rout a cove on the other edge of the boards. You can cut your boards to length before you run them through the router or leave them at full length and cut them to final length after routing.

8 ATTACH THE CLADDING

Set the tub assembly on sawhorses to make it easier to work on. The first cladding board is the most important. Place the board under the lip of the stock tank. Then use a carpenter's square to check that the board is fully square to the platform. Attach the board to the edge of the platform with finish screws.

Work your way around the tub, keeping the bead on each board tight to the cove of the preceding board. Check for square as you go. The very last board may need to be custom cut and routed again to fit tightly.

9 ADD THE PIPING

Drill a ¼-in. pilot hole from the inside of the tank through the tank's drain plug and through the cladding. Using the pilot hole as a guide, drill a 1¼-in. hole through the cladding from the outside. Wrap the thread of a pipe nipple with plumber's tape and thread it into the drain plug hole. Next, attach the coil to the pipe extension with a rubber coupler.

10 SECOND HOLE

Thread a pipe nipple onto the upper end of the coil and mark on the cladding where to drill the top hole. Again, drill a ¼-in. pilot hole, only this time through the cladding into the stock tank. Remove the board and drill a 1¼-in. hole at your pilot hole into the board. Remove enough insulation to make space for the drain plug, then drill a hole to fit the threads of your drain plug and install it.

11 ATTACH THE COIL

Reinstall the bored cladding and, as before, wrap the thread of a pipe nipple with plumber's tape and thread it into the drain plug. Then attach the coil to the pipe nipple with a rubber coupler—then enjoy your tub.

11